THE CINEMATIC
CONNERY

THE CINEMATIC
CONNERY

THE FILMS OF
SIR SEAN CONNERY

A.J. BLACK

POLARIS
PUBLISHING

This edition first published in 2022 by

POLARIS PUBLISHING LTD
c/o Aberdein Considine
2nd Floor, Elder House
Multrees Walk
Edinburgh
EH1 3DX

www.polarispublishing.com

Text copyright © A.J. Black, 2022

ISBN: 9781913538842
eBook ISBN: 9781913538859

British Library Cataloguing-in-Publication Data
A catalogue record for this book is available on request from the British Library.

Designed and typeset by Polaris Publishing, Edinburgh
Printed in Great Britain by CPI Group (UK) Ltd, Croydon, CR0 4YY

To Dad
The first man I believed was a superhero

CONTENTS

NOBODY DID IT BETTER

THE NEWS CAME in the winter of 2020, on 31 October, a night more commonly remembered for the celebration of Halloween. Sir Sean Connery, the most iconic Scottish actor in cinematic history, had passed away at the grand old age of 90.

It soon became apparent that Connery had been suffering for some time with the cruel blight of dementia. By the end, he struggled to recognise even close family members. Yet, as good friend Sir Jackie Stewart recounted in his obituary, even in those final days Connery had flashbacks to the cinematic career that had spanned six decades.

'He told me he wanted to watch Sidney Lumet's *The Hill*, his favourite film in which he'd acted. That role meant more to him than all the Bonds. The next day, he asked me again if I'd like to see it as if he'd never asked me before. And so, we did.'

Connery's choice of *The Hill* as the performance he loved the most speaks to the dichotomy within an actor who defined the marquee name. He was an actor who became defined by one of *the* primary characters in 20th-century popular culture history, yet always aspired for more. When the world wanted him to be 007, Connery hoped they would seek out Trooper Joe Roberts.

While he might have raised a sardonic eyebrow at his branding as James Bond, Connery will forever be remembered as the defining face of that character on the silver screen. But this obscures a deeper truth about the actor's impact. Connery was a performer who worked across not just a diverse, evolving era of cinema but during a social, political and cultural maelstrom. He was as symbolic to the 1960s as Andy Warhol, The Beatles and the Mini Cooper.

Yet his beginnings were inauspicious, with no indication of the life and legacy that would help to shape the cultural conversation for half a century.

*

Though young Thomas Connery, known colloquially as 'Big Tam' for much of his early life, was for a time destined as much for a life in professional football, a working man's trade or even Charles Atlas-style body-building, the boy who would be Sean developed a keen interest in the cinema of his youth.

Connery was born into a tough world, on 25 August 1930, to a hard-working father, Joseph, and devoted housewife, Effie, who had barely ever set foot beyond Fountainbridge, their harsh corner of Edwardian-era Edinburgh, let alone imagined travelling the length and breadth of the world as their son would later do.

His father earned two pounds a week in a rubber factory, while his mother occasionally worked as a cleaner. With money extremely tight, Tam's first job was a milk round in a horse-drawn cart for four hours before school. 'I started aged nine at Kennedy's Dairy,' he recalled. 'I worked there every day and would then go to Bruntsfield School.

'I used to walk to work in the dark; my mother went to work at the same time. And then I used to go straight from there and go to school. And if you got wet, you had to sit in wet clothes at school.'

His brother, Neil, was born in December 1938, and the usual meals of porridge and potatoes had to be stretched four ways. Once a week, if the family had sixpence to spare, Tam would walk to the public baths. When he was 63, he told an interviewer that a bath was still 'something special'.

'Fountainbridge evokes so many crazy memories,' he said. 'We had gaslights in the stairs and the building had six or seven floors. The flats were small, and some had nine in a family – I don't know how they all fitted in. There was no hot water in the whole street. We had to go to the swimming baths to get clean – which is why we were all strong swimmers!

'In 1940, the schools started to close down because of the threat of bombing from the Luftwaffe and they began moving kids out into the country, evacuating them. I was supposed to go to Australia but one of the ships was sunk, so my father said, "No, you're not going." So we were moved out of the schools and into private houses – and I never went back to school. From '42/'43 onwards we were in people's houses, and a lot of people didn't want certain kids in their houses. And I was one of them. For them it was okay for me to deliver the milk but it wasn't the same to go in and be taught [by them]. I never went back to school. I just left. And it was only later that I regretted how much I'd missed out.

'The war changed everything. I left school at 13 and it was straightforward economics: you had to do what you could do. I got a horse and cart and I used to deliver the milk and coal and all that kind of stuff. I never had a sense of us being poor. People talk about hardships, but you don't know anything else. What do you compare it with? And so you get on with it. It was only when I went away and joined the Navy at 16 that I was really conscious of how different everything was in other places. How much better it could be.'

Despite, or perhaps due to, these early privations, he indulged in the fantasy and escapism of cinema as soon as he was able. 'The cinema was so formative in my childhood,' he told Michael Parkinson in 2003. 'You used to see the feature, the second feature, the trailer, the news . . . you could spend a week there! My parents would say, "Go to the pictures," and they'd get rid of you. You'd come back four hours later.

'I was limited by circumstance. I had many jobs, but none of them were as a brain surgeon. For people from my background, the target was just to get out.'

Connery would one day become part of the Hollywood establishment, but he would first play a role in enlivening a British film industry that suffered a significant downturn in the post-war period.

In contrast, during the 1940s in which Connery grew up watching the global conflict from afar through the wireless and Pathé news reels, British cinema was experiencing a 'golden age', the like of which it has never quite experienced since. Numerous polls over the decades have ranked the films of dynamic directorial duo Powell and Pressburger as among the greatest British films ever made, notably *I Know Where I'm Going!* (1945), *A Matter of Life and Death* (1947), *Black Narcissus* (1947) and *The Red Shoes* (1948). David Lean was at his peak with *Brief Encounter* (1945) and *Great Expectations* (1946), Ealing comedies were hitting highs, and J. Arthur Rank formed the Rank Organisation, which would produce, distribute and exhibit a vast amount of seminal British pictures for decades to come. During the war, the Ministry of Information began to deploy cinemas for propaganda, out of which came a range of ambitious filmmakers producing outstanding work, such as Humphrey Jennings, whose short films have resonated through the decades. (Alfred Hitchcock also directed two short films for the Ministry; unfit for military service due to his age and weight, he felt compelled to contribute to the war effort.)

Film historian Michael Brooke summed up the decade in two films released five years apart: 'Laurence Olivier's ambitious big-budget Technicolor *Henry V* [1944] was simultaneously the first great Shakespeare film and a vital contribution to the war effort, with the rousing battle scenes providing a huge morale boost. By contrast, Carol Reed's crepuscular *The Third Man* [1949], set in divided Vienna and with a multinational cast portraying characters primarily looking out for themselves, brilliantly caught the post-war mood, one of feverish, scurrying uncertainty about what lurked around the corner.'

What lurked around that corner, the world Connery came of age into, was a sense of lingering anxiety combined with a tentative hope that the devastating conflicts that had defined the first half of the 20th century would be consigned to history. The fall of Nazi Germany and the end of the Second World War resulted in significant changes for the United Kingdom, with Winston Churchill's wartime coalition being replaced by Clement Attlee's Labour government. They came to power in 1945, ushering in reforms such as the National Health Service that gave the British people access to free healthcare and better living standards on a scale never before seen in ages of nobility, monarchy and, before that, serfdom.

The Scotland, the Britain, in which Connery grew up was transforming in ways unimaginable to his parents and the generations before them.

*

When Connery unofficially retired from acting after 2003's CGI-heavy action extravaganza *The League of Extraordinary Gentlemen*, it would have been hard to imagine that such a venerable titan of the silver screen started, five decades earlier, in the most unlikely of productions after he travelled to London to take part in a body-building competition with a friend (where he took third place in the Tall Man class, according to most accounts). After three years in the Navy, he was forced out on medical grounds after developing ulcers.

'I was quite skinny,' he recalled. 'Wiry. I started doing body-building.' He worked as a lifeguard at Portobello swimming pool in the summer, and in the winter, 'I worked as a model at the art college in Edinburgh,' he said, 'for which I used to get . . . I don't know, one pound something an hour. You posed for 45 minutes. It wasn't nude; you wore a pouch thing, but that was it. It was very arduous – quite a good discipline. And on the back of that I went down to London for the Mr Universe competition, representing Scotland in the Tall Man's class.'

While in London he saw an advertisement in an evening paper for 'strong looking youths for an interesting job'. When he went to the address in Soho he found himself in an audition room. A company was about to tour *South Pacific* around the country and the producers, keen to feature muscular extras, were looking for chorus boys.

'They were going to go out on tour for a year, which sounded pretty good to me,' he said.

Connery sang a hesitant rendition of 'I Belong to Glasgow'. 'They then asked me to do some handsprings and handstands. And one had to look like an American, which I suppose I could pass for.' He was cast on the spot. He was, as *The New York Times* later recognised, 'back in the Navy again, as one of the chorus of American sailors.' Of that experience, Connery simply reflected: 'That was it. I couldn't think of any job but show business again. I was hooked.'

Connery doesn't recall where the nickname 'Sean' came from, but it was the handle he answered to when he joined *South Pacific*, and when asked how he wanted to be billed, he decided on Thomas Sean Connery. 'They said it was too long. I didn't know if I was gonna stay an actor, so I used Sean – Sean Connery. And it's stayed.'

This was 1953, and Connery was still a decade away from the iconic status afforded him by James Bond and global stardom, but it marked the beginning of the remarkable journey he would undertake from humble Scottish origins to near-mythic status, a journey in which his life and career would parallel and adapt to an ever-changing cinematic and global landscape.

'I was always very conscious of the fact that I didn't have a formal education as such,' Connery remarked. 'I remember being greatly impressed when I was on tour with *South Pacific* with actors and writers and directors that seemed so brilliant and seemed to know everything – and I thought I was so stupid. As I got older I realised that they weren't so smart, but it was a great hurdle for me to overcome.

'I remember being on a break after the first run of *South Pacific* and was playing football in Manchester. As far as childhood aspirations went, it was all about football. In the summer a crowd of us would play football in the Meadows [in Edinburgh] *all day*, run home for a piece [sandwich] and then run back. We built up an amazing stamina.

'When I was 23, Matt Busby offered me a trial at Manchester United. Robert Henderson, an actor in *South Pacific*, said that 23 was pretty late to become a footballer – by the time you're 25, if you haven't done something, you're over the hill – but as an actor you can work for life.

'I'd never really considered it before as a career and I talked it through with him. He was the first person in my life that I'd ever had genuine guidance from, a sense of direction.

'I asked him, "What will I have to do?" And he said, "You'll have to be a bit of a contradiction to what you are now. You have to be able to look as though you could work in a mine *and* read Proust." He gave me a whole list of all this stuff to do. So I went, "Okay," and I went to work with him and went on tour with *South Pacific* for another year.'

'During the tour, I spoke to this Connery about Ibsen one day,' said Henderson. 'He didn't know who it was and I told him: "Ibsen is a playwright. You should read his plays." In principle, it was a waste of time: the chorus boys were not hired for their intellect. But a few weeks later Connery had read them and he had come to talk to me about them. I was amazed. I told him that with his physique, if he also had a cultural background, he could have a great career.'

'Everywhere we went I visited the local library,' said Connery. 'And by taking on a year in the libraries of Great Britain, I went through a whole course in literature – Shaw, Shakespeare, *War and Peace*, *Remembrance of Things Past*, *Seven Pillars of Wisdom* . . . a whole conglomerate of books. And coming out the other side, half of them

I didn't understand, but the fact that I had made that jump was very important for my own confidence; it's a part of your identity. And that's why I'm not too easy on people who have had a very good opportunity with a very good education who rather dismiss it.'

The post-war domesticity and frugality of 1950s Britain was being eclipsed by the economic boom and social changes rippling across the United States, with the birth of rock'n'roll, the formation of the civil rights movement and the concept of the 'nuclear family' living in the shadow of the atomic bomb and Mutually Assured Destruction. Connery was yet to reach the heights of the Hollywood he venerated as a teenager, but he would dabble in the glamour, in films such as *Another Time, Another Place* (1958) alongside Hollywood legend Lana Turner, a far cry from the 'British New Wave'-leaning existential grit of his supporting role in *Hell Drivers* (1954) or first major starring role as an over-the-hill heavyweight boxer in TV movie *Blood Money* (1957). He remained, during this decade, fully an actor of two worlds: post-austerity Britain and booming, countercultural America.

It was the 1960s when he fused the two together as an icon of British cinema shot through with Hollywood excess. Connery managed to transform Ian Fleming's dour 'blunt instrument' James Bond into Albert 'Cubby' Broccoli's colourful, swaggering symbol of post-colonial confidence. Particularly in *Goldfinger* (1963), the James Bond movie that established the template that the entire franchise would follow for the next forty years, Connery was a towering force of smouldering masculinity. The Swinging Sixties had fully arrived, with class barriers breaking down under Labour's resurgent socialist rule, and Connery managed to merge his working-class origins with the establishment bulwark that was 007 with effortless style. He now served to epitomise, in movies that dominated the decade, a new, youth-centred, popular culture.

By the 1970s, edging into middle age and now an established star largely abandoning the baggage of Bond, Connery adopted a serious tone in places to reflect a more introspective era. The optimistic brio of the 1960s was replaced with the shock and disillusionment of the calamitous mistake of the Vietnam War and the subsequent release of the Pentagon Papers that led to the Watergate scandal, seriously damaging faith in American democracy, and in Britain, seismic economic depression as post-war Keynesian thinking gave way to neoliberal insurgency and, ultimately, the rise of Thatcherism. Connery's projects veered from the traditional fare of *Robin and Marian* to the questionable colonial imperialism of *The Wind and the Lion*, through to his intense, hard-boiled performance in *The Offence*, a neo-noir film that served as a response to the 'American New Wave': countercultural, auteur-driven cinema designed for grown-up audiences seeking creative nuance and expecting no easy answers.

Connery nonetheless felt more comfortable in the 1980s, when Reagan's conservative Americana tracked alongside the blockbuster era, in an age of power ballads, vivid fashions and teenage dirtbags as the MTV generation built on what the baby boomers inherited. Having battled through the 1970s to prove his chops as an actor, eschewing the iconic space in pop culture in the process, Connery relaxed into this age of excess. He returned for one last, laconic outing as 007 in *Never Say Never Again*, won his first Academy Award in a scene-stealing turn in Prohibition-era crime epic *The Untouchables*, chewed up the scenery as a Spanish immortal in the Queen-soundtracked stylistics of *Highlander*, and won a BAFTA for his role in the medieval whodunnit *The Name of the Rose* (1986). By the time he sent up his suave heroic persona as a bookish history professor in *Indiana Jones and the Last Crusade*, Connery seemed to understand his place in a world which had always wanted him to be James Bond *and* Sean Connery.

In his last full decade as a star of the big screen, the 1990s, Connery took his place as an emeritus icon of cinema: a gentleman star ageing gracefully and able to switch between accent-defying roles as a Russian submarine commander one minute and a dogged corporate detective on the other. *The Rock* allowed him to update

James Bond to slick 1990s action cinema, while *The Avengers* saw him playing a literal Bond-style supervillain who would not have been out of place three decades earlier. Connery's security amidst crowd-pleasing, charismatic roles and dramatic fare complemented the unipolar safety of the post-Cold War world, as 'Cool Britannia' allowed for a re-evaluation and nostalgic reverence of the 1960s.

When the illusion of 21st-century security was shattered by the existential trauma of 9/11, Connery seemed to understand that the time had come for a new age. In his final film, *The League of Extraordinary Gentlemen*, set in the dying days of Victorian England as shadowy forces beyond the comprehension of his colonial protagonist Allan Quatermain conspire to disturb and unseat the established order, Connery's jaded establishment figure, hauled out of retirement for one last adventure, felt strangely appropriate. 'May this new century be yours, son . . . as the old one was mine,' he tells American gunslinger Tom Sawyer.

Connery passed on two batons here: Quatermain's and his own.

*

The intention of this book is to explore the career of Sean Connery as it spans these decades and look, in detail, at the pictures that defined him and the cultural zeitgeist he, in turn, defined.

While the story of the post-war era is not encapsulated completely in cinema, the complex ebb and flow of these decades is reflected in the careers of actors such as Connery, performers whose roles and influence on culture form part of our collective experience through multiple generations, helping to shape the world we live in today.

This is not the story of Sean Connery's life, or his passing. This is the story of the world he inhabited, the world he left an indelible mark on, and what that story means to us.

ONE

SKIRTING THE NEW WAVE

'BIG TAM' CONNERY became an actor in the 1950s, but it was *Sean* Connery who became a star in the 1960s.

Connery entered a post-war cinematic landscape that reverberated with the shock and trauma of over half a decade of total war. His first credited appearance, as an extra in Herbert Wilcox's Errol Flynn and Anna Neagle vehicle *Lilacs in the Spring*, came in 1954 when Winston Churchill was approaching the end of his second term as prime minister, rationing was still in place, Queen Elizabeth II was only a year into her reign and the towns and cities of the United Kingdom still displayed the ravages of conflict. Yet change was on the horizon, first signalled a year earlier across the pond.

László Benedek's 1953 *The Wild One* immortalised the image of a youthful Marlon Brando as the leader of a motorcycle gang. Brando's anti-establishment attitude, leathers and detached cool would pave the way for James Dean's *Rebel Without a Cause* and the rock'n'roll explosion spearheaded by Elvis Presley that would define the decade and help form the countercultural revolution of the 1960s of which Connery would end up a major, transatlantic symbol.

For now, however, Connery was plying his trade in minor roles on television – such as *Dixon of Dock Green* or *The Jack Benny Program* – and in films of little note or substance – such as *No Way Back*, directed by Montgomery Tully, and Gerald Thomas's condensed feature *Time Lock*. 'I never felt comfortable in that sort of BBC situation because I wasn't part of the old-boy network,' said Connery of this period. 'I didn't go to any of their public schools, I did not particularly appear "English", but I could have played hundreds of parts that never came my way.'

The parts that he *did* land were neither showcases for his talent nor cultural touchstones for cinema of the 1950s, and rather positioned Connery as a toiling B-movie presence remarkable for little more than his lithe physique and rough good looks.

'That was my Too period,' he said. 'Whenever I went for a job, I was either too tall or too broad or too Scots or too young or too dark. Nobody wanted to know.'

Things began to change in 1957, however, when he won roles in a collection of films that not only built his profile but began to shape the actor that the world would come to know, and love, as Sean Connery.

Hell Drivers was the first film in which Connery truly makes any kind of mark. A crime drama directed by Cy Endfield, the film is a remarkable who's who of future stars who would influence British cinema and television in striking ways for decades.

Though Connery was not top-billed for *Hell Drivers*, and indeed the part he played was relatively incidental, co-star Herbert Lom would later recount how Connery would ultimately put the rest of the cast in the shade. 'We had what was then called a star-studded cast – Stanley Baker, Pat McGoohan, Peggy Cummins, Dickie Attenborough, myself and a few others and, of course, Sean Connery's name was never mentioned anywhere,' he said. 'I saw the picture advertised recently for a rerun on television and it said "*Hell Drivers* . . . starring Sean Connery". Full stop. I suppose that is a compliment and fame indeed, and those of us who have worked with him are proud of that.'

Connery played Johnny Kates, a lorry driver within a haulage company with ties to organised crime, part of a crew run by Patrick McGoohan's tough and swarthy Red, but the role is strictly secondary to Stanley Baker's unwitting protagonist Tom Yately, an ex-con dragged back towards the murky world of crime when he gets a job at the company, despite trying to go straight.

Aged 26 at the time of filming, Connery's Johnny was a formidable, towering presence; broad-shouldered and taller than most of his compatriots, he conveyed a physicality that was reserved primarily for japes and boorish pranks with the rest of the crew. Connery was graced with relatively few lines in the film, but he nevertheless stood out amidst the fray to successfully mark his presence on the big screen for the first time.

Later that year, he was cast in *Blood Money*, a British remake of *Requiem for a Heavyweight*, which had been originally released as part of an anthology series of feature-length dramas called *Playhouse 90* on the American network, CBS. The script for *Requiem for a Heavyweight* had been written by Rod Serling, who would subsequently write the hugely influential *The Twilight Zone*, and starred Jack Palance as Harlan 'Mountain' McClintock. McClintock was a washed-up boxer suffering from 'punch-drunk syndrome' – brain damage – that would prevent him from taking part in the only sport he has ever known and escaping from a world embroiled with organised crime after his reckless manager bets the wrong way on a McClintock fight and now owes a fortune to the Mafia. It was a harsh and challenging piece of drama, with added dramatic weight and authenticity given Serling and Palance's previous boxing experience.

After winning Emmy and Peabody awards, *Requiem for a Heavyweight* not only put Serling on the map as a creative force, thereby helping to pave the way for *The Twilight Zone*, it also encouraged him to engage in a British remake a year later, with a televised play renamed *Blood Money* that would go out live on the BBC's *Sunday Night Theatre* programme on 31 March 1957. It would star, almost out of nowhere, Sean Connery.

Though some misgivings existed about Connery's ability to portray a heavyweight boxer in *Blood Money*, he was considered visually appealing to a female audience and his accent, also initially a possible barrier, served as an effective way of depicting the 'punch-drunk' innocence and tragedy of McClintock's character. Though a somewhat clichéd potboiler of a story, heavily influenced by American melodrama, *Blood Money* served to establish Connery as an actor capable of portraying protagonists with a flawed, haunted edge.

Sadly, *Blood Money* was one of the many *Sunday Night Theatre* episodes that did not survive the traditional purges of an era that did not value televised performance as it did celluloid, or cherish the theatrical experience, but Rakoff did, in 2014, reveal that he had recorded, for posterity, the audio of the performance, from which only still images survive. 'I had suddenly thought,' Rakoff told the BBC, 'maybe this is an important piece.'

To the history of television, perhaps not. Yet to the career of Connery, this was formative. It suggested acting talent beyond his physical presence and charisma, both of which he would marry in his cinematic career as a leading man.

Connery may not have ended up working heavily in television during his career, but following this breakthrough he nevertheless took on a number of television roles; these included classic parts such as Shakespeare's *Macbeth* (in the title role), Tolstoy's *Anna Karenina* and Terence Rattigan's *Adventure Story* as Alexander the Great, as well as appearances in a variety of anthology series which brought together the burgeoning British New Wave of talent with accessible stories for the working-class viewer.

Though he skirted the movement in some of his projects, Connery was never considered a key player in the British New

Wave as the 1950s gave way to a very different 1960s – unlike one of the major contemporaries of his era, Richard Burton. Mutual friend Robert Hardy commented on the similarities and differences of the two men: 'I looked at him and thought to myself then how much like Burton he was – not in looks; I think it was that sort of nationalism that they both had, and the retained accent, which crystallised my view. There was something about Sean that reminded me of Rich in that, though they were both from different national backgrounds, they were startlingly similar in their speech and movement.'

'My strength as an actor, I think, is that I've stayed close to the core of myself,' reflected Connery years later, 'which has something to do with a voice, a music, a tune that's very much tied up with my background experience.

'I always thought a reason Richard Burton was successful was that, even when he played English kings, his tune was unmistakably Welsh. It didn't detract from his quality, it enhanced it, because it meant his emotions could be interpreted and understood. When I was younger, I used to go to the Old Vic to watch Shakespeare, and I couldn't get the actors' emotions or even understand them because their voices were so far removed from normality. When they said, "Haw naw, mah lahd of Buckingham," they might as well have been saying "jungbutpooahbo". It was like a different language.'

Burton was, crucially, considered for the role of James Bond more than once during the 1960s, and was indeed a favourite of Ian Fleming – who famously took time to warm to Connery as 007 – and it serves as a key comparison simply for how Connery, with the slightest nudge, theoretically could have been the star of John le Carré's brittle *The Spy Who Came in from the Cold* in 1965 instead of Burton. In no small part, it is an 'anti-Bond' film in its revelation of precisely how grubby, technical and nihilistic Cold War espionage was in le Carré's world as opposed to Fleming's post-colonial, sexually charged adventures. In advance of the game-changing role of 007, Connery rarely ventured into waters Burton, or another of the 'angry young men' of his ilk, often trod – with one intriguing exception.

The Frightened City (1961), directed by John Lemont, sees Connery in the substantial, if still not top-billed role, of Paddy Damion, a cat burglar drawn into the organised crime world of 1960s London by seedy mobster Harry Foulcher (Alfred Marks), in part to help provide for his crippled partner Wally (Kenneth Griffith), injured in a robbery that Paddy in part feels responsible for. Along the way, Paddy seduces Anya (Yvonne Romain), the moll of slick, ice-cool businessman-turned-gangster, Waldo Zhernikov (Herbert Lom), and is ultimately dragged into a turf war between two villains who have London in their terrified grip, while the dogged, maverick Inspector Sayers (John Gregson) works to bring them down.

With distance, *The Frightened City* might appear cliché-ridden but it was released at a time when British life, particularly in London, was consumed by the glamour of gangster culture. This was the era in which the Kray twins and their 'Firm' ran the East End, and their savage level of organised, criminal brutality sat uncomfortably alongside the glitz of the entertainment world and the burgeoning Swinging Sixties.

In a sense, the glamorisation of 1960s gangster culture exists in step with the changing dynamics of British life. *The Frightened City* fails to have a lingering effect on the viewer by bringing to life the vicious, tawdry glitz of that era, but it does suggest a growing fascination with a criminal underclass who seemed as exotic as they were dangerous. Lom, who also appeared on screen with Connery in a very different role in *Hell Drivers*, has the makings of a Bond villain in Zhernikov – quietly menacing, intelligent, cunning and from 'elsewhere', with a glamorous girl at his side, and pulling the strings of hoodlums lacking his nous.

Connery, as Paddy, is a small-time crook who ultimately retains enough conscience to help bring down the amoral gangster 'supervillains'. It is a role that is as close to his breakout 007 moment as he would get in his pre-Bond career. Many of the visual touchpoints of Bond feature in *The Frightened City* – Connery showing off his physique in the shower after a boxing match before later appearing in a variety of immaculate three-piece and lounge suits, and displaying the balance of athleticism and controlled violence that would become a hallmark of his Bond.

Many a 007 has a signature role that stood out as an unwitting audition for the James Bond role. Roger Moore spent years as a suave master of disguise in *The Saint*; Pierce Brosnan glided his way over television as the smooth Remington Steele; Daniel Craig exuded menace in *Layer Cake*. For Connery, it is hard to see beyond *The Frightened City* as the picture that might have convinced Eon Productions that he was their man. For the first time he melds together the towering strength, and vulnerability, witnessed in *Blood Money* and the vibrant and furious, even raucous, edge of *Hell Drivers* to craft Paddy as a convincing antihero, and a formative, dynamic early 1960s role for Connery as a man of action, as well as substance.

As the pallor of the Second World War hung over the 1950s, so too was British cinema particularly consumed with replaying the conflict in a litany of pictures made across the decade. Films such as *The Dam Busters*, *Sink the Bismarck!*, and David Lean's epic *The Bridge on the River Kwai* helped entrench this, but the era was already providing challenges to the post-war examination of the global conflict. *Another Time, Another Place* (1958) is a curiosity in that regard for many reasons, placing the focus on a female character and her relationship to the man she loves in an unusual context, and looking at the consequences of war through a feminine, at points melodramatic, prism.

Directed by Lewis Allen, *Another Time, Another Place* principally serves as a vehicle for Hollywood starlet Lana Turner, playing Sara Scott, an American reporter working in London at the tail end of the war, in 1945. She falls in love with a British war reporter named

Mark Trevor (played by Connery), despite being in a relationship with her American boss Carter Reynolds (Barry Sullivan). As she anguishes over which man to choose, fate intervenes: Mark is killed in an air crash while reporting in Europe, and Sara, taking a pilgrimage to his hometown in sleepy Cornwall, discovers he was married with a young son to Kay (Glynis Johns). In befriending Mark's widow, Sara must decide whether to tell her the truth about her relationship with Mark.

The great film critic of her age, Pauline Kael, once wrote of Connery: 'Connery looks absolutely confident in himself as a man. Women want to meet him, and men want to be him. I don't know any man since Cary Grant that men have wanted to be so much.'

Another Time, Another Place was the first example of Connery placing his mark on the cinematic landscape in his first signature big-screen role, even though he wasn't afforded top billing as the male co-star. His character dies just under halfway through the film, yet Connery's presence continues to dominate; in part thanks to how Mark Trevor's death serves as the catalyst for Sara's own journey and casts a shadow over the narrative, but also for Connery's instinctive matinee-idol charisma that, while still unrefined, is present in his scenes with Turner. They turn somewhat stilted, melodramatic material into compelling viewing.

'I liked her enormously, I must say,' said Connery. 'But the press made such a thing about the fact that she was 42 and I was 28.'

Connery's on-screen chemistry with Turner turned the concerned head of her then-boyfriend Johnny Stompanato, a bodyguard and enforcer for the influential Mickey Cohen crime family. Convinced the pair were having an affair, Stompanato stormed on set at Borehamwood Studios in England and threatened Connery with a gun, telling him to stay away from her. Connery, according to legend, grabbed the weapon, twisted it out of Stompanato's hand, and laid him out with a single punch. Subsequently, on heading for Los Angeles to film Disney's *Darby O'Gill and the Little People*, Connery is reputed to have been advised to keep a low profile as certain mobsters were looking for him to exact revenge for his treatment of Stompanato.

These kinds of salacious details are the stuff of gossip and hard to verify, but they are of interest in the context of Connery and the eras of cinema he spanned. Audiences, retrospectively, have wanted the story of Connery facing down a real-life gangster with iron will to be true to reinforce his depiction of raw masculinity in the wake of his career-defining role as James Bond. Connery might have had the youthful look of a Cary Grant or Rock Hudson but he was coming of age and had developed an intensity, fire and arrogance that would carry him into Bond and beyond. Not that he was without moments of trepidation on set, as Lana Turner recounts: 'It was one of Sean Connery's first films, and he often missed his marks or forgot his key lights, to the annoyance of the director. Because I was co-producer, I had to work to smooth things out to ensure that the schedule went ahead as planned.' This does not sound like the Connery who would go on to become such a towering presence on and off screen and suggests, as was already becoming apparent, that his dalliance with Hollywood melodrama did not befit the screen persona that lay beneath the surface. Just before his breakout role, another very different film set during the great second conflict of the century would make this crystal clear.

Four years after *On the Fiddle* was released in the UK, and three years after Connery's rampant success as James Bond began in *Dr. No*, *On the Fiddle* was given an American theatrical release under the curious title of *Operation Snafu* and promoted to look and sound more akin to a 007 adventure than an amiable, wartime British comedy. There was a cynicism to this move, of course. By 1965 Connery was established as a signature cinematic name while *On the Fiddle* was an archaic example of wartime, and 1950s, British culture. The 1960s was moving headlong into swinging counterculture, and colourful adventures and bawdy romps such as the *Carry On* films. *On the Fiddle* belonged, aesthetically, to the 1950s and perhaps even earlier.

The film sees Connery given second billing to Alfred Lynch, who played Horace Pope, a wartime spiv – a proto-Del Boy Trotter – who, after falling foul of the law while trying to con army recruits, ends up billeted (by court order) into the forces where he meets the gentle giant Pedlar Pascoe, played by Connery, who Horace (or 'Popey' as Pedlar calls him) drags into his get-rich-quick schemes amidst Second World War trouble and strife. Pedlar, in hindsight, could represent the kind of role that Connery might have been straitjacketed into if *Dr. No* hadn't propelled him into a different stratosphere. Not for the first time, Connery is the tall, strong comic foil for a less charismatic presence in Lynch, who would serve a role-reversal just four years later in *The Hill*, the same year *Operation Snafu* debuted to a somewhat underwhelmed American press. Reaction was typified by Howard Thompson's *New York Times* review: 'This is the old wartime romp about two British pals, brain and brawn, who goldbrick and profiteer their way through the ranks, fleecing everybody in sight until the inevitable whitewashing climax when the two operators, good boys at heart, turn hero and squash some Nazis. The wonder is that a picture with a story already done, gag by gag, a hundred times is so easy to take. It is, though – flip, friendly, brisk and a wee bit cynical in its take-it-or-leave-it jauntiness. The film is familiar and trifling, but it's perky.'

Connery choosing to play two roles of questionable moral fortitude in *The Frightened City* and *On the Fiddle* serves as an intriguing coincidence. Trevor is a love cheat, albeit a bland one, who pays for his indiscretion with death. Pedlar is a loveable lunk who stands by Pope's side through thick and thin, even into the jaws of death. Released initially in the same year, both pictures stand as testaments to Connery's determination to stand out and be counted as more than just a comedy sidekick, a bland lover written out in the first act, or a rough-and-ready gang member in the company of the New Wave rebels. He wanted to be noticed, and one moment in *On the Fiddle* adds to the building blocks of his path to Bond. In war-torn France, fighting a German platoon in the forests, Pedlar stands and shells the Nazi forces with artillery fire from a powerful machine gun. His expression is stony and fixed. The moment isn't played for laughs. This is a warrior and, for a flicker of a time, a movie star in the traditional sense. It is no wonder *Operation Snafu*, once Connery had 'made it', sought to capitalise on this.

*

In 1958, after completing *Another Time, Another Place*, Connery flew to Los Angeles to appear in a film produced by a name that pervaded cinematic and popular culture then and now: Walt Disney.

At the end of the 1950s, Walt Disney Pictures were cresting the wave of changing American social and political attitudes following the Second World War and imbuing the values of the 'nuclear age' into their films and television shows through stories of fairy tales and magical kingdoms, *Darby O'Gill and the Little People* being a key example.

Directed by Disney favourite Robert Stevenson, and adapted from the original 1900s stories by H. T. Kavanagh, the film stars Irish actor Albert Sharpe as the titular Darby O'Gill, the playful old caretaker of a rich man's estate in a small 19th-century Irish town, who lives with his beautiful, homely daughter Katie (Janet Munro) and spends his time desperately trying to catch Brian (Jimmy O'Dea), King of the Leprechauns, convinced he will lead him to a pot of gold and riches. But when he's replaced by the handsome and kindly Michael McBride (Connery), Darby plots to capture Brian and gain three wishes to ultimately save Katie from an untimely demise.

Stevenson's film has, to put it mildly, become something of an artefact through a modern lens. Filled to the brim with Irish stereotypes, from the toothless villagers speaking in broad Gaelic, brawling and drinking in taverns to the quaint gender roles inhabited by Katie and Michael, its mischievous portrayal of Irish myths and legends has ended up subsumed in cliché.

One of the instances of violence directly involves Connery's character, who otherwise stands as an example of the traditional, stock matinee idol Connery had portrayed in *Another Time, Another Place*, only with even less nuance. Mark Trevor's moral compromise is absent in Michael McBride, who charms Katie, befriends Darby, fights, and bests the town bully, Pony Sugrue (Kieron Moore), and even sings a jolly Irish tune.

'I had so little experience singing that it was a nightmare to learn the song and go and make the record – which we had to do before we did the movie,' recalled Connery. 'Janet [Munro] and I went down to record it, and a guy called Tutti Camarata was the conductor, and there was this great big orchestra. Fifty-piece or whatever it was. I was at one pedestal and she was at the other, and suddenly it was my turn to sing and nothing came out. So we had to stop. And then after a few stops and starts they realised that I had absolutely no experience of what to do at all. So they realised that they had to take a recording and I would do it against the recording. And then the nightmare came when they said, "Now we'll do the other side of the record," which was a song called "The Bally McQuilty Band", which I had to learn there and then and sing. And with the help of some vodka and from Janet, we did it.'

While on the one hand McBride fills the traditional Disney role of the handsome prince who charms the fair maiden, Connery's visible brawn is used for violent ends in what acts less as a climax and more of a needless, audience-pleasing flourish.

Connery's appearance in *Darby O'Gill* further suggests the pre-Bond, pivoting zigzag of a career that was already international, spanning both British cinema and his burgeoning Hollywood profile, yet he remains an anaemic secondary presence in a picture which references little more than whimsy through the prism of all-American Disney. It is far from his finest performance, yet it served as an unexpected calling card for his future as 007. Dana Broccoli, wife of Bond super-producer Albert 'Cubby' Broccoli, asked to test Connery for *Dr. No* on the strength of *Darby O'Gill*.

Michael McBride, in that sense, serves as the flipside of the two characters Connery, in his journey to James Bond, inhabited across these early, pre-breakout pictures. The angry young man existed in *Hell Drivers* and *The Frightened City*, but so does the icon, the romantic ideal, the charismatic totemic force. Even in lesser pictures such as *Darby O'Gill*, pictures that would not signify Connery's journey as an actor in any way, those dualities also exist.

The last picture to place him in the role of supporting actor in a film reflecting a different age was as O'Bannion in 1959's *Tarzan's Greatest Adventure*, the latest in a running series of pictures based on the well-known Edgar Rice Burroughs creation, featuring Gordon Scott in the title role. Connery would play a boorish, drunken thief amidst a gang of bandits, who ends up dead before the end of the film, and while his role in *Darby O'Gill* is more substantial to the narrative, it still serves as a waste of his talents – though Scott was certainly complimentary about Connery and seemingly aware of his impending ascent to a greater level of global fame and reach: 'Connery was marvellous,' he recalls. 'He and I had some good giggles when we got back to Shepperton. They wanted to use him in the next *Tarzan*, even though he gets killed in this one, because he was very good. He said okay, but he had to do this thing for Broccoli and Saltzman – and that was *Dr. No*. We couldn't touch him after that.'

Connery would do his fair share of adventure pictures and period pieces across his career, but they would be on his terms. He might never have achieved this, however, were it not for another supporting role in 1957's *Action of the Tiger*, helmed by future director of three Bond pictures, Terence Young. Starring Van Johnson, Martine Carol and Herbert Lom (tethered repeatedly to Connery in this era), the film revolves around a young French girl attempting to rescue her brother from imprisonment in Algeria.

Connery plays Mike, the sexually charged mate to Johnson's ship's captain Carson, and again demonstrated the magnetism of his future role as 007. This further marries together Connery's duality between the upper-class redolence that the James Bond series so caricatured – from an American perspective – and Connery's working-class origins that aligned him with individuals such as Richard Burton, Richard Harris and Albert Finney, who were emerging in the same era. Young saw something else though in Connery, something that stood apart.

'He was a rough diamond,' Young remembered. 'But already he had a sort of crude animal force, you know? Like a younger Burt Lancaster or Kirk Douglas. The interesting thing is that Martine Carol, who was a very famous French actress at the time, said, "This boy should be playing the lead instead of Van Johnson. This man has big star quality."'

The movie was a damp squib. 'A *terrible* film,' said Young, 'very badly directed, very badly acted – it was not a good picture. But Sean was impressive in it, and when it was all over, he came to me and said, in a very strong Scottish accent, "Sir, am I going to be a success?" I said, "Not after this picture, you're not. But," I asked him, "Can you swim?" He looked rather blank and said, yes, he could swim. "What's that got to do with it?" he asked. I said, "Well, you'd better keep swimming until I can get you a proper job and make up for what I did this time." And four years later, we came up with *Dr. No.*'

TWO

THE SECRET OF THE WORLD

LET ME SET you a challenge. Try to find an obituary of Sean Connery that doesn't mention James Bond in the subject title, or even one that does not refer to him as 'James Bond actor' Sean Connery. They are few and far between. It is likely that Connery would have been dismayed at such a legacy. His relationship to the world's most legendary secret agent was extensive, complicated and, at times, mired in resentment and bitterness. As Michael Caine observed, 'If you were his friend in the early days, you didn't raise the subject of Bond. He was, and is, a much better actor than just playing James Bond, but he became synonymous with Bond. He'd be walking down the street and people would say, "Look, there's James Bond." That was particularly upsetting to him.'

It is possible, however, that Connery underestimated what his portrayal of Bond meant not just for cinema but for Western culture in the formative decade of the 1960s. It was as transformative and populist as Beatlemania, and as iconic – if not more so – than anything audiences had seen on film to date. Connery's arrival as the character in *Dr. No* birthed more than just another action hero, as Peter Bradshaw, the *Guardian* film critic, attests: 'It is the most famous self-introduction from any character in movie history. Three cool monosyllables, surname first, a little curtly, as befits a former naval commander. And then, as if in afterthought, the first name, followed by the surname again. Connery carried it off with an icily disdainful style, in full evening dress with a cigarette hanging from his lips. The introduction was a kind of challenge, or seduction, invariably addressed to an enemy. In the early 60s, Connery's James Bond was about as dangerous and sexy as it got on screen.'

'Timing had a lot to do with it,' explained Connery when asked about the phenomenal success of the books and films in a 1965 interview with *Playboy.* 'Bond came on the scene after the war, at a time when people were fed up with rationing and drab times and utility clothes and a predominantly grey colour in life. Along comes this character who cuts right through all that like a very hot knife through butter, with his clothing and his cars and his wine and his women. Bond, you see, is a kind of present-day survival kit. Men would like to imitate him . . . or at least his success . . . and women are excited by him.'

Bond had been written as a 'Hoagy Carmichael figure' by Ian Fleming – smooth and sophisticated with a deep seriousness and, indeed, a cruelty redolent of a trained killer. Fleming took the name of his protagonist from an American ornithologist who was an expert on Caribbean birds; it was a name expressly designed to be functional and unassuming, to blend into the background.

'I quite deliberately made him rather anonymous,' Fleming said. 'This was to enable the reader to identify with him. People have only to put their own clothes on Bond and build him into whatever sort of person they admire. If you read my books, you'll find that I don't actually describe him at all.'

Little of Connery's swaggering, towering cool played into the formative vision Fleming had of a character designed to be a proxy of his own post-war adventure fantasies. Nor did any of this matter to Connery when he auditioned for the part. With other actors in the frame, director Terence Young advised Connery to come in wearing a suit, but the actor turned up in what was described as a 'lumber jacket'. This immediate bullishness to do things his way, this unwillingness to compromise, would mark Connery's tempestuous reign as James Bond, which was filled with contract disputes, audible frustrations at the limits of the character and the repetitive nature of the films, and the clash between the actor he wanted to be – that hybrid child of the British New Wave, matinee idol and Hollywood contract-player – and the global phenomenon James Bond turned him into.

When the journey began, however, Connery had no idea just what *Dr. No* and *From Russia with Love* would do to his career, his life, and his entire future. A symbol for a generation was about to explode onto the silver screen.

*

Dr. No is both a film completely of its time and yet ever so slightly removed from the early 1960s in which it was made. This was an intentional choice made by the screenwriters Richard Maibaum, Johanna Harwood and Berkely Mather when they deviated from Fleming's source material and aligned Doctor No with the criminal organisation SPECTRE (Special Executive for Counter Terrorism, Revenge and Extortion) rather than the Soviet Union. This distanced *Dr. No* from being overtly political, although Terence Young's treatment is deeply rooted in the psychology of the continuing Cold War.

Ian Fleming's novel, *Doctor No*, was published in 1958, just three years before Eon Productions – under the joint auspices of Hollywood producers Cubby Broccoli and Harry Saltzman – secured the rights to the Bond series and, in so doing, created one of the most legendary working partnerships in cinematic history.

One of the reasons *Dr. No* stands out from every other Bond movie (even *From Russia with Love* which edges closer to the blockbuster template established in *Goldfinger* that would be replicated, more or less, for the next five decades) is that Bond is as much a detective as a secret agent. He is no Sherlock Holmes making incredible deductive leaps, but *Dr. No* has him investigating, questioning and steadily putting the pieces together of what No is doing, and quite how he is doing it, for the entire first hour of the film before he heads to Crab Key for the final act. In latter films we become used to seeing Bond slide from one action set-piece to another as he edges closer to exposing and confronting the villain, but *Dr. No* devotes an entire scene to Bond's spycraft as he places a piece of hair over a potential entry point in a room as a detection measure in case of an intruder. It does not tick off the more comedic Bond beats that would become formulaic, even expected, certainly by late in the Roger Moore era. It is less casual.

That is not to say that Sean Connery doesn't take to the role like a duck to water because, well . . . he does. Cubby Broccoli's wife, Dana, famously remarked that Connery 'moved like a panther' and there is no doubt that she was right; though intimidating physically, Connery moved with a lithe grace that fashioned the cinematic 007, immediately, into a different animal to Fleming's protagonist.

As mentioned, it was Connery's performance in *Darby O'Gill* that convinced Dana Broccoli that he was worth testing for the role of Bond. Cubby Broccoli rang his secretary and asked what else Connery was doing. She told him he had just finished a repertory run in *Macbeth*. 'Christ, we're looking for a James Bond, not Banquo's ghost,' said Broccoli. But he and Saltzman nevertheless agreed to the test.

Describing how he came to the role, Connery recalled, 'Broccoli called and said he had this Fleming film and thought I might fit the part. He asked me over, and after we discussed it a bit further I said I would be interested provided they put some more humour into the story. I felt this was essential. He agreed, then said, "When can you test?" I asked, "What test?" He said, "A film test." I said, "Sorry, but I'm not making tests. I'm well past that. Take it or leave it but no test."'

Connery's bullishness, particularly at the initial meeting with Broccoli and Saltzman, immediately endeared him to a role which would rely on charm and strength but which was also aligned to the changing cultural wind in the Western world. Under Fleming's pen, Bond represented a Britain clawing at the last vestiges of empire. There is certainly far less brevity in Fleming's *Doctor No* and Eon's *Dr. No*, and their alternative spelling almost underscores the contradiction: this film may have adapted Fleming's work, but it was approaching James Bond from an alternative vantage point, one aware of changing cultural mores. Broccoli and Saltzman were gregarious American moguls, big men who lived well, smoked cigars and, certainly in Cubby's case, had a deep love of British culture. With the Bond series, they stamped a definitively American feel to the way Fleming's hero was brought to the screen – which remains present to this day under the command of his daughter Barbara and brother-in-law Michael G. Wilson, who were both born in the United States.

'In 30 minutes, he sold us both,' said Broccoli. 'It was the sheer self-confidence he exuded. I've never seen a surer guy. Every time he made a point he hit the desk with that great fist of his, or slapped his thigh. It wasn't just an act, either. When he left we watched him through the window as he walked down the street. He walked like the most arrogant son-of-a-gun you've ever seen – as if he owned every bit of Jermyn Street from Regent Street to St. James's. "That's our Bond," I said.'

James Bond was a level of wish-fulfilment for Fleming, who took certain aspects of his own experiences as a liaison officer during the war when he worked with the Secret Intelligence Service (more popularly known as MI6), the Special Operations Executive (SOE), of which his brother, Peter, became a member, MI5 (the counterespionage department) and Combined Operations. Fleming spliced these experiences to create Bond, an educated operative who owed more to the colonial Etonian set than Connery's own working-class Scottish background.

Fleming wasn't initially keen on Connery's portrayal – which dials back the elitist establishmentarianism and injects Bond with a gallows level of dry wit – precisely because it was less in tune with his 1950s creation. Connery seemed to understand, however, as did Broccoli and Saltzman, that you had to *like* the man going around sleeping casually with beautiful women and executing people for hire if you wanted men to want to be him and women to want to sleep with him. Connery's Bond was cold but accessible, unflappably graceful and magnetic. He was catnip for the lens. 'He is really a mixture of all that the defenders and the attackers say he is,' said Connery about the character. 'When I spoke about Bond with Fleming, he said that when the character was conceived, Bond was a very simple, straightforward, blunt instrument of the police force, a functionary who would carry out his job rather doggedly. But he also had a lot of idiosyncrasies that were considered snobbish . . . such as a taste for special wines et cetera. But if you take Bond in the situations that he is constantly involved with, you see that it is a very hard, high, unusual league that he plays in. Therefore, he is quite right in having all his senses satisfied . . . be it sex, wine, food or clothes . . . because the job, and he with it, may terminate at any minute.'

Connery also believed, as did his wife at the time, Diane Cilento, that the script and story needed fun in order to move successfully from the page to screen. 'I took the role seriously on one level,' said Connery, 'which was that one had to be menacing, one had to be strong enough to do all this stuff, or seem old enough to do it. And the humour was one element that was missing from the books of Fleming himself, but which we felt was important to add in.'

Dr. No presents, almost fully formed, a post-colonial British hero for the 1960s and the remainder of the Cold War era. Bond is cool, calm, deadly and enviable, despite an emotionally empty existence filled with pain, death and, ultimately, sorrow – yet Connery was able to humanise the character, often with just the glint of his eye. It was partly this playfulness that led to the witty one-liners that would come to define the series across the decades. This was first witnessed in *Dr. No* when Bond kills his fake driver on arrival in Jamaica and deposits the corpse outside Government House with a droll 'Sergeant, make sure he doesn't get away.' Connery was at ease both with Bond's rough-edged urbanity and his calculated deadliness. While No may describe him as 'just a stupid policeman', Bond is also very distinctly a 00 – a trained assassin. The entire inclusion of Professor Dent (a character that doesn't appear in the book) allows the audience to see Bond's calmness under pressure; after a firefight, Bond breaks his cover and reveals that he has counted the number of shots Dent has fired. 'It's a Smith and Wesson,' says Bond coldly. 'And you've had your six.' That could, indeed, be the moment James Bond is born on screen – for all the charm, quips and heroism, Bond is, at heart, a killer.

This alone sets Bond apart as an action icon for the 1960s, and particularly in how he became a *Boy's Own* pin-up for a generation of hero worshippers with far less moral compunction than those who may have enjoyed the derring-do of Errol Flynn or Douglas Fairbanks Jr in the dawning age of colour, or the haunted, post-war nobility of John Wayne or Gary Cooper as the ageing gunslingers of the Old West seeking solace or redemption. All Bond seeks is the warm bed of the nearest girl, a dry Martini (shaken, not stirred) and the clinical satisfaction of protecting Queen and Country in glamorous global locations. What wasn't attractive about such a life? Beatlemania was less than a year away from *Dr. No*'s release. New British heroes were being born by the day.

The Bond we know is shaped in *Dr. No*, forged through *From Russia with Love*, and truly emerges in *Goldfinger*. In a moment taken directly from *Doctor No*, Bond is gifted his traditional Walther PPK by SIS's armourer (Peter Burton, a proto-Q before Desmond Llewellyn arrived in the next film), with M insistent that his trusty Beretta is a gun better suited to a woman (the film is much less sexist than Fleming's novel, but some elements still creep in). This is like Arthur being given his Excalibur.

James Bond is presented, right from the off, as a superhero. Not in the literal sense as portrayed in DC Comics or Marvel (about to make its stamp across this decade by creating characters that still thrive to this day), but still a character from fantasy. He is strong, witty, effortlessly charming and fights villains too cunning and strange for local law enforcement to deal with, all in exotic settings. He also appears, through *Dr. No*, totally unencumbered by the tragedy or pain seen in established comic-book heroes such as Bruce Wayne becoming Batman or Peter Parker becoming Spider Man.

'I think the most important thing in the whole Bond series, apart from Fleming himself, was Terence Young,' said Connery. 'I think he was the greatest influence. Terence had very much identified with the idea of being the grande senior; he was always a great *bon vivant*. He was very much up on the latest shirts and blazers and was very elegant himself – whether he had money or not – and all the clubs and that kind of establishment.

'And also he understood what looked good – the right cut of suits and all that stuff, which I must say was not that particularly interesting for me. But he got me a rack of clothes and, as they say, could get me to look convincingly dangerous in the act of playing it. He took me on the trip to get the clothes and it was a real eye-opener – the budget on the clothes was astronomical in relation to the film. But he was right, Terence, because there was a look about him [that we transferred to Bond]. The shoes were handmade at Lobb's, he had no cufflinks and instead had a special fold-back button, he used a very small Windsor knot [on his tie].'

'I had a very clear idea of what an old Etonian should be,' said Young. 'I was a [Royal] Guards Officer during the war, and I thought I knew how Bond should behave. So I took Sean to my shirtmaker, my tailor and my shoemaker, and we filled him out.

'He knew this was a big chance, and he made no mistake about it. But don't forget – he was a damn good actor by then. He'd had stage success; he'd appeared in *Macbeth*, and he'd been brilliant in a Jean Giraudoux play called *Judith*, which played in the West End for about six months. Besides, four or five years had elapsed since *Action of the Tiger*. He'd matured, he'd become a better actor – and when the chance came, he was ready for it.'

'*Dr. No* was a very, very poverty-stricken production in terms of finance,' said Connery. 'It had a $1 million budget that was then worth less by the time we started shooting because the dollar devalued. Amazingly, in fact, it came in under budget. I remember before we filmed the sequence with Ursula [Andress] coming out of the sea, we had Cubby Broccoli and Harry Saltzman out with spades digging the sand up to bring the sea back a bit. So we were hand-moving the sand; that's how much money we had.'

Connery also had to do many of his own stunts, and in one scene he was asked to drive a small sports car between the giant tyres of a construction crane, which very nearly ended in disaster.

'He was very lucky to be alive,' recalled Young. 'We damn near killed him. When we rehearsed it, he drove about five or ten miles an hour, just to see if he could go under it, and he cleared it by about four inches. But as we were shooting it, he was coming at 40, 50 miles an hour – and he suddenly realised the car was bouncing two feet up in the air, and there he was with his head sticking out. It so happened that the last bounce came just before he reached the thing and he went down and under – or he would've been killed.'

'If I remember correctly, going under the crane was Cubby Broccoli's idea,' said Connery. 'Maybe he'd paid very heavy insurance beforehand . . .'

'The film came in the wake of the kitchen-sink dramas,' reflected Connery later. 'So you wanted to have something that was still backgammon, chemin de fer, and good food and beautiful girls and marvellous cars and rather luxurious locations.

'He [Bond] was popular with men and women, which was kind of unusual. But anybody who said that it was going to be one of these immeasurable successes was lying.'

Dr. No marks the beginning of Connery's Bond – the perfect hero to fight the colourful, dastardly villains who lay ahead.

*

From Russia with Love, according to legend, was the last movie screened for JFK at the White House before he left for his fateful appointment in Dallas. He was already a fan of Ian Fleming's books and championed the source material as one of his favourite novels. JFK, it is alleged, even discussed ideas of how to overthrow Castro with Fleming. Why would a hero like Bond appeal to the President of the United States in such a way? Quite apart from his own charm and well-known reputation with women, JFK perhaps sensed an underlying Americanism in the character brought to bear in the transfer from book to celluloid, a move away from Fleming's distinctly British creation.

Between 1959 and 1960, amidst completion of his seminal horror masterpiece *Psycho*, the great auteur Alfred Hitchcock came close to directing what would become *Dr. No*, when the initial project from Broccoli and Saltzman looked set to be Fleming's *Thunderball*. Though he is associated historically as the director of twisted, often psychosexual, thrillers and darkly comic crime pictures, Hitchcock had directed *North by Northwest* in 1959, featuring Cary Grant as an advertising executive pulled, thanks to a case of mistaken identity, into an international espionage plot involving a sinister organisation. *From Russia with Love*, unquestionably, owes a debt to Hitchcock's American spy caper in how it captures the fading glamour of the previous decade. If *Goldfinger* serves as the first Bond film to truly encapsulate 'the Sixties' as an entity, *From Russia with Love* is the last to echo the 1950s in which Fleming first wrote the majority of 007's adventures.

'I had $2 million for *From Russia with Love*,' said Terence Young, who once again directed. 'That was a good budget, and it was, in my opinion, the best of all the Bond films – because it was the best of the Bond books.'

Dr. No crafted an espionage agent built from film noir: a glamorous, post-Imperial detective able not just to defeat the crimes and misdemeanours of powerful supervillains but, unlike his archetypal ancestor Sherlock Holmes, one whom the fairer sex found irresistible. James Bond truly becomes a spy in *From Russia with Love* and begins to exist as more than just man. He is becoming myth.

Connery, although he was in the midst of contract wranglings over returning to play the character, and rueing the fact he had signed a multi-picture contract, still found joy in performing in the role. 'I suppose the Walter Mitty in every man makes him admire someone like Bond a little,' he said. 'Ian Fleming told me he studied psychology in Munich before the war. Perhaps that's why he seemed to know such a lot about the hidden yearning in men and women.'

The character of Bond, remarkably, does not appear in the book until almost halfway through, with Fleming instead casting an early focus on SMERSH, the nefarious Russian spy organisation. Aware they are losing ground in the ideological war against the West and in need of a symbolic victory, SMERSH choose to lure 007, through the promise of Russian spy technology and the sexual allure of a beautiful woman, to his death. Chess is a visual and metaphorical theme throughout the film as the antagonists look to manipulate Bond to their will.

It is interesting that in *From Russia with Love*, despite the presence of Sylvia Trench (Eunice Gayson) – who also appeared as one of Bond's paramours in *Dr. No* – M's secretary, Miss Moneypenny (Lois Maxwell), Tatiana (Daniela Bianchi) and the Romani girls (Aliza Gur and Martine Beswick), sex often plays second fiddle to Bond, certainly compared to later films in the franchise, including *Goldfinger*. He appears chiefly focused on exposing what is largely considered by MI6 to be a Russian plot to discredit them, before uncovering the hand of SPECTRE as the puppet-masters influencing proceedings when he meets his nemesis, Red Grant (Robert Shaw). The detective we saw in *Dr. No* still exists here, tempered as he is by the old-world enigma of Istanbul and the *Orient Express*, where he plays his own game of psychological chess with Grant. Grant is SPECTRE's own blunt instrument, looking to settle a score against Bond for his defeat of Doctor No (this marks the only continuation of a plot line from one film to another until Daniel Craig's iteration in the 2010s).

Grant and Bond's relationship is, in microcosm, an example of what *From Russia with Love* is looking to explore: the enduring Cold War tug-of-war between equally matched superpowers at a point of American dominance. If Bond represents the Western establishment entering a new phase of social freedom, Grant exists as the bulwark of Eastern fear and repression. Robert Shaw essays a thinly penned character supremely well as an instrument of order. He might be an agent of SPECTRE but he is, in truth, an expression of controlled chaos, although Young's film dials down the psychopathy of Grant in Fleming's book (in which he is a serial killer harnessed into an assassin).

Guy Burgess and Donald Maclean were two of the most infamous British defectors of the Cold War – Cambridge graduates turned Russian spymasters who managed to slip away to Moscow having stolen an enormous amount of state secrets from the 1930s to the 1950s. Fleming was unable to fathom why they would betray Queen and Country for the bleakness of life beyond the Iron Curtain. Red Grant feels like an expression of that anxiety, and his moniker 'Red' is not incidental – he is a living, breathing 'Red Scare'. He is, in some way, unknowable and that adds to his menace as a Bond villain. We may learn that he escaped Dartmoor prison and was recruited into SPECTRE in the film (a poorer backstory than his chilling Irish origins in the book) but the effect is the same.

From Russia with Love begins with the 'death' of James Bond. We see Connery, in full tuxedo, Walther PPK drawn, stalking an enemy. This is Bond of the 1960s at his most virile and deadly. Yet he is slaughtered, strangled by Grant from behind, and cast aside. We soon learn that the corpse belongs to a stooge in a mask – part of a SPECTRE training drill for Grant as he prepares to take on the real Bond – but it instantly shows the audience that Grant is an enemy to be fearful of.

Grant runs counter to Bond in almost every way, despite how they might in other circumstances be cut from the same cloth. Grant is stiff, public-school educated and hard-edged. Connery is the effortlessly debonair, working-class lad play-acting at aristocracy, reflecting American values on the world stage as much as British ones while maintaining a unique distance all his own.

What Connery brings to Bond, despite these trappings, is a refusal to be straitjacketed by convention. Fleming sees a kinship between Bond and Kerim Bey in the book which is, to an extent, repeated in the film adaptation, perhaps seeing the head of MI6's station in Turkey and loyal ally (Pedro Armendáriz Jr), as an example of the roguish freedoms Bond struggles to attain.

For Americans, their new world began with the assassination of John F. Kennedy, just one month after *From Russia with Love* was released for British audiences to see. What followed was a decade of social and cultural fire, trauma, love, sex and death that eclipsed anything the 20th century – even the decades of world war – had seen thus far. The world needed not just wartime heroes, or post-colonial spies and detectives, but superheroes, larger-than-life representations of global confidence, prosperity and aspiration. Connery's James Bond, reborn after surviving SPECTRE's chess game, was about to give them their first one.

As Britain struggled with its waning global power, Bond became myth – the most famous 'secret' agent in human history.

*

Goldfinger presents 007 as the first on-screen superhero of the 1960s, and perhaps, from a contemporary perspective, of all time.

Bond might not have supernatural powers, but he has expertise, intuition and an aptitude for luck that goes far beyond mortal man. He often wears a costume, such as a perfectly tailored tuxedo (indeed he dons a white one for *Goldfinger's* pre-credits sequence) or a diving suit, carries with him gadgets and accoutrements that give him an advantage over his foes, and displays the swagger of a man who believes himself invulnerable. When the Mexican girl he charms at the start of *Goldfinger* asks him why he wears his gun, Bond jokes, 'I have a slight inferiority complex.'

For the first time, with this third outing for Bond, Eon Productions grasped just how successfully they had translated Fleming's novels into a worldwide cinematic sensation, and they played to the gallery in a way that neither *Dr. No* nor *From Russia with Love* had done. Screenwriter Richard Maibaum, who adapted Fleming's novel, summed up the thinking: 'We dared to do something seldom done in action pictures: we mixed what was funny with what was serious.'

Connery was by now completely comfortable in the Bond role, not to mention fairly chuffed about the financial benefits the role afforded him. '[Bond's] going to make me rich depending on how the tax works out,' he commented. 'Rich enough to retire, I suppose. I've a contract to do three more Bond movies in the next three-and-a-half years and I'm perfectly happy about it. It gives me security for that time and also leaves me free to make other films for a great deal of money.'

By this stage he understood both how to play the character he had established while also injecting a deeper playfulness and humour into the performance – something that had already been woven into the final version of the script. The film's director, Guy Hamilton, summarised the approach: 'Terence [Young] had understood a lot of things from the audience reaction to *Dr. No*. [Sean] matured rapidly, and the difference between *No* and *Russia* is vast. Myself, Sean and the team – we all knew what we were aiming for. Bond was sweetened, I suppose, by the perfection of formula.'

It was a formula that shifted, almost immediately, into a clear division between the films and the source material. Broccoli and Saltzman were already heading that way with *Dr. No* and *From Russia with Love*, but they stayed closer in tone to what Fleming had devised, even if they softened much of Fleming's 'sex, snobbery and sadism' (as Paul Johnson of the *New Statesman* had accused the novels of being in the 1950s) to appease a mass audience. *Goldfinger* represented the biggest change from book to screen, while retaining the core shape of Fleming's central plot, in what is arguably one of his strongest 007 novels and a compelling, pacy read.

The plot of *Goldfinger* reveals a significant anxiety about the state of the global economy, and particularly that of the British economy, which was in flux. Britain's post-Suez colonial power was declining and its status in the so-called 'American century' more diminished than that of the United States. It was experiencing a domestic boom that was driving low employment and a strong sense of social democracy, but on a global scale the country was in a slump. One can read Fleming's novels as something of an elegy for empire, with Bond as the dashing imperialist who would compare drinking unchilled Dom Perignon to 'listening to The Beatles without earmuffs'. Indeed, the inclusion of that line sits at odds with Bond's position as an iconic figure of the 1960s and suggests the dichotomy between the character Fleming had created and the world that he now inhabited.

This is clear in how Bond, and by extension Connery in his performance, challenges Goldfinger's insecurities through various means. Bond seduces the woman, Jill, who the villain has paid to appear as his lover, and exposes him as a card cheat. In a sequence taken from one of the strongest passages in Fleming's book, and which inspired a lifelong passion for the sport in Connery, Bond takes on Goldfinger in a game of golf, again revealing him as a cheat (if not openly) and besting him. Goldfinger later counters this humiliation by threatening Bond's greatest weapon as a superhero – his manhood – in perhaps the most iconic sequence in the entire

Bond series – the laser beam travelling up towards Bond's crotch – and inspiring the immortal exchange, 'Do you expect me to talk?' 'No, Mr Bond, I expect you to die.' (Incidentally, the lines were not taken from Fleming's text, nor indeed is the laser beam.)

If *Goldfinger* is the peak of Bond's swaggering masculinity, with even the affirmed lesbianism of Pussy Galore in Fleming's work (as homophobic as it now is to modern eyes) dialled down to ensure she plays into the emerging 'Bond girl' template, then the film is Connery at his absolute peak in his most famous role. *Thunderball* might be the actor at his most smouldering and, perhaps, most assured, but it also marks the beginning – mirroring Fleming and Bond's own malady – of his apathy for the role. In *Goldfinger*, he was still enjoying the work and finding a way to be enriched playing the world's greatest secret agent.

'In *Dr. No* the character was established,' he said. 'By the end of the second film, the audience had thoroughly got hold of him. After that the interesting thing was to surprise people who thought they knew how he was going to react to a situation. You'd play the reality, play the humour, have a bit of playful repartee with the audience, and do something unexpected. For instance, play up the ageing, the fact that the fights are getting exhausting. But there was only so far this process could go.'

Connery was becoming synonymous with James Bond in a way he simply didn't appreciate, particularly given what he had long considered the meagre remuneration for his services by Eon. (For Alfred Hitchcock's *Marnie*, he was paid almost eight times the fee he received for *Goldfinger*.) He was under contract for two more Bond films, but he was losing patience – rapidly. He didn't bother showing up for the London premiere of the film in August 1964. The honeymoon period was over.

Yet for the character of James Bond, *Goldfinger* truly was the beginning of his becoming a cultural sensation that threatened to overshadow the actor playing him and hinted at a reality no one at the time would have believed – that 007 would be able to outlive

Connery on screen. Fleming, who died in 1964 and did not live to see the final product, would doubtless have been less than impressed with the direction Bond was heading: away from the deadly, often humourless establishment figure of his novels and towards the kind of colourful, comic and outlandish superhero who confronted villains such as Auric Goldfinger or, to come, Ernst Stavro Blofeld, with their ever more earth-shattering schemes, festooned with an increasing array of gadgets to aid his cause.

It would be thirteen years before Carly Simon sang of the character 'nobody does it better' – a charge that would be levelled at Connery's successors – but even then, Connery wanted little of it. He wanted fame and fortune, but he also wanted respect.

Sean Connery wanted to be more than James Bond.

THREE

PROVING GROUND

THOUGH HIS PERFORMANCE as Bond dominated Connery's career during the 1960s, he made a concerted effort to avoid being typecast. 'I don't want to be Bond all the time,' he declared. 'It riles me when people call me Bond off the set . . . that's why I'm making pictures like *Woman of Straw*, in the hope audiences will accept me in other parts.'

Connery had such aspirations before *Dr. No*, but they were harder to realise as a character actor who struggled to break through in even minor British or transatlantic films, often produced, written or directed by minor figures on the cinematic landscape. It is immediately telling that, following the success of *Dr. No* and *From Russia with Love*, he started working with more varied creatives – Sidney Lumet (who would become a regular collaborator), Irvin Kershner, Edward Dmytryk and, particularly, the master of suspense, Alfred Hitchcock.

Eon Productions, sensing Connery's restlessness, wanted to keep their star as close to their chest as possible, even though Connery had stressed in interviews that he would play 007 for no more than seven films – a tally he stuck to, if perhaps not in the manner or in the length of time he originally envisioned.

Eon's manoeuvring was designed to maintain a sense of control over an actor already blooming into an icon rarely seen in the world of cinema. In turn, the films Connery made around his appearances as Bond showed a deliberate effort to evolve beyond the role.

His appearance in *Marnie*, Hitchcock's 1964 picture, showcased a darkness the Bond movies had hinted at but without the glamour or validation of working for the secret service. He plays Mark Rutland, an arrogant, controlling manipulator and a rapist.

A similar sinister vein runs through his role as Anthony Richmond in Basil Dearden's *Woman of Straw* in the same year. Heir to a fortune, he coerces maid Maria (Gina Lollobrigida) into seducing and plotting against his rich uncle. Bookended by his appearances as Bond, these two roles mirror and flow into one another, cementing Connery as a defiantly singular actor in an era of changing cultural and cinematic tastes. Connery is both Bond and what is often termed a 'character actor' at the same time, the powerful and seductive idol balanced with an edgier screen presence.

As the 007 adventure begins to ebb away, he displays a detached taciturnity in pictures such as *The Hill* and *Shalako* and appears in films that are a combination of period Hollywood adventure, colonial British affairs and even a European arthouse film, *The Red Tent*.

He is *more* than Bond, and in his 1960s offerings beyond the franchise, Connery is determined to prove it.

*

When Eon became aware that Connery was turning down roles within their company that were not James Bond, they asked him what director he would like to work with. Connery replied with the answer many in the early 1960s would likely have given: Alfred Hitchcock.

Hitchcock was, by this point in his career, a living legend. He was emerging from what many consider his golden run of films made in the United States; from 1954's *Dial M for Murder* and *Rear Window* through to *Vertigo* (1958), *North by Northwest* (1959), *Psycho* (1960) and *The Birds* (1963), the master of suspense was, without doubt, at the very top of his game.

However, *Marnie* has been described as both his last masterpiece and the beginning of his decline as a filmmaker. His output would exponentially drop across the 1960s and 1970s, through to his final picture – 1976's *Family Plot*. Beyond *Marnie*, critics rarely discuss films such as *Torn Curtain* or *Topaz* in the same breath as his earlier output. *Marnie* was a critical and commercial failure at the time, as the documentary maker and writer Tony Lee Moral discusses: 'Early reviewers declared *Marnie* old-fashioned and technically naive. Many were critical of Hitchcock's use of a highly expressive *mise en scène*, which included painted backdrops, the dependency of studio-bound sets, conspicuous rear projection, stylised acting, and red suffusions of the screen. These devices alienated audiences and critics alike, in what amounts to a constant assault on the boundaries of cinematic realism.'

Marnie rests as the apogee of expressions concerning women, voyeurism and obsession that Hitchcock spent a career – particularly during the years he spent in the United States – telling stories about. Obsessed with the image of the icy, beautiful blonde who contained hidden psychological depths, Hitchcock was drawn to the story of Marnie Elmer, as depicted in Winston Graham's 1961 novel of the same name. Marnie is a sexually repressed loner who robs Mark Rutland (Connery), a successful businessman who, on learning of her deception, blackmails her into marriage. So begins a tempestuous relationship based on control and submission.

Intended as a return starring role for Grace Kelly, who had appeared previously in Hitchcock's *Dial M for Murder*, *Rear Window* and *To Catch a Thief* before retiring from acting following her fairy-tale marriage to Prince Rainier of Monaco, *Marnie* was precisely the kind of material that was manna from heaven for a director of Hitchcock's tastes.

The director's fascination with American female repression is clear across his finest American-made pictures, as are his methods of punishing that ideal. From Janet Leigh's blonde thief being slaughtered in the shower in *Psycho* to Tippi Hedren being attacked by murderous avian hordes in *The Birds*, Hitchcock uses the extremities of his tense narratives to exploit the weakness he finds in this female ideal. Hedren, who suffered her own level of psychological and sexual abuse from Hitchcock while making *The Birds*, would take the role of Marnie and turn in a powerful performance of a tormented woman.

Connery, as Rutland, is the toxic and abusive figure who victimises her. Despite actively seeking to work for Hitchcock, Connery nevertheless did not take on the role sight unseen. He asked to read the script, quite taking aback Hitchcock's London agent, who claimed that not even Cary Grant had made such a request. 'Well, I'm not Cary Grant, and I'd like to see the script,' Connery retorted. Hitchcock blinked and duly obliged – not to mention providing a pay day that made Connery one of the highest earners in Hollywood at the time.

Hitchcock liked to take established actors with clearly defined personas, expected by moviegoing audiences, and twist them against type into amorphous and sinister creations. This was particularly bold in the Hollywood studio era, where leading men and matinee idols could make or break a picture. In Connery, despite being at the beginning of his career, audiences in the two years before *Marnie* strongly associated the actor with an urbane British man of action.

In *Marnie*, Hitchcock sabotages those audience expectations. Connery might retain his casual drawl, dress in fine suits, and stroll around the picture with rampant sex appeal, but the character he plays psychologically deconstructs, with savage brutality, and later moves to rape Marnie by tearing her clothes from her body after she denies him sex.

Connery was asked many years later by Mark Cousins what he made of such controversy and working with the great director: 'I don't think I was that concerned about these kinds of issues at all,' he said before swiftly diverting to the film-making process. '[Hitchcock's] preparation to moviemaking was second to none in terms of what he wanted in the script and what he'd visualise . . . I never had too many problems discussing anything with him but he would just say [affecting Hitchcock impression], "Oh, it's just a movie."'

In an interview following its release, Hitchcock said, 'The meaning of *Marnie* is that you have a girl who is a criminal but the circumstances that make her a criminal come from an accident in her childhood. It's an almost Freudian situation.

'The suspense in this picture is: what is the mystery behind a girl who is a thief, who is very strange? She cannot bear to see red flowers against white or any red against white. She has a mysterious background. And the leading man in the picture is interested in her because she is a thief and he wants to marry her and he is therefore strange himself. So you have two very strange people. And the suspense must come from "how do these two people get together?"

'I saw her [Tippi Hedren] in television doing a commercial,' continued Hitchcock. 'She had never acted before and I cast her in *The Birds* and that was the beginning for her. For this particular picture I wanted Grace Kelly, but because Grace wasn't able to do it I thought that Tippi could. I like actresses that have a coolness, an aloofness. I do not like women who have sex hanging on them like jewellery. I like to have it concealed like a mystery, to find out what sex is like underneath.'

'I think he only gave me two directions the entire time we made the film,' said Connery. 'He was very humorous. We had to do many retakes because he was producing and directing, we had technical problems with the blue screen and trying to do back-projection. And one time – I have a bad habit of when I'm listening to somebody with my whole attention my mouth opens – and I didn't realise I was doing it, and he said after the take that he didn't think anyone in the audience would be interested in my dental work. And I also have a habit of talking too quickly when getting really up into a scene and after the take he said, "I think we will go one more time and perhaps we'll inject some dog's feet," which meant pauses. And apart from that, nothing. He was terrific.'

The Bond franchise, certainly in the 1960s, had more than its fair share of questionable scenes from the perspective of sexual behaviour, but Connery's 007 would never have gone so far. Hitchcock sensed the potential in Connery's portrayal of Fleming's character for a level of coercion and brutality.

There is little doubt that *Marnie* would be attracted to a man like Mark. What the film observes, and perhaps why *Marnie* as a picture resonates more strongly in the 2020s than it has done in previous decades, is just how much she is broken down by the sheer force of male entitlement to 'own' her as much as consider her an equal. Marnie at one point compares herself to an animal Mark has caged rather than a woman he loves and Mark snaps, 'That's right – you are. And I've caught something really wild this time, haven't I? I've tracked you and caught you, and by God I'm going to keep you.'

'It's a story about a girl who had had a terrible time; her mother had been a hooker,' explains Connery. 'I played a very wealthy Boston type. She comes as a secretary and steals money and I go after her.

'It was my first introduction to the "perfecto" of Hollywood. I think they really wanted someone like Cary Grant. The hairline had to be perfect with the piece, the make-up guy had a special way of doing my eyebrows, and there could never be even a suggestion of stubble or having your shirt hanging out. That was the mode of Hollywood then . . . And in that movie we had some major problems because he was producing and directing, blue-screen stuff was not working, and we had to do things three times, and he had quite a lot of flak from stuff that was not going well, and the woman who wrote the film, Jay Presson Allen, a marvellously dynamic woman, she kept coming and watching, and I think put

Tippi off quite a bit. And it came out in a funny way – it had later recognition for being a certain type of movie.'

There are visible similarities between Mark and the character of Don Draper, the suave advertising executive majestically portrayed by Jon Hamm in Matthew Weiner's ABC series *Mad Men*. Draper, like Rutland, is dark, handsome and successful, and capable of capturing women in his thrall, yet *Mad Men*'s deconstruction is not of the women Draper psychologically tortures; it is of the tortured soul of Draper himself.

Therein lies the difference. This is not to denigrate *Marnie*, which as a film contains flashes of rather sadistic brilliance, but Connery never looks entirely at home in decrypting the magnetic power that his screen performance as Bond contains. There is a fearlessness lacking in his performance and a restraint that suggests Connery had, even subconsciously, one eye on protecting a character and performance that he was building his reputation on.

A decade later, by the time of *The Offence*, such fear would be gone.

*

In the wake of filming *From Russia with Love*, Connery signed up to Basil Dearden's *Woman of Straw* – script unseen (a decision he would later regret after being disappointed in the film) – in order to play the playboy nephew of ailing tycoon Sir Charles Richmond, who hatches a scheme with the beautiful hired nurse Maria to inveigle her way into the old man's affections, seduce and marry him, before plotting his demise and sharing his fortune together. The film was based on Catherine Arley's 1954 novel *La femme de paille*. The so-called 'woman of straw', common parlance in the early 20th century to denote a woman of loose morals acting contrary to common expectations of society, is Maria: she is the whore, the betrayer, who corrupts an ailing elderly man in order to be with her young, handsome steed.

There are many similarities between *Marnie* and *Woman of Straw*. The roles of Mark Rutland and Tony Richmond are separated by the thinnest of gossamer; both are charming, wealthy, psychological manipulators, even if Dearden's film lacks any of the projected forward-thinking nuance of Hitchcock's. *New Yorker* critic Eugene Archer was particularly scathing at the time: 'What could be more archaic than the sight of James Bond himself, Sean Connery, stalking glumly through the very type of old-fashioned thriller he usually mocks? That is exactly what we have in *Woman of Straw* . . . For, despite the fancy trappings laid on by the respected old producer-director team of Michael Relph and Basil Dearden, this handsomely colored exercise is the kind of pseudo-Victorian nonsense that Alfred Hitchcock long ago laid to rest.'

Yet the project appealed to Connery as it afforded him the chance to work with two actors of different kinds of renown. Gina Lollobrigida had risen to prominence in the 1950s and 1960s to become one of European cinema's most vibrant actresses and international sex symbols, rivalled only by Sophia Loren and Claudia Cardinale. After a decade working in Europe following a contractual wrangle with Howard Hughes and RKO Pictures that prevented her working in American cinema until the 1960s, she was edging towards the end of her career peak just as Connery was on the rise. He was especially thrilled to be working with Ralph Richardson, one of Britain's most established and renowned Shakespearean actors whose Falstaff was considered definitive, saying of the actor: 'An audience is never safe with him. You don't know what he's going to do next.'

Connery also felt comfortable with Dearden, who had directed him several years earlier, pre-stardom, in *On the Fiddle*, in an extremely different British film project. Dearden's film is, essentially, a stagey melodrama in which the audience struggles to find sympathy for the victim given how bitter and hateful Charles Richmond spends the entire film being. Maria, treated and portrayed as the harlot, is at the mercy of Tony's magnetism.

Tony is, ultimately, the villain of such a story, but Dearden's film contains the clear associations with Connery as James Bond without the same acerbic sense of distance that was apparent in *Marnie*. Connery might not have been ready to deconstruct that, but Marnie intended, at least, to try. *Woman of Straw* merely reinforces such toxic masculinity by suggesting everyone will be better off without the ghastly, rich old visage of a dying world, of colonial Britain crumbling around the Swinging Sixties.

If there was a level of real-world toxicity on the set of *Marnie* thanks to Hitchcock, rumours circulated for the first time of such issues around Connery himself on *Woman of Straw*. Lollobrigida was reportedly 'temperamental' on set, and tabloid gossip swirled at the time around whether Connery had slapped the actor for real during a scene where Tony manhandles Maria, less than impressed with her talent and her attitude. Connery claimed the slap was 'mistimed' and the truth will always remain elusive. Reports such as this nevertheless fuel the idea that *Woman of Straw* was buying into the blurring between Connery and Bond, which was happening in the world around the actor, to his chagrin, and becoming visible on screen.

Connery did not help matters when, in 1965, he gave a notorious interview to *Playboy* that haunted him for decades afterwards, in which he said: 'I don't think there is anything particularly wrong about hitting a woman, although I don't recommend doing it in the same way that you'd hit a man. An open-handed slap is justified if all other alternatives fail and there has been plenty of warning. If a woman is a bitch, or hysterical, or bloody-minded continually, then I'd do it.'

It is crucial to place comments such as these in the context of the era they were said, and Connery subsequently raked over the comments (while never recanting them) in further interviews years later, but part of the reason Connery thought in this way could have concerned his position, in the eyes of the audience, as an example of red-blooded masculinity. Well beyond *Woman of Straw*, we see instances in Connery films of him showing violence towards women – or intended violence. It is easy to forget that Connery rarely played entirely virtuous characters, with even the heroes he portrayed flecked with a range of issues from emotional inaccessibility to bitterness and beyond. Connery's Bond might be visualised as an archetypal hero, but he is in essence a cold-blooded assassin. Connery was creating his own archetype on screen during this period, with pictures such as *Marnie* and *Woman of Straw*, which bought into the idea of male strength and control.

'I have a temper, a violent side which I use as an actor,' he reflected years later, 'though whether it's been ammunitioned by childhood or other factors, I'm not absolutely sure. I only became fully aware of the unfairness of it all when I got out [of Edinburgh] and had something to compare it with. In some ways it's easier to relate to the things that happen later in life than earlier: setbacks, trusting in people who turn out to be absolute swine, the death of a good friend, the death of a parent. I know for instance that the death of my father had an absolutely devastating effect on me.' All that, he believed, found its way into his view of reality, and from there into his acting.

'They [United Artists] gave me all kinds of approval,' Lollobrigida revealed. 'Script approval. Director approval. And, of course, actor approval. Now they wanted very badly Sean Connery. "Sean who?" I asked. So several of them came to Rome to talk to me, try to convince me. They didn't say to me that he was not very well known, that he was a very good actor, or that he was handsome. No. Nothing of that. No, they said to me, "He's a re-e-e-al man."'

James Bond might have transformed him into a hero, but *Woman of Straw* was reaffirming Connery's intention never to be simply one, recognisable mould. One of his next pictures would confirm this, underscoring a fascination with exploring modern relationships in the fast-changing 1960s.

*

Before he starred in *A Fine Madness*, however, Connery turned down a film that would have cemented his iconoclastic role in the era's culture, even beyond the role of Bond: that of the lead in Michelangelo Antonioni's *Blow-Up*.

The role of London photographer Thomas, who believes he has unwittingly captured a murder on film, eventually went to David Hemmings, and the film won the Palme d'Or at the Cannes Film Festival, and inspired works as varied as Dario Argento's *The Bird with the Crystal Plumage* (1970), Francis Ford Coppola's *The Conversation* (1974) and Brian De Palma's *Blow Out* (1981). Connery, burned by his experience on *Woman of Straw*, asked to see the script as he had before *Marnie*, but unlike Hitchcock, Antonioni took offence to the request and cast Hemmings instead.

Film critic Roger Ebert described *Blow-Up* as a film about a character 'mired in ennui and disgust . . . Much was made of the nudity in 1967, but the photographer's cruelty towards his models was not commented on; today, the sex seems tame, and what makes the audience gasp is the hero's contempt for women.'

Perhaps Antonioni's style, his neo-realist lack of active direction for his stars and psychedelic focus on mood and artistic function, would have been a step too far for Connery. He never did work for visual artists who encouraged improvisation and expression over storytelling and structure, with rare exceptions such as John Boorman with *Zardoz*. Across his career he tended to plump for directors who provided a very clear, linear base to work from, often rejecting pictures that he didn't intuitively understand. *Blow-Up* was likely one such picture and, for Connery's career, whether it was a shrewd long-term choice is open to question.

A Fine Madness, directed by Irvin Kershner (George Lucas's mentor who would later make *The Empire Strikes Back* and, with Connery, *Never Say Never Again*), was no Antonioni masterpiece that would cascade down the decades to shape modern attitudes, in cinematic terms, to the 1960s. Indeed, it is largely forgotten, and perhaps with good reason. Kershner's film brings out the worst toxic qualities inherent in the archetypal masculine figure Connery was fashioning.

In the film, based on the 1964 novel of the same name by Elliott Baker, Connery plays Samson Shillitoe, a volatile, tortured artist living in New York's Greenwich Village with his long-suffering wife Rhoda, played by Joanne Woodward. He is being pursued by a debt collector for unpaid alimony to an ex-wife while belligerently battling depression as he struggles to find the inspiration to complete his latest poem. His wife seeks out psychiatrist Dr West (Patrick O'Neal) to try to cure him of his malaise. Along the way, Samson begins seducing West's bored wife Lydia (Jean Seberg) as all his chickens come home to roost.

When asked to conjure up an actor who might best portray a poet filled with existential torment over his art, Connery would not necessarily be first among the names one might suggest. But Samson does not exist in a world of Byronic romance: he lives in a sweltering New York City at the height of sexual liberation. Women fall at his feet at every given opportunity.

Seberg, meanwhile, is a symbolic representation of feminine sex appeal in the 1960s. She had been immortalised as a pioneer of the Nouvelle Vague movement for her appearance in Jean-Luc Godard's *À bout de souffle* (1960) and had dabbled in Hollywood productions across the decade before her political activism and affiliation with the Black Panthers saw her blacklisted as part of the FBI's infamous COINTELPRO project. Seberg apparently committed suicide in August 1979. She was found in her car near her Paris apartment, having been missing for several days, and her death was ascribed to a massive overdose of barbiturates and alcohol.

Connery's Shillitoe is a loathsome character, filled with self-interest and prone to angry diatribes, including against the agents of women's liberation who have asked him to perform and realise him to be a misogynist: 'Spine snappers! You don't want my poetry. You want my liver!' Shillitoe barks. He spends the entirety of *A Fine Madness* railing against the power and influence of women, while refusing the psychoanalysis his wife (who loves him despite his philandering and abrasive nature) tries to employ to deal with the demons within. This is hardly a direct parallel with Connery, quite happily married as he was at the time to his first wife Diane Cilento (the mother of his actor son Jason), but it suggests Connery was attracted to roles during this period that both traded on the James Bond persona he was all too keen to escape from while at the same time rejecting motions to unpack what the persona meant, both to him as an actor and to his career.

A Fine Madness was relatively well-received at the time, and *Films and Filming* even made one of the first references in print to Connery's unique accent, noting how it was becoming ever more engaging film by film: 'When you hear him, you can trace the story of his life . . . of metropolitan Scotland, the showbiz drawl of London, the transatlantic snarl of New York; without losing any of its origins, the accent gets richer and more delightful with each new venture.'

The glamour of roles in which Connery utilised echoes of James Bond were only part of the picture in how he engaged, beyond that franchise, with cinema in the 1960s. The international nature of his accent would be tested in roles that saw Connery adopt different shades to his persona – the taciturn protagonist, the ensemble player and even, in the rarest of exceptions, both actor *and* director. There was a space between toiling as the well-meaning comic foil in *On the Fiddle*, the solid leading man in crime pictures such as *The Frightened City* and the explosive, star-making success of *Dr. No* where Connery faced the possibility of career oblivion when it came to the big screen.

Under contract with 20th Century Fox, Connery had spent several years being recalcitrant when it came to accepting roles Fox attempted to place him in, and by 1962 he had not made one film with them. Increasingly frustrated by his contract with the company, Connery found himself cast in the first of two Second World War ensemble pictures he would make at very different points in his career: *The Longest Day*.

Directed by Ken Annakin, Andrew Marton and Bernhard Wicki, who unusually shared responsibility for directing exterior shots depending on their geographical location, and adapted with Romain Gary by Cornelius Ryan from his 1959 novel of the same name, *The Longest Day* tells the story of the D-Day landings in Normandy in 1945, detailing both the prelude to and aftermath of the climactic battle that was the beginning of the end of the Second World War, utilising a 'docudrama' style that was rare in an era of cinema festooned with battle tales from a conflict that had defined Western society in the 20th century.

Though *The Longest Day* benefits from a truly stellar ensemble cast of American, British, French and German actors, including megastars of the age such as John Wayne, Robert Mitchum and Henry Fonda, respected British thespians such as Kenneth More and Richard Burton, and even Connery's villainous future sparring partner in *Goldfinger*, Gert Fröbe, the film suffers from a lack of dramatic intensity. The picture aspires to evoke accuracy in its docudrama style but it is at the expense of any sense of character, despite the enormous and talented cast involved, many of whom were household names.

The film works in bringing Normandy to life to stunning effect: one tracking shot of Allied soldiers attacking a factory off one of the beaches is an incredible feat of golden era moviemaking and is rarely matched even now. It spares no expense (it cost, adjusted for inflation, a solid $150 million to make) in vividly bringing the landings to life, even while it refrains from depicting the horror of war in the manner of later films such as *Saving Private Ryan* – perhaps an acceptable trade-off for a movie designed by Fox to appeal to audiences of all ages. (The studio was losing colossal amounts of money during this period thanks to the nightmare that was the Elizabeth Taylor–Richard Burton vehicle, *Cleopatra*, a film which killed the Hollywood historical epic for decades to come.)

Connery's role in *The Longest Day* is minuscule. He appears on screen for less than two minutes as Private Flanagan, a soldier on one of the many landing craft on Sword Beach, in a role opposite Kenneth More and Norman Rossington which is comic in nature, despite the darkness of the setting, and feels particularly in line with the Pedlar Pascoe role Connery played in *On the Fiddle* – the loud, boisterous foil that seems so contrary to the deadly cool of 007. Flanagan leaps from the landing craft bellowing to the Germans shelling the beach, 'Come out, ya dirty slobs!' as bagpipes play, signalling the arrival of the Allies. It almost serves as a symbolic motif for Connery's cameo, and a sign of the direction his career might have taken if not for Bond – forever cast as the forgettable comic lunk, perhaps plying his trade more in television than on the big screen.

It would be easy to pass *The Longest Day* by when discussing Connery's career, given how slim his role is within an ensemble filled with stars of the past rather than, by and large, the future, but it is an important footnote. War pictures such as this were a dying breed by 1962, in the wake of epics along the lines of *The Dam Busters* (1955) or *The Bridge on the River Kwai* (1957). As American cinema took hold in the 1960s, and cynicism grew following the Vietnam conflict, war movies took on different complexions (Connery's small yet more notable role in a similar picture, 1977's *A Bridge Too Far*, would be one of the last black-and-white pictures he ever appeared in as the age of colour on both sides of the Atlantic became ubiquitous).

The Longest Day was a huge success and has gone down in history as, arguably, one of the greatest war films ever made, but in terms of Connery it is a paradox – a film in which a future megastar lurks in the tiniest and most anonymous of roles, an actor who would shine far brighter in cinematic history than most of those around him.

The Longest Day serves as an intriguing companion piece to *The Hill*, a very different kind of picture set during the Second World War, in which he would appear not as part of the faceless ensemble, but as the star. A film that could scarcely be more different from *The Longest Day*, but one also filmed in stripped-back monochrome, and for the first time one that gave Connery a role that was not stylised, flippant or contemporary, but serious, bleak and harrowing.

Written by Ray Rigby, based on the play by R. S. Allen, and set in the Libyan desert at the tail end of the conflict, *The Hill* revolves around a military prison known as a 'glasshouse', where conscripts charged with offences such as insubordination, going AWOL or petty theft are brought to suffer punishing drill routines in the extreme heat as punishment. Here, the sadistic Staff Sergeant Williams (Ian Hendry) makes the convicts repeatedly climb a large man-made hill at the heart of the camp. Connery plays Trooper Joe Roberts, convicted of assaulting his commanding officer and whose rebellious rejection of authority sees him clash with Williams as conflict breaks out for control of the prison and how it is to be run.

Aside from *The Hill* being Connery's personal favourite of his entire career, it also ranks as among his best in terms of execution and performance with his most consistent directorial collaborator, Sidney Lumet. Though already renowned for his adaptation of *Twelve Angry Men*, one of the greatest pictures not just of the 1950s but the twentieth century, Lumet was yet to reach his 1970s purple patch within the American New Wave of socially aware, politically driven cinema. In a way, *The Hill* could be seen as a companion piece to their later collaboration, 1973's *The Offence*, as they were the only examples in five collaborations where Lumet truly challenged the breadth of what Connery could do as an actor.

'In his early films,' observed the novelist and filmmaker Michael Crichton, who would later direct Connery in *The Great Train Robbery* (1979), 'Connery exudes a rich, dark animal presence that is almost overpowering.'

Connery discussed at the time how enthused he had been making *The Hill*: 'That's the first time, truly, since the Bond films that I've had any time to prepare, to get all the ins and outs of what I was going to do worked out with the director and producer in advance, to find out if we were all on the same track. Then we went off like Gang Busters and shot the film under time, and it was exciting all the way down the line. Even before being shown, *The Hill* has succeeded for me, because I was concerned and fully involved in the making of it. The next stage is how it is exploited and received, and that I have absolutely no control over; by the time *The Hill* is out, I shall be involved in *Thunderball*. You get detached; a film is like a young bird that has flown from its nest; once out, it's up to the bird to fly around or to fall on its arse. When *Woman of Straw* was shot down, I wasn't entirely surprised. But whatever happens to *The Hill*, it will not detract from what I think about it.'

Lumet recalled an initial conversation with his star for *The New York Times*: '"I'm going to make brutal demands of you, physically and emotionally", and he knew I'm not a director who has too much respect for "stars" as such. The result is beyond my hopes. He is real and tough and not at all smooth or nice. In a way he's a "heavy" but the real heavy is the Army.'

'I had lunch a couple of times with Sydney [before agreeing to do *The Hill*],' remembered Connery, 'because I didn't honestly believe that an American could make a film about the British Army or the British Services. I didn't think that they could have a grasp on the various idiosyncrasies of discipline in a British institution. Having been in the Navy myself and knowing something about the military, and having been exposed to the American side of the Navy, which I was when I was in Plymouth, I couldn't see how he could get such a handle on it. And of course, a rare occasion, I was wrong. He made an extremely good film, very well cast. But people tend to forget that that film was a total failure at the time. It was well reviewed but nobody saw it.'

The Hill boasts an impressive cast of talented British actors beyond Connery's star power who Lumet is unafraid to cast in challenging or indeed repulsive parts. Hendry, who the same year would appear in another acclaimed and challenging mid-1960s picture, Roman Polanski's *Repulsion*, and was otherwise best known for camp television work such as *The Avengers*, gives perhaps a career-best performance as the loathsome Williams, and Harry Andrews, in a role originally intended for Connery's later sparring partner in *The Offence*, Trevor Howard, is equally vicious as the commanding Regiment Sergeant Major Wilson. Connery is otherwise surrounded by stage and screen legends such as Michael Redgrave, and emerging talents including Roy Kinnear, Ian Bannen and Alfred Lynch, to whom he was previously second-billed as the sidekick in *On the Fiddle*.

Lumet's picture is the first film in Connery's résumé which truly distinguishes him from the role of Bond. Despite how intense, loud and expressly colonial it frequently becomes, Lumet's picture is an exercise in contained tension, repression, fury and failure. Just three years after the release of *The Longest Day*, *The Hill* displays the kind of cynicism inherent in military conflict and the psychological trauma of conscription that later films, grappling with Vietnam and the broader cost of the Second World War and warfare generally, would have built into their DNA. It is hard to imagine the existence of films such as *Platoon* or *Full Metal Jacket* without *The Hill*, which serves to typify the natural rejection of authority that was becoming apparent in Connery's own career choices and general conduct.

'He is one of the most complex men I've ever known,' said Lumet of Connery. 'He was using himself [in his character in *The Hill*]. He was really using his own inner self: it wasn't character. That kind of a rebel, that kind of totally balanced man – in the sense of "this is just, this is unjust" – that very clear line that that character draws in terms of his behaviour and other people's behaviour. And Sean is like that.'

There are no women in *The Hill*, and it is one of the first projects for Connery where he does not employ his natural, powerful charm towards the opposite sex to carry his magnetism. Roberts exists in the least glamorous circumstances possible, in which men quite literally die at the extreme whims of men such as Williams or Wilson, who barks, 'No one is going to pin a medal on us!' Lumet's 'glasshouse' is not only a prison for the convicts – it equally imprisons the guards – and *The Hill* explores this confluence. 'There really isn't a lot of story,' noted Lumet. 'It's all character – a group of men, prisoners and jailers alike, driven by the same motive force – fear.'

Connery was too young to have served in the Second World War, but as a listless young adult in late 1947 he joined the Royal Navy as a cadet, leaving Edinburgh for Portsmouth on the English south coast. He struggled as a cadet with what he believed was the incompetence of his superiors, the inherent class structure which came with British military service and his innate difficulty with figures of authority. 'I don't like anyone telling me what to do,' he explained. 'Put it another way, I don't so much mind being told what to do provided I have respect for the person who is telling me, but there is nothing more boring, more annoying, more maddening than being told to do something by someone who is incompetent.'

'Class!' he would say later. 'It's ridiculous to say there are no class barriers in this country. I try to ignore class now. But there were times when people wouldn't let me.'

In 1964, Connery's director on the first two Bond movies, Terence Young, was trying to convince him to work with his wife Cilento on what would have been familiar ground for his talents – *The Amorous Adventures of Moll Flanders* – following in the footsteps of Albert Finney's romping early 1960s adaptation of Daniel Defoe's other major work, *Tom Jones*. But once he received Rigby's screenplay for *The Hill* – which was based on some of his own wartime experiences – Connery was drawn to a tale which reflected his own deep-seated issues with class, authority and an archaic system of rule. Yet it was the Wilson role, later played by Andrews, that Connery coveted.

Though frequently we might associate Connery as an actor with action man roles, in considering the broader scope of his career, there are just as many instances of films in which he does not resort to violence, or considers taking up arms only as a last resort. For example, in *Outland*, he is the reserved sheriff on a deep space mining colony forced to protect his home from assassins; in *Robin and Marian* and *Cuba* he is the middle-aged man who seeks a quieter life; and as William of Baskerville, in *The Name of the Rose*, he is a reflective monk. Connery's career is not just diverse but filled with examples of stories in which he interrogates his own feelings concerning the application of violence. He and Lumet will explore this with a different intensity in *The Offence*, Connery's darkest hour, and he will later win an Academy Award in a more populist examination of the means of violence in *The Untouchables*.

Once again, as Connery with one hand looks to escape the shadow of James Bond, in films such as *The Hill* he is equally trying to understand and unpick what drew him, fame and fortune aside, to the role of such a questionable hero who became *the* pop culture icon of his generation, a role many people see so differently from what Ian Fleming wrote and who Connery helped define on screen. Perhaps part of why Connery so often rejected being defined by 007 lay in his disgust of the establishment James Bond reinforced with his defence of Queen and Country, reporting to the kind of old white men in rooms who, in other circumstances, could have ended up as twisted and embittered as the men Roberts faces up to in *The Hill*.

Connery did appreciate, however, just how much the success of Bond had helped him make *The Hill* in the first place. 'It had everything to do with it, of course,' he admitted. 'As a matter of fact, it might not have been made at all except for Bond. It's a marvellous movie with lots of good actors in it, but it's the sort of film that might have been considered a non-commercial arthouse property without my name on it. This gave the producers financial freedom, a rein to make it. Thanks to Bond, I find myself now in a bracket with just a few other actors and actresses who, if they put their names to a contract, it means the finances will come in.'

Lumet's eventual film presaged the filmmaking movement he would end up defining in the following decade, discussing techniques with Connery, including a forerunner to Steadicam which auteurs such as Stanley Kubrick would later embrace, techniques that broke from the mould of what people might expect from war cinema. 'We even use a special sort of film that gives a rough, documentary look,' Connery enthused. 'There are no little lights under your face to take away lines; in fact we use natural lighting as much as possible.'

What he describes is a verité style of filmmaking that finds roots in both the French and British New Wave cinema designed to depict reality, a style Connery – reared on the artificiality of the decaying studio system – would fuse with a populist one-man brand as he moved into the 1970s, becoming the kind of star who, even without Bond, could command the very creation of a film. He claimed as much of *The Hill*, and he would have to bargain with MGM years later over returning to the role of 007 as a means of seeing *The Offence* realised. *The Hill*, nevertheless, is an example of the kind of picture Connery wanted to make, free of contracts and studios working to mould him into something he was not.

Feted by critics, submitted as the British selection for the illustrious Cannes Film Festival, *The Hill* struggled commercially. Perhaps this was due to the ugly brutality of Lumet's subject matter; amidst the colour and boom of the 1960s, audiences were perhaps unwilling to engage with the dark truths about masculinity, war and empire that *The Hill* portrayed. Equally, audiences were unprepared, between the global sensations of *Goldfinger* and *Thunderball*, to see Connery so unlike the figure they knew – harder-edged, lacking the toupee that concealed his early bald spot and replete with the heavy moustache he would employ in most of his subsequent films over the decades.

Yet if Connery's fans, and critics, believed *The Hill* was a career left turn, they had no idea what was coming next – namely the only film he ever directed.

*

The Bowler and the Bunnet is a remarkable addition to Connery's career given its timing and how idiosyncratic and unique it is in comparison to the rest of his work.

A one-hour documentary aired on Scottish television in July 1967, presented, narrated and directed by Connery (and written by Clifford Hanley), it is a stark, black-and-white examination of the so-called 'Fairfield Experiment', carried out a year earlier at the Fairfield Shipbuilding and Engineering Company in Glasgow. Industrialist Sir Iain Maxwell Stewart's initiative was financed by George Brown, the First Secretary in Harold Wilson's Labour cabinet, who provided £1 million to enable the trade unions, management and shareholders at the company to try different forms of industrial management. The title refers to the shipyard managers who wore bowler hats while the labourers wore cloth bonnets (aka 'bunnets'), highlighting the class division between the two sectors.

'The idea was to break down the barrier between labour and management,' said Connery. 'It was way, way ahead of its time.'

Connery was, at this point, an established transatlantic star. The same year would see the release of *You Only Live Twice*, the last of his peak as James Bond, if not the final time he would play the character. He was now able to move between genres, be it the sex comedy of *A Fine Madness* or the Western period heroics of *Shalako*. The last thing anyone would have expected was for him to make an unashamedly political commentary on the class system in British society centred around the Clyde shipyards. He would tell Mark Cousins in 1997's *Scene by Scene* that he played football relentlessly as a young man in and around Edinburgh's shipyards and 'what that documentary did for me in personal terms was to make me realise that part of me belonged to that kind of background. I thought I'd left it all behind me. I thought I'd been liberated from that claustrophobic, John Knoxian narrow environment. Well, I had in a way, because of the lifestyle associated with the Bond films, but I know I just couldn't turn my back on it completely.'

Learning of the events at Fairfield awoke in Connery less a nationalism – though he would in later life become vocally committed to Scottish independence and back the party of the later disgraced Alex Salmond – but rather a personal sense of responsibility to the country from which he hailed. Early in his career, Connery had played several working-class characters, from Pedlar Pascoe to Johnny Kates in *Hell Drivers*, through to Private Flanagan, not to mention minor television roles, but they had been washed away by the glamour of Bond, or the affluence and sex appeal of Mark Rutland in *Marnie* and Tony Richmond in *Woman of Straw*. The higher Connery's star rose, the further his roles moved from his upbringing.

Connery's anxiety around this, of losing touch with those roots as class divides began to erode across the 1960s thanks to an incumbent Labour socialist government and the growing power of unionism in workforces, is clear all the way through to the press release he asked Warner Brothers to publish as part of his actor's biography: '[Not long] ago, the establishment was in complete control. On stage and screen, the monopoly was held by actors who reflected the fads and foibles of the so-called upper classes. An actor had no chance unless he was the stereotype gentleman. Ronald Coleman, Noël Coward, Rex Harrison and Leslie Howard projected this image. Great actors, I admit, but they hardly typified the average Englishman.'

In the same biography, Connery aligns himself as a 'non-hero' style of performer, able to emerge in the wake of a 'rebellion' against class distinction, a comment which sounds strikingly aligned with the class fervour of the exponents of the British New Wave he had skirted, as previously mentioned, and neatly in context with *The Hill*, a picture in which class rebellion lurked just beneath the surface. Connery was never part of the New Wave club, but now, with success at his door that afforded him a career beyond Scotland

(and the UK), working with the world's biggest actors, directors and most glamorous women, Connery believed that perhaps he *should* have been. That within him was a natural rebel against authority who did not want to be pigeonholed and did not see himself in the vein of a classic English 'gentleman' who was no longer representative, in cinematic terms, of the modern British male. This tracks with his rebellion against typecasting, particularly as James Bond, and his refusal to allow himself to be solely defined in such a way.

If *The Bowler and the Bunnet*, a film directed with charm and passion by Connery – even if it doesn't suggest a burgeoning documentarian or filmmaker waiting in the wings – was an outlet for a sense of rebellion against class, against definition and against the established English norms that threatened to straitjacket his career before the unique cultural tinderbox of Bond, then the saddest factor is that his efforts in raising awareness of his friend Iain Stewart's support of the Clyde shipyards came to naught. Just a few months after the documentary was broadcast, the government nationalised the country's shipyards and consolidated them into several centrally located sites, leaving behind Stewart's progressive management techniques.

One wonders if the disappointment of Connery's efforts to look at contemporary Scotland as a mirror of class struggle saw him retreat into exploring the past, as his career at the tail end of the 1960s would focus almost exclusively on building a presence filled with period detail.

*

Since becoming a star player after the success of *Dr. No*, all of Connery's non-Bond appearances were based in contemporary settings, save for *The Hill* which took place in the autumn of the Second World War, a not-too-distant historical setting from the late 1960s.

From 1967, that began to change. Connery would eschew contemporary-set stories for most of the next two decades, choosing frequently to appear in both British and American productions which spanned a range of genres and historical locations, with his infamous accent becoming an anachronistic trademark, whether portraying a 16th-century Spanish immortal or King Agamemnon of Ancient Greece.

The first example of this career choice was *Shalako* in 1968, an unusual beast for several different reasons. Directed by Hungarian-born Edward Dmytryk, it was an American Western co-produced as a British-German film. Largely filmed in the arid deserts of Spain, rather than New Mexico, its cast was decidedly European, including Shakespearean actor Jack Hawkins, comedian Eric Sykes (one of Connery's closest friends and golf buddies over the decades), Honor Blackman (her second film with Connery after her turn as Pussy Galore in *Goldfinger*) and renowned French beauty Brigitte Bardot.

Based on the 1962 novel of the same name by Louis L'Amour, Connery plays Shalako, a former US Cavalry officer who saves a hunting party of European aristocrats when they stumble onto Apache land.

By the late 1960s, audiences of Western films had grown familiar with two modern approaches. The 'revisionist Western' had emerged from the embers of McCarthyism, the 'Second Red Scare' hearings that took place from the late 1940s which saw much of the Hollywood entertainment industry persecuted and blacklisted. Pictures such as 1952's *High Noon* (directed by Fred Zinnemann, who would make his last movie with Connery three decades later) was an early example amidst a sea of traditional cowboy movies. Come the abolition of the restrictive Hays Code in the 1960s, which had for decades forced Hollywood into conservative, repressive rules about what could and couldn't be depicted on screen, filmmakers such as Sam Peckinpah, Robert Altman and George Roy Hill immediately set about recontextualising the established rules of the Western at a time when the civil rights movement and greater social mobility resulted in modern Americans questioning their own national mythology and cultural history.

The other subgenre that was changing the American Western during the 1960s was the so-called 'Spaghetti Western' – an Italian movement that was subverting the classic Western with its Mediterranean settings, violent amoral antiheroes and cheaper budgets. Filmmakers such as Sergio Leone, who produced what would become the seminal example of the Western for modern audiences in the late 20th century with the *Dollars* trilogy starring Clint Eastwood, rose to prominence in a subgenre that attracted both European and American audiences, and pulled in several American stars such as Henry Fonda, Rod Steiger, Eli Wallach and James Coburn.

It is easy to understand why Connery would have been tempted by a project such as *Shalako*. Here was something that would allow him to edge further away from the threat of stereotyping as the suave secret agent or ladies' man and position himself as more of an archetypal hero in the mould of stars he would have watched growing up, shot through with the modern sensibility of cultural awareness and the cool swagger of the Spaghetti Western. This could enhance his star power. Beyond Connery's portrayal of Bond, there is no more iconic screen performance in the 1960s than Eastwood as the 'Man with No Name' in *A Fistful of Dollars*, after all.

Unfortunately, *Shalako* turned out to be a rather old-fashioned and somewhat dull example of what the genre could do. There is little in *Shalako* that stands the test of time, from either a performative or directorial perspective. Unlike in *The Hill*, or even *Marnie*, where Connery was pushing the boundaries of how audiences might perceive him, *Shalako* is Connery's first significant, post-007 attempt to place himself in the standard vein of a leading man who could slot into conventional adventure fare. It was a misguided endeavour for two reasons.

First, Connery was already proving that he was unconventional, both on and off screen. He turned down overtures from Eon

Productions to play Bond again for 1969's *On Her Majesty's Secret Service* (more on that later) and agreed to *Shalako* for a hefty $1 million dollar profit share from the $5 million budget. *Shalako* producer Euan Lloyd had first courted the much older Henry Fonda for the role, but investors had little interest in backing a film with an actor considered over the hill – ironically, Fonda would turn in a remarkable performance for Leone around the same time in the far superior *Once Upon a Time in the West*, so he undoubtedly had the last laugh. Connery was not the tailor-made star for *Shalako*, and it showed.

Second, *Shalako* was a late example of a traditional genre of Western that was dead on arrival. Lloyd asked Connery to shave the thick moustache he had sported in *The Hill*, in *The Bowler and the Bunnet* and would carry into future films. Moreover, audiences were not even granted the pleasure of seeing Connery in a clinch with Bardot, arguably one of the greatest screen sirens of the age, when they *had* been afforded this when he was partnered with Lollobrigida and Seberg.

Connery talked about his experience working with Bardot with a cheekiness that did not necessarily overlap onto the screen in this instance. 'She was absolutely professional in everything she was contracted to do,' he recalled. 'The professional side was absolutely splendid and the personal side, we had a marvellous time. Very humorous. A lot of laughs. She worked hard. No, I didn't find anything extraordinary, and you know if I really did, I'd doubt very much if I'd say.'

Shalako worked to neuter everything audiences wanted from Connery and, more broadly, from the modern, introspective, sharper, and insightful Western, one that would challenge the preconceived notions of American mythology that JFK's assassination and the horrors of Vietnam had put in doubt.

It is worth considering that *Shalako* was produced in 1967, the very same year the American New Wave began with a period picture that understood precisely how you subvert and startle audiences who wanted contemporary storytelling – Arthur Penn's *Bonnie and Clyde*. Compared to that film, *Shalako* was a relic at least a decade out of date before it hit the screen, and audiences knew it.

Film critic Roger Ebert was unimpressed: 'The story shows signs of having been inspired, if that is the word, by Paul Newman's *Hombre* (1967). Both films deal with experienced Westerners who get stuck with the job of guiding a bunch of tender fools to safety . . . Connery's situation is simpler: he saves a European aristocrats' hunting party, I guess, simply because he's after BB.'

The film was Connery's first, true big-budget flop. The only time he would dabble again in the Western would be 1981's *Outland*, a much better film, and a clear example of how the genre had evolved with the times. Unlike the man *Shalako*, Connery managed to outlive the death of America's frontier mythology on film.

*

In July of 1969, America took one of the most significant steps in human history, and certainly for its own sense of national achievement, when NASA's Neil Armstrong took 'one small step for man, one giant leap for mankind' and immortalised the *Apollo 11* moon landing that captivated billions across the planet.

Though the film didn't emerge until 1971, once the global moment had passed, one wonders how audiences might have reacted to the next period piece Connery agreed to star in, *The Red Tent*, had it arrived when it was originally intended. As a film about doomed explorers seeking a new frontier in the inter-war period, *The Red Tent* itself was perhaps as doomed an endeavour from the start, although for Connery it was in many ways a loss leader; despite his top billing, Connery only appears on screen for just over ten minutes.

Directed by Russian filmmaker Mikhail Kalatozov and based on the 1960 novel of the same name by Yuri Nagibin, the film depicts the real-life crash of the airship *Italia* in 1928 while heading for the

North Pole and the subsequent effort to rescue aviator and Arctic explorer Umberto Nobile and others from the crash before they freeze to death. English-born Australian actor Peter Finch starred as Nobile, while Connery – in little more than an extended cameo – appears as Norwegian explorer Roald Amundsen, one of the key historical figures in Polar exploration, who despite the rescue of Nobile and others tragically disappeared in the *Italia* rescue attempt. His remains were never discovered.

The Red Tent is unusual for the fact that Kalatozov frames the structure of the film around Nobile's regrets regarding his actions during the mission and rescue as an older man, in Rome, where he imagines himself on trial and visited by the 'ghosts' of those who lost their lives. Through this narrative device, we then see events play out in flashback, though we must consider the reality of the 'unreliable narrator' to proceedings given the picture is filtered through Nobile's prism. Nobile himself, by then an old man, gave the film and Finch's casting his blessing; perhaps the story provided him with a sense of closure and absolution for his failings.

The Red Tent, more than either *The Molly Maguires* or *Shalako* before it, sees Connery looking to shake off the building blocks on which he established his fame. Amundsen is white-haired, bookish and calm in nature; indeed he resembles the character of Henry Jones in *Indiana Jones and the Last Crusade*, without his comic element.

Sadly, *The Red Tent* did little for Connery's post-Bond career. Finch, an established character actor who would go on to win an Academy Award for his excoriating turn in 1976's *Network* (for Sidney Lumet) before passing away unexpectedly that same year, is the true star in a film populated by European and international stars of substance – Hardy Krüger and Claudia Cardinale in particular. Here, Connery fails to radiate the kind of star power visible earlier in the decade. It feels almost as if it is a deliberate attempt on Connery's part, in seeking to distance himself from his own mythology, to actively sabotage his own career.

Though not a terrible film by any stretch, it is perhaps to Connery's favour that no one remembers the dour, introspective and haunting nature of *The Red Tent*, even if it presages the creeping darkness of the 1970s across Western culture when the euphoria of mankind's leap into the stars was counteracted by scandal, corruption and economic austerity. *Shalako*, for all the faults of a picture out of time by the late 1960s, did at least see Connery work to cast himself as the archetypal hero, even if it was never a suit that he wore well across his career. *The Red Tent* sees him play the noble hero lost to tragedy, but he possibly began to sense that, after James Bond, he would struggle to fit the kind of uncomplicated good-guy protagonist who was no longer particularly realistic for those times.

One exchange in *The Red Tent* does resonate. As the imagined Amundsen recalls the details of his own crash – the true facts of which have been lost to history – he describes how after the death of his pilot, a scarcity of food and not even a fire to keep him warm, he found solace in a book to keep him company. A fellow aviator, Lundborg, suggests the book is a theatrical touch.

'Oh, and for whom would I have been performing?' Amundsen asks. 'For yourself,' Lundborg retorts. 'But that's not theatrical, it's necessary,' Amundsen replies. 'The trick is to choose a good part.'

Is this Roald Amundsen talking? Or Sean Connery?

*

The Molly Maguires should have been the film, all things being equal, that transformed Connery into the post-007 star he wished to become. It was designed that way, yet it turned out to be far from the case.

Directed by Martin Ritt, who had not long ago worked with Connery's wife Cilento on *Hombre* (the kind of revisionist piece *Shalako* did not turn out to be), and written by previously blacklisted screenwriter Walter Bernstein, the film was based on

Arthur H. Lewis's 1964 novel *Lament for the Molly Maguires*. Set in 1876 – around the same time period as *Shalako* – it explores a very different side of America's post-Civil War national story. Taking place in Pennsylvania, Ritt's film concerns a detective, James McParlan (Richard Harris), who is sent undercover into a coal mining community in order to expose the 'Molly Maguires', a secret society of Irish-American miners led by 'Black Jack' Kehoe, fighting back against their exploitation by the wealthy mine owners.

Immediately, it becomes clear why Connery would have been attracted to the role of Kehoe. The man is a born rebel fighting against the imposed American structures of big business that took advantage of the working class, which is precisely what *The Bowler and the Bunnet* had examined from a contemporary Scottish perspective. It was a story based on true events, much like the wartime experiences in *The Hill*, with the Irish-American experience of the time described in stark terms.

The central conflict between big business and unionised workforce is distilled into the roles played by Connery and Harris – Kehoe and McParlan. The former represents the common man and the interests of the community, and the latter is the weapon sent in by the wealthy corporate entities seeking to protect their companies from the power of community action. Connery, unusually, accepted second billing after Harris to play Kehoe, keen as he was on a role that reflected the liberal, working-man sensibilities he felt powerfully connected to. It was, in a sense, the perfect part for Connery: gruff, impassioned, charming and unconventionally heroic, depending on your point of view.

Ritt believed that audiences, in failing to embrace the film, had not understood that Kehoe, despite technically being a murderer, was the true hero of the film: 'I wanted to show that the villain in the film was the informer, a man who wormed his way into the graces of his fellow workers and then turned them in. To me that is a villainous act. And in the American tradition, an informer is a villainous person, although those ethics have been somewhat undermined by the hysteria of the Communist scare.'

It comes as no surprise to hear Ritt voice these links to the anti-Communist hysteria that had resulted in the film's writer, Walter Bernstein, being blacklisted. Ritt had directed Richard Burton several years earlier in one of his finest roles, as John le Carré's Alec Leamas in *The Spy Who Came in from the Cold*. As mentioned earlier, it was almost an 'anti-Bond' film, even more than *The Ipcress File* in which Michael Caine played reluctant espionage agent Harry Palmer. Leamas was an over-the-hill, embittered agent in a grubby, opaque world far removed from the colourful exuberance of Ian Fleming's post-colonial heroic fantasies – precisely the opposite to what Connery did with Bond – and it leaves you wondering how different 007 might have been had Burton played the character in *Dr. No*. Nonetheless, Ritt believed, as Connery did, that the revolutionaries favouring unionised equality in *The Molly Maguires* were the heroes of the story, rather than the capitalists.

Richard Harris, an actor of Irish heritage, played what would have been considered the more conventional leading-man 'hero' role, but the edge to the detective as the spy who, come the conclusion, we are meant to consider a traitor is more in line with the equally unconventional career the actor had. While Connery could be difficult, single-minded and somewhat outdated in some of his opinions, Harris was a complete hellraiser both off and sometimes on set and, arguably, his career had peaked following his turn in Lindsay Anderson's *This Sporting Life* in 1963.

Harris is the actor who engages in the conventional budding romance with Samantha Eggar's beautiful local girl Mary, but their relationship has no happy ending. McParlan is scorned by the community after his actions lead to Kehoe's arrest and intended execution. Yet he, like Harris himself, is fiery and embittered. 'I'll see you in Hell,' is his final line in the climactic confrontation between McParlan and Kehoe, and it brings the curtain down on an uncompromising portrayal of hard lives in austere times.

Ritt's film, like his depiction of the Cold War, has nothing of the glamour witnessed in some of the pictures Connery and Harris cut their teeth on, in previous decades, and *The Molly Maguires'* conviction that the true heroes would be crushed by the forces of big business was too bitter a pill to swallow. Audiences stayed away in their droves.

A lifelong friendship with Harris was one of the few aspects of *The Molly Maguires* that came out favourably for Connery, whose experiment in recasting himself as a heroic period-drama figure had, at this point, floundered. Though his performance as Kehoe is solid in an otherwise workmanlike picture, it was one of Connery's biggest box-office failures to date – and he had failed to score on the big screen as his own leading man beyond the Bond franchise.

The 1960s had been a remarkable decade for Connery. Plucked from supporting-role obscurity and a possible career of primarily television roles, he had been thrust into the most iconic film role of the decade, one of the most potent of the century, and had surfed the wave of social, cultural and political upheaval in Britain and the United States to place himself as an international superstar. Tethered directly to neither country but just as well known in both, he had not quite escaped the shadow of the role that made him. He was neither forged by the British New Wave nor folded into the American New Wave, and as *The Molly Maguires* bombed at the box office in 1970, he faced a choice as his career and star power threatened to fade.

After *The Longest Day*, there was a risk that he might become a performer trapped in the studio era. Connery was *more* than Bond, but now the choice was simple: would he embrace the character that made him a star and return to the role everyone wanted to see him continue to play – or not?

FOUR

NEVER AGAIN

'WHAT WILL IT take to satisfy this man?'

It was a question asked by a source close to Cubby Broccoli, as Ian Fleming's already enormously successful series of novels had, thanks to *Dr. No*, *From Russia with Love* and especially *Goldfinger*, turned the character into an icon and Connery into a worldwide star.

Throughout the 1960s, Connery had flexed his dramatic muscles in a variety of roles. Some had been successful, some less so; all of them had been creatively interesting and challenging, but by the mid-1960s few had strayed far from the image Connery had cultivated as 007. *Woman of Straw*, *Marnie*, *A Fine Madness* – they all contained clear aspects of the Bond template; even *The Hill* – despite being a very different kind of film – had the same accusations thrown at it, in terms of Connery's performance.

By the production of *Thunderball*, Connery wanted out, and his co-star in *Goldfinger*, Honor Blackman, sensed as much during the making of that earlier movie: 'I knew very well that he was an excellent actor by then and could easily have been a very good classical actor. He'd already done lots of superb theatre work. And on *Goldfinger*, I could see quite definitely another Connery trying to get out, but he never let on.'

A major issue for Connery was just how much he was being tailored by Broccoli and Saltzman to prop up the character he played rather than the other way around. The emphasis, quite deliberately, was on James Bond as opposed to Sean Connery, even if his name was emblazoned on posters. They loved him as Bond, but would they appreciate him as more than 007? On the evidence of the other pictures that he made during this decade, it was a difficult pill for audiences to swallow. Connery was dangerously close to, if not already cursed with, the kind of typecasting he despised.

Connery compared fame to growing into a piece of merchandise or a 'public institution', given he had experienced everything from junket interviewers calling him 'Mr Bond' to fans scaling the walls of his home. 'Well, I don't intend to undergo that metamorphosis,' he declared. 'This is why I fight so tenaciously to protect my privacy, to keep interviews to an absolute minimum, to fend off prying photographers who want to follow me around and publicise my every step and breath.'

The end of Connery's life as Bond was very clearly in sight. Having completed filming on *Thunderball*, he had two remaining pictures on his contract. One was *You Only Live Twice*, which for a time he believed was the last Bond film he would ever make, and the other was *On Her Majesty's Secret Service*, a film that was intended originally to be the third Bond movie instead of *Goldfinger*. Connery made only one of the two remaining films he was contracted for and the story of why, and of the last two Bond films he made in the 1960s at the height of his cultural popularity, is next.

For now, Sean Connery was James Bond, whether he liked it or not . . .

*

As Connery geared up for his fourth outing as 007 in *Thunderball*, the popularity of the Bond franchise was going through the roof. *Goldfinger* had been released over the holiday period and had proved to be an enormous hit in Britain, the United States and beyond, with the dark glamour of Bond's world rippling across continents. Sales of Ian Fleming's original books were skyrocketing as fans looked to enhance their knowledge and awareness of 007's world, and merchandising under Eon's aegis was producing financial results rarely seen in the wake of a film before.

Fans could emulate Bond's sartorial style in specially designed dinner jackets, neckties and shoes, and smell like him with aftershaves, perfumes and colognes. They also helped John Barry's jazzy *Goldfinger* score and Shirley Bassey's iconic theme song rocket up the charts on both sides of the Atlantic. For children and teenagers, there were action figures, model Aston Martins complete with ejector seat, secret agent attaché cases with gadgets, watches, replica guns, drawing kits . . . and for adult drinkers, there was even a revolver-shaped 007 vodka pouring device.

Moreover, the success of the first three Bond pictures spawned a legion of imitators and complementary projects, in cinema and television, that sought to profit from the public's widespread interest in the world of espionage. Len Deighton's Harry Palmer spy novels were soon adapted for the big screen, with star Michael Caine delivering a more prosaic aesthetic to 007's international glamour – produced by none other than Harry Saltzman and featuring a soundtrack by John Barry.

Aside from the natural audience predisposition in the West for action-packed, exciting narratives populated by heroes and villains, what drove the boom in spy fiction triggered by the successful Bond series? A key factor was the ever present thread of Mutually Assured Destruction which hovered over audiences during the 1960s, especially after the Bay of Pigs fiasco and the Cuban Missile Crisis. The choice of *Dr. No* as the film to launch the Bond series was not a direct reaction to the near miss of nuclear conflict though; neither were *From Russia with Love* or *Goldfinger* responses to the assassination of JFK. *Thunderball*, however, is the first film to tackle the chief geopolitical anxiety of the decade – nuclear weapons.

In *Thunderball*, one of Fleming's most celebrated James Bond novels, 007 is sent to Shrublands, a wellness retreat in the English countryside, to improve his fitness by order of M. While there, he connects a fellow patient, Count Lippe, to a criminal organisation. Investigating further, Bond discovers Lippe's connection to one Giuseppe Petacchi, a NATO pilot involved in a plot to steal two atomic warheads under the auspices of SPECTRE. Its 'number 2', Emilio Largo, works in the Bahamas to plant the bombs as SPECTRE extort world leaders for hundreds of millions of dollars. Bond, with the help of Largo's lover and the betrayed Petacchi's sister Domino, must work against the clock to find the warheads and stop Largo and SPECTRE before their deadline expires.

The Cuban Missile Crisis occurred just a year after the publication of Fleming's novel, and by the release of *Thunderball*, in 1965, there was renewed anxiety about the clash between superpowers who were far from the point of *perestroika*. However, Broccoli and Saltzman deliberately avoided invoking the Cold War chess match between empires by depicting the villains Bond would face in *Thunderball*, even those tethered to Russia more specifically, as rogue entities connected to SPECTRE.

Thunderball, therefore, from a cinematic perspective, represented the biggest danger to date for Bond in terms of world-destroying stakes and high-concept supervillains. It was, as mentioned, designed to be the first film in the James Bond series, with a script penned by Richard Maibaum the same year as Fleming's book was released. A complicated legal suit subsequently ensued between Eon Productions and film producer Kevin McClory that resulted in the film rights to just *Thunderball* as a story, including the characters within, slipping away from Broccoli and Saltzman into the hands of McClory. It forced them to engage directly with McClory, after the success of *Goldfinger*, to make *Thunderball* 'in house' rather than have McClory produce a rival Bond picture with a different lead playing 007.

Much has been written – entire books, no less – about the complex legal tussle between Eon and McClory that started with *Thunderball* and lasted for decades. Ultimately, both parties came together to make Fleming's grandest 007 novel at the zenith of the series' popularity within the 1960s. For Connery, however, the sheen of playing the most popular character in cinema history had worn off. As he described, rather pompously: 'The problem is to get across the fact, without breaking your arse, that one is not Bond, that one was functioning reasonably well before Bond, and that one is going to function reasonably well after Bond. There are a lot of things I did before Bond – like playing the classics on stage – that don't seem to get publicised. So, you see, this Bond image is a problem in a way and a bit of a bore, but one has just got to live with it.'

Yet, in many ways, *Thunderball* presents Connery's Bond at the very height of his prowess and allure, before he began to look tired and just a little past-it come *You Only Live Twice* – even if the film itself was unable to capture the swagger and insouciance he would display in *Goldfinger*. Witness him approaching the Bahamian casino as John Barry's elegant 'Mr Kiss Kiss Bang Bang' theme drifts across the water, in full tuxedo, stepping off the boat with a power and cool that would be near impossible to replicate. A restlessness nonetheless accompanies his performance as Bond in *Thunderball* that becomes apparent in several ways.

Though we witnessed misogyny in *Goldfinger*, at numerous points Bond's sexual magnetism and charm morphs into a distinctively aggressive control of the woman he less romances and more overcomes in *Thunderball*. He sexually harasses Shrublands health worker Patricia Fearing (Molly Peters) into sex under threat of exposing her hand in his treatment of Lippe. He coldly utilises villain Fiona Volpe (Luciana Paluzzi) for sex to gain information, in the first instance on screen where he seduces a woman he knows to be corrupt for his own gain. His romance with the main 'Bond girl', Domino Petacchi (Claudine Auger), is built on a broader need to inveigle himself with Largo, and she is one of the most psychologically vulnerable woman Bond encounters – a more complex Honey Ryder.

Can we correlate this casual sexism with the countercultural revolution that was underway? Terence Young described Bond girls of the 1960s as 'women of the nuclear age, freer and able to make love when they want to without worrying about it'. Are the women in *Thunderball* truly exercising their own agency in an era of social and sexual change? Or does Connery's Bond represent in this film, more perhaps than in any of his others, a colonial-era 'superhero' keeping women sexually subservient to his whims as he helps an assortment of old white power brokers maintain the global order that SPECTRE seeks to snatch away? The fusion of actor and character in the mind of fans that so infuriated Connery would only continue to be amplified thanks to the misogynistic comments he would make while filming *Thunderball* to *Playboy*, and there is a sense that Connery's frustration during *Thunderball* ripples over into the character.

The film itself hints that Connery's tenure as Bond, perhaps even the character, cannot last forever. The pre-titles sequence, arguably the most comic-book and child-friendly introduction to the films to date, opens on a coffin and the death of a man with the initials 'JB' before Bond straps on a jetpack to escape gun-toting bad guys. This does not come from Fleming, who would experiment with the 'death' of Bond in *You Only Live Twice* instead, but *Thunderball* – even unconsciously – seems to understand that, five pictures in, Connery will not be around forever, even as he sits as comfortably in the tuxedo of 007 as he ever will. This feels like a different approach to the 'death' of Bond we witnessed at the beginning of *From Russia with Love*. This suggests less the demise of one incarnation and the birth of another and instead the acceptance that Connery's Bond might be poised for his final mission.

'Mind if my friend sits this one out? She's just dead!' Bond quips after allowing Volpe to fatally take bullets meant for him, in a memorably callous moment of disregard for another woman who has died to save Bond. 'Just dead' certainly reflected Connery's approach to Bond at the time, even while the series and his performance were at the height of their cultural and commercial popularity. Connery was, nevertheless, said to be charming, patient and indeed comical on set, performing Groucho Marx-style walks and generally larking about. While filming, he seemed to be in a positive state of mind concerning the future too, as he discussed in an interview at the time when asked what he did when not making movies: 'I don't know. When I'm not working, I seem to be trying to make some preparations for work. I really have to be involved in work or something physical . . . I've now taken up golf, which seems to be a splendid compensation. I normally play soccer, but I can't always find 21 other fellows who want to play. And I play chess and I read a lot, you know. And I have a fair collection of records . . .'

Nevertheless, a torpor about 007 was beginning to form, and as Connery took roles beyond Bond that stretched him, the writing was on the wall.

*

If we are to accept the history of James Bond on screen in 'official' terms, representing only the series produced by Eon Productions, then 1967 saw only one 007 film – what for a while would be Connery's final performance as the character – in *You Only Live Twice*.

That, however, is not quite the whole story. The year 1967 provided two films that owed a great deal to the James Bond character and franchise while being wilfully distinct from what audiences had come to know through Connery's depiction of the character: both would define the rampant 'Bondmania' of the Swinging Sixties.

Casino Royale, the first Bond novel written by Fleming, in 1953, had only ever been adapted as a live television recording, in 1954, starring American actor Barry Nelson (technically the first actor to play 007), as well as a radio adaptation with *Blockbusters'* own Bob Holness in the main role, and the rights to produce Fleming's debut Bond story were not owned by Eon Productions. Fleming had earlier sold the rights directly to Gregory Ratoff, a producer of Russian extraction, whose widow, on his death in 1960, passed the rights to make *Casino Royale* to Charles K. Feldman. In 1967, Feldman mounted an adaptation so unusual it would stray close to the realm of apocrypha.

Aware that Connery's portrayal of the character was a cultural and commercial sensation, Feldman had unsuccessfully attempted to negotiate to produce the film with Eon as a further Connery vehicle, but Connery's response was appropriately abrupt. 'I'd only do it for a million dollars,' he stated bluntly. Too high a price, so that put paid to Feldman's aspirations. He decided that seven 007s would be better than one and crafted a psychedelic satire from Fleming's straight-backed story. Adorned with recognisable faces as versions of Bond, including David Niven, Peter Sellers and Woody Allen, not to mention a range of supporting actors from America and Europe (including Orson Welles as villain Le Chiffre), it stands as a colourful example of 1960s excess. It also establishes that, by the late 1960s, James Bond was now ubiquitous enough as a cinematic presence to be spoofed and lampooned.

Though in almost no way loyal to Fleming's source material, *Casino Royale* is nonetheless evidence of just how deeply Connery's portrayal of Bond had permeated the cultural subtext of the 1960s, and although Feldman might have aspired to position it as a *Dr. Strangelove*-esque satire, the film falls much closer to a surreal portrait of everything Bond as a character represented. Cultural historian Robert von Dassanowsky goes as far as to suggest that *Casino Royale* is a 'metafilm' that comments on the style of the 'real' Bond films, 'which, beginning with *Goldfinger* and *You Only*

Live Twice, updated and altered Fleming's original novels until only character names and vague plot directions were employed. Ultimately, even the titles ran out, but this 1967 film is far more *Weltanschauung* than spy narrative. Feldman, in his belief that he could make a Bond to break all banks, went to extremes to cover up the lack of two major elements in this "Bond" film – Sean Connery and the James Bond theme. Instead, the film was stocked with in-stars, in-jokes, and an in-style that would surpass not only the grandeur of the original series and its penchant for outrageous cold-warrior escapades, but in turn, influence the megalomania of the "real" Bond series.'

If *Casino Royale*, released just two months before *You Only Live Twice*, presents the scope of Bondmania in American terms, and how Hollywood processed the phenomenon, in Europe during the same year, we see an altogether different lampoon of Connery's 007 which, in terms of Connery himself, cut much closer to home. The film was *Operation Kid Brother* aka . . . *O.K. Connery*.

Whereas Sean had spent the 1960s travelling the globe as the biggest movie star on the planet, his younger brother Neil remained in Edinburgh, working as a plasterer. The story of how Neil, who had never acted a day in his life, came to headline an Italian-made spy caper playing a facsimile of James Bond, is genuinely remarkable, even decades on.

Having been sacked for losing his tools, Neil ended up – thanks to his association with his famous brother – discussing it on British radio, which Terence Young heard. Struck by how similar Neil sounded to Sean, he said as much to Italian film producer and friend Dario Sabatello, inadvertently leading Neil into an unusual, if not ultimately life-changing, opportunity. Sabatello offered Neil a $5,000 lump sum to headline what would become *Operation Kid Brother*. Given Neil had been earning £7 to £8 an hour as a plasterer, and wasn't even earning that now, it was a no-brainer. He said yes.

The film's director, Alberto De Martino, has talked about the unexpected nature of Neil's casting: 'This film is a real miracle, because we had to meet the almost impossible challenge of using poor Neil Connery. Not only was he the opposite of an actor, he looked like nothing. My father, who was a make-up artist, took care of him, and did it again from head to toe. He was losing his hair, so we put a wig on him; he had bad teeth, so he had dentures; he had a dull face, they put a beard on him; he had small eyes that gave nothing on the screen, we put adhesives on his temples to pull his eyes out and make them stand out more . . . We had invented him a character of a hypnotist doctor: he had therefore only to wave his hands to hypnotise people, and he spoke as little as possible. Other than that, he was doing what he could, but I consider it a tour de force to have managed to make the film stand up.'

Operation Kid Brother was also titled *O.K. Connery* in Italy because it was a term that the producers kept using when Neil was doing his screen test, and it stuck; indeed, it was even fashioned into the title of a warbler sung by Christy and composed by the great Ennio Morricone called 'Man for Me (O.K. Connery)', which, it has to be said, is quite the ear worm. Nonetheless, the rationale for using such a title speaks to how powerfully Sean Connery had broken through into the global cultural consciousness. The blur between actor and character is visible in a film where Neil plays a plastic surgeon with his own name, and frequent allusions are made to his 'brother'.

O.K. Connery is even more of a cinematic footnote than Feldman's adaptation of *Casino Royale* the same year, but it was only possible to make due to the star power of Connery. Sabatello even managed to marshal numerous actors from the Eon Bond series to cross over and play facsimiles of the roles they portrayed previously or were still playing – Bernard Lee and Lois Maxwell essentially portray M and Moneypenny twice in the same year. Indeed, Maxwell claimed she had a bigger pay day on the Italian film than all of her Eon appearances combined over twenty-five years. Moreover, Daniela Bianchi (Tatiana Romanova in *From Russia with Love*), Anthony Dawson (the voice of Blofeld in several films) and Adolfo Celi (villain Emilio Largo in *Thunderball*) all appeared and – bizarrely for Bianchi and Celi, who were Italian – ended up dubbed.

Connery, to put it mildly, was unhappy about the entire project and, no doubt outraged as Lee, towards the end of the film, speaks dialogue to Neil's Bond such as: 'You were fantastic . . . you should have seen your brother's face when he heard of it.' Connery understood that he was dealing with a blatant attempt to cash in on his fame, after Sabatello had been unsuccessful in luring the man himself to appear in an Italian-made version of the Bond series. 'Neil is a plasterer, not an actor,' he later reflected. 'Still, they put him in a film over in Rome – gave him the lead, too! It's a typical example of the way some people do things. It doesn't matter whether the person can act or not. What matters is one happens to be one's brother.'

Not that Bond producer Harry Saltzman was especially concerned by such ploys: 'We have stopped several kinds of imitations that were harmful already. We try to protect ourselves. There are nine Italian motion pictures being made, quickies, they're made in ten to twelve days. They don't hurt us – people know they aren't Bond pictures.'

It did, however, matter to Connery, who was already determined that the global perception of him as little more than James Bond should come to an end. His sixth outing as 007, in *You Only Live Twice*, would be, he announced at the time, his last. 'There's no time for anything else. And I spent a session in the hospital between 'em once. [He injured his back during a fight scene with Oddjob.] I don't intend to do that again.'

He was still contracted to appear in two more Bond pictures after *Thunderball*, but along with a reduced schedule, Eon allowed him out of the contract in the hope that they could tempt him into a seventh film with a deal more to his liking. The intended plan, to film *On Her Majesty's Secret Service* after *Thunderball* – which would have been in line with the Fleming novels – was ditched to make a film described as 'less gimmicky and more realistic' by Broccoli, a film grounded in a deeper sense of humanity than *Thunderball* or *Goldfinger* before it. This was, in no small part, a measure of appeasement to keep Connery in a role he was vociferously looking to detach from, frustrated, for one thing, by the intrusion on his personal life, which his wife Diane described as living inside a 'frenzied fishbowl'. 'It's an invasion of one's privacy,' he ranted, 'and I don't believe in any of that rubbish about the price of fame and all that sort of jazz.'

You Only Live Twice, ultimately, ended up much less grounded than Connery or anyone else might have envisaged, as the Bond franchise reacted to the growing cinematic reality that bigger meant better. A decade before the proliferation of what we now understand as the blockbuster, *You Only Live Twice* raised the stakes for 007 and the franchise to a degree greater even than the stolen nuclear warheads of *Thunderball*. It became the signature example of Cold War tension, pitting superpower against superpower.

After faking his death in Hong Kong, Bond is dispatched by M to solve the mystery of who is capturing American and Russian orbital spacecraft, heightening tensions between the two superpowers. This takes Bond principally to Japan and the corporate Osato organisation, into partnership with a capable Japanese agent called Aki (Akiko Wakabayashi) and, ultimately, on the trail of a resurgent SPECTRE and the man behind the plot, Ernst Stavro Blofeld (Donald Pleasence). Along the way, Bond immerses himself in Japanese culture and falls for the charms of local girl Kissy Suzuki (Mie Hama), before seeking out Blofeld inside his hollowed-out volcano den.

Though it does not stand as the greatest Bond film of all time, *You Only Live Twice* remains one of the most influential. Pleasence's Blofeld became the Machiavellian weasel template for decades' worth of Bond villains; Ken Adam's Oscar-winning production design was an astounding feat; Lewis Gilbert would largely repeat the same narrative a decade later in directing Roger

Moore in *The Spy Who Loved Me*, as would Roger Spottiswoode twenty years after that in *Tomorrow Never Dies*. *No Time to Die* borrows numerous elements from both the film and Fleming's original source material, including a poison garden and an island lair, not to mention Bond's siring of offspring.

Eon, for the first time here, chose to jettison a great deal of Fleming's novel, in part for practical reasons. Set directly after *On Her Majesty's Secret Service*, it features emotional undercurrents and certain characters – such as henchwoman Irma Bunt – from that previous book. The choice also reflects the growing political anxieties of the era. Broccoli and Saltzman chose to ramp up the storytelling while Fleming's novel pulled it down; his *You Only Live Twice* is one of the most poignant and low-key Bond novels, jettisoning much of the global travelogue as 007 embraces Japanese culture after the murder of his wife, befriends Tiger Tanaka, and even conceives a child with Kissy as he trains to infiltrate Blofeld's 'Garden of Death' within the ancient Japanese castle he has bought. He is on a mission to gain revenge. It even ends on a cliff-hanger that the Bond series has not dared to attempt – 007, unable to remember who he is, heading off to Russia for answers.

You Only Live Twice instead chooses to place Bond within Blofeld's manipulation of the Cold War chessboard for his own ends. Space – just two years after the first spacewalk of astronauts in 1965 – and just two years ahead of the *Apollo 11* mission to the moon – becomes the staging ground for nuclear annihilation. Though never explicitly stated in the script, it is heavily intimated that Blofeld is being bankrolled by Red China, keen to see the Americans and Russians destroy each other to their advantage. Beyond their manipulations in *Goldfinger*, this is the only point in the 1960s that we see the Bond series attempting to depict the Chinese as a shadowy menace employing agents of chaos such as SPECTRE to tip the balance of the Cold War.

This was the last time for a decade that the Bond franchise attempted to portray the ideological struggle of the Cold War in such stark Third World War-baiting terms, and by the time the Roger Moore era returned to those waters it would increasingly frame the conflict in the vein of escalating *détente* rather than growing fear. As the decade came to an end, and the immediate effect of both the Cuban Missile Crisis and JFK's death started to wane, the Bond series edged further into colourful adventures designed to reflect cinematic trends rather than reflect the state of world politics.

Connery perhaps sensed this change and wanted little part of it. There is an irony that the last Bond film he made in the decade that forged his career, a film he hoped would provide a semblance of dramatic weight to his time as Bond, would actively avoid content from the original novel that might have given Connery what he desired from the role. He considered himself second fiddle to the gadgetry as the films grew progressively more over the top, and coupled with the relentless press and public intrusion during filming, everything built during *You Only Live Twice* to a conviction that his time as 007 had more than run its course. Connery also didn't have his own publicist at the time to field the range of these intrusions, saying later: 'It was around the same time as The Beatles. The difference was that they had four of them to deal with it!'

The promise of character development in Fleming's novel simply never came to pass in a finished article which, much like *Thunderball*, favoured visual theatrics and spectacle over dramatic weight, and with, as we have seen, his performance as Bond not only wearing thin but being open to personal and specific parody, he knew the time had come to say, as Blofeld does during the climax of the film, 'Goodbye, Mr Bond.'

'This is the last one. The sooner it's finished, the happier I'll be,' Connery grumbled to gossip columnist Sheilah Graham before he started work on *You Only Live Twice*. As it turned out, however, though he might have been done with James Bond, James Bond was not quite done with him.

*

Sean Connery IS James Bond.

So exclaimed the posters for *You Only Live Twice*, affirming the consistent overlap between star and character. Connery's resentment lay in a lack of identification beyond the character, and in the eyes of the public, no one else could be identified as 007 after five films and five whirlwind years. This was before it became common practice for actors to eventually relinquish their licence to kill and pass the baton over to a younger star for a new generation.

Broccoli was irked by Connery's reticence: Saltzman was convinced that they could get him to sign on for the next film, which was definitely going to be *On Her Majesty's Secret Service*. 'Has anyone ever asked us if we would want him to do it?' said Broccoli. 'Would you want anyone to do a film if he kept telling everyone he doesn't want to do it?'

The producer was convinced that the *character* of James Bond, like Edgar Rice Burroughs' Tarzan, was the star as opposed to the actor, and was durable enough to survive a casting change. Despite how strongly Eon had encouraged audiences to identify Connery so completely with the role, this had, as much as financial reasons, driven Connery's rejection of the whole endeavour. 'I will only do things that passionately interest me for the remaining thirty-five years of my life,' Connery declared at the end of the 1960s, underestimating his personal longevity by at least a decade.

Nonetheless, Eon did enter into negotiations with Connery, following his performance in *Shalako*, to return as 007 for the next film. In 1969, the year *On Her Majesty's Secret Service* came out – starring George Lazenby as Bond in his memorable but only appearance – the landscape of cinema was in flux. It was beginning to reflect the cultural climate of the decade and reshape itself on both sides of the Atlantic. The big, self-assured pictures were losing out to more provocative, left-field movies such as Dennis Hopper's

Easy Rider and Ken Russell's *Women in Love*. Connery might have been wiser to have doubled down and stuck with what he knew.

Eon offered him close to a million dollars up front with a gross point percentage, closer to the financial terms he might have appreciated from the beginning, but he declined the offer. He later explained, at around the time he did eventually return for *Diamonds Are Forever*, his reasoning: 'I'd been frigged about too much on other Bond pictures. There's so much bullshit that comes from bad decisions being made at the top. I admire efficiency: like watching a good racehorse or the way Picasso works: where everything functions perfectly within its capacity. But talking to some of these moguls about it is like trying to describe to someone who has never taken exercise what it is like to feel fit when you do exercise. They don't understand.'

Lazenby took the role, for a fraction of what Connery was offered, and went on to appear in what has been cited as not just one of the strongest James Bond films, but one of the most influential. In Daniel Craig's last outing as 007, fifty years on, in *No Time to Die*, we see him fall in love and at one point quote the key line from *On Her Majesty's Secret Service*: 'We have all the time in the world.' The strings from John Barry's seminal score to Peter Hunt's movie were also featured.

For many Bond and Connery fans, and cinephiles generally, Connery's absence from *On Her Majesty's Secret Service* – what could have been his crowning glory as James Bond – is one of the great missed opportunities in filmmaking. The critical reaction to Connery's absence, and the drive to bring him back as Bond for *Diamonds Are Forever*, suggested the brand would struggle to survive without him. The two had a symbiotic relationship. After relatively disappointing box-office returns for *On Her Majesty's Secret Service* and lacklustre critical notices, it appeared that the hype of Bondmania – at its peak in the mid-1960s – was actually beginning to die down. Without Connery, was the series in danger of becoming a relic of the past?

Diamonds Are Forever was an attempt at a rallying call, as what would become a challenging, gloomier decade for the Western world arrived with a thump after the energy and excitement of the 1960s.

The return of Connery was no foregone conclusion, however. Lazenby was quickly frozen out, with the actor reticent to jump back into such an expectation-laden part, but United Artists were keen to find a way to revitalise the brand. Production, for the first time, would be moved to the United States given the story's key setting in Las Vegas and the Nevada desert. And numerous actors, British and American, were interviewed – everyone from Ralph Fiennes' distant cousin, explorer Ranulph Fiennes, to Robert Wagner, through to John Gavin, an established actor who had appeared in Hitchcock's *Psycho* and Kubrick's *Spartacus* among other films, and who was a favourite of Broccoli's wife Dana. Roger Moore, who would take the role in 1973's *Live and Let Die*, was mooted but remained under contract with TV series *The Persuaders*.

Ultimately, UA president David Picker knew there was only really one option: 'We had to get Sean back. I saw Sean; he revealed to me his unhappiness. The only way I could get him back was to make a series of conditions that would enable him to do the film on the terms that he felt comfortable with. Harry and Cubby really were smart enough to realise that the only way to save the series was to have Sean.'

Plenty of stops were pulled out to draw him back in. Vast sums of money were discussed. His first Bond girl, Ursula Andress, was even drafted in from Paris to convince him. The subsequent result was a unique deal, one highly lucrative for Connery, and one that would help shape the direction of his career across the 1970s. He was given a $1.25 million salary plus a whopping 12.5 per cent of the film's gross profit. They also offered to back two projects Connery wanted to make, sight unseen – only one of which, 1973's *The Offence*, ended up being produced. Connery ended up giving his salary to the Scottish International Educational Trust, of which he was a co-founder alongside lifelong friend Jackie Stewart amongst others, reaffirming his determination to support Scottish interests with his global success. The money he made helped to fund his divorce from Diane Cilento.

Connery was pleased with the financial arrangement. 'I've been three years in the process of setting up my own trust,' he explained. 'I'm sure that in the film business again there'll never be that opportunity to make that kind of money. Doing the other five [Bond] pictures was a constant conflict to get a better deal. Now, after three years away, the climate has changed and they've come around to agreeing. It's as simple as that.'

The climate in this case was the nervousness by studio executives about Bond's appeal without Connery and the importance of Bond remaining popular as cinematic trends began to change. Richard Maibaum and Tom Mankiewicz's script, in contrast to how slavishly *On Her Majesty's Secret Service* cleaved to Fleming's work, differs enormously from Fleming's 1956 novel. The essential story concerning diamond smuggling remains, but whereas Fleming centres the villainy around New York gangsters the Spangled Mob, and brothers Jack and Seraffino Spang, the screenplay jettisons many characters and elements from the novel in order to position Blofeld (recast here for the third time in a row with Charles Gray, who previously played the small role of MI6 contact Dikko Henderson in *You Only Live Twice*) as the primary villain with a much more outlandish, world-destroying scheme concerning the smuggled jewels.

Broccoli qualified this at the time: 'Like most of the Ian Fleming stories, they need updating to make a film. You can't just take them now, as we were able to in the early days with *Dr. No*, and more or less get a script right out of the book.'

Such choices inform how, by the early 1970s, the Bond series had truly evolved into a separate entity from Fleming's more nihilistic 1950s source material, a change that arguably began with the establishment of the blockbuster formula in *Goldfinger* that Connery so quickly tired of. *Diamonds Are Forever* does, in many respects, stick to the same repeated formula – gadgets, girls, henchmen, arch-villains – but there are quirky and discernible differences that make the film not a little strange, and incredibly of its time in a manner other Bond films, even earlier ones, have avoided. Connery, interestingly, considered it 'the best [script] they've had, certainly construction-wise with a beginning, middle and an end of a story'.

James Chapman, a professor of film studies at the University of Leicester, suggests Connery's performance fits a deliberately over-the-top, camp Bond picture wherein comic situations and unusual characters are at the forefront:

'Bond almost being cremated at a funeral parlour, Bond using a piton-gun to climb around outside his hotel while clad immaculately in a black dinner jacket, and Bond being knocked around by two athletic women called Bambi and Thumper. The film even sends up the myth of Bond as superman. When Bond kills one heavy and switches his own wallet for the dead man's, Tiffany Case (Jill St John) is incredulous: "You've just killed James Bond!" she exclaims. "Is that who it was? Well, it just goes to show nobody's indestructible," Connery replies with comic irony.'

Quite apart from the fact that such an exchange belies the idea of 007 as a 'secret' agent, it also prefigures a trend that would continue across the Roger Moore era of a self-knowing Bond, a sense of his being a recognised myth in society (lest we forget Moore's Bond in 1985's *A View to a Kill* telling a San Francisco cop he's a British agent, who replies, 'Well, I'm Dick Tracy and you're still under arrest!'). It also establishes Connery's propensity for bringing the audience in on his performance. This will be writ large in *Never Say Never Again* just over a decade later – in the film's title alone – but even here Connery is encouraging us not to take his return all that seriously. The script helps in this regard – take Bernard Lee's M commenting to Connery as much as Bond: 'You've been on holiday, I hear?'

In truth, *Diamonds Are Forever* is the least handsome Connery has ever looked as Bond. Though just forty years old when the picture was filmed, Connery arguably looks older here than when he filmed *Never Say Never Again* at fifty-two; a bit schlubby, weary-looking, and indeed tipping into the leery viciousness he will soon demonstrate in *The Offence*.

The film begins with Bond hunting down Ernst Stavro Blofeld as a means of revenge. He chases him from Cairo, beating up goons along the way, tracking him down to a hideout where Blofeld is undergoing facial reconstructive surgery – this explains how he can look like Charles Gray rather than Telly Savalas. 'Welcome to Hell, Blofeld!' Bond declares as he submerges his nemesis in a vat of hot mud, seemingly killing him in the process – but there is no mention of Tracy, his murdered wife, and little sense of his fury beyond Blofeld now being fully established as the villain of the Bond series. Had Connery's Bond experienced the pain that Lazenby's Bond had suffered, Broccoli and Saltzman might have found a way to give *Diamonds Are Forever* an entirely different stylistic approach.

Instead, this would be Blofeld's final appearance in the Eon Bond films – notwithstanding a bizarre cameo in the pre-credits sequence of 1981's *For Your Eyes Only* and discounting the Kevin McClory-produced *Never Say Never Again* where Max von Sydow played the character – until 2015's *Spectre* when Christoph Waltz reinvented the role for a new era. Nor would the Bond series truly explore the concept of Bond falling in love, losing his beloved, and going on a crusade of vengeance until the Daniel Craig era decades later. It could have been the kind of dramatic and emotional punch that Connery found so lacking in the Bond series, the kind of storytelling that could have convinced him to return for more than just buckets of cash.

After the film premiered in December 1971, Connery was asked by a reporter if 007 had had his day: 'Possibly,' he admitted. 'I wouldn't know. It's perfectly possible the cycle has ended. I came back for the one, that was the understanding. I've got other things I want to do.' As it turned out, Connery wasn't quite done with James Bond in the 1970s, nor indeed in the 1980s, but that's another story. In terms of the Eon-produced films from Broccoli and Saltzman, *Diamonds Are Forever* would be the last time Sean Connery was James Bond.

He was free of the character, for now, and he had other things to do. And for better, and sometimes worse, he was about to make good on that statement.

FIVE

OFF THE BEATEN TRACK

THE 1970S WAS a decade of two distinct halves for Connery, perhaps to a greater degree than any other in his career.

One half was the man of adventure who understood that while he often sought to challenge himself in roles that pushed what he was capable of on screen, audiences recognised in Connery a certain brand that satisfied them when they went to see him at the movies.

The other half was the aspirational star who wished to be taken seriously as more than just a stock, archetypal hero in outlandish adventures coasting on his charisma. To that end, early in the decade, he started Tantallon Films, with the intention of producing the two pictures for which he had been promised financing from United Artists in exchange for appearing in *Diamonds Are Forever*. Although he admitted that he had very little idea about the complex economics involved in being a major producer, he wanted to emulate the success that the likes of Elizabeth Taylor and Richard Burton had enjoyed (both artistically and economically) in the role.

Connery having the clout to position himself with such a deal attests to both the star power he still wielded (even if it remained so thanks to James Bond) and his ability to break the mould of British actors in establishing himself in the same sphere as the auteur directors and powerful independent producers in the so-called 'New Hollywood' who, at the turn of the 1970s, were bursting out of the studio system to produce some of the finest examples of American cinema in history – *The Godfather*, *The Exorcist*, *Nashville*, *Taxi Driver*, *Five Easy Pieces*, *Klute* . . . the list goes on.

Various possibilities swirled around what might become of the two-picture deal, the first being *The Offence*. Connery wrote his own version of Shakespeare's *Macbeth*, which went nowhere after the muted reception to Roman Polanski's 1971 version starring Jon Finch (and a young Keith Chegwin). Connery had designs on the film further enhancing Scotland's international cinematic profile: 'It's a known fact in Scotland that we export more people than any other country in the world. Because basically there are so many ideas – and no money. But you can't build a wall and keep people in. You've got to give them something to do. And that gave me the germ of an idea. It's to start our own renaissance.'

We were never gifted the cinematic version of Connery's *Macbeth*, for better or worse. It was a period when Connery was struggling to break out of the box audiences had placed him in as the 1960s ended.

He was free of Bond, but was Bond free of him?

*

Anxieties about the pervasive nature of electronic surveillance and technology are now, in the early 21st century, part of the fabric of modern existence. WikiLeaks, drone warfare, the dark web, digital currency, the Cambridge Analytica scandal and the rapid development of A.I. would have seemed unfathomable fifty years ago.

In 1970, such concerns about technology were in their infancy. Yet events that would precede, and follow, Sidney Lumet's adaptation of Lawrence Sanders' 1970 novel, *The Anderson Tapes*, bore witness to how the decade would politically and socially reflect growing concerns revolving around government intrusion and surveillance in America.

Connery's next film arrived at the beginning of this febrile conflux of government distrust, conspiracy at the highest levels of power and the growing importance of electronic surveillance.

In *The Anderson Tapes* Connery plays John 'Duke' Anderson, a master safe-cracker fresh out of prison who immediately decides to stage the heist of an upper-class Manhattan building where he is staying with his girlfriend Ingrid (Dyan Cannon). Robbing the building with the support of the Mafia, he assembles a team (including future Bond villain Christopher Walken, in his first screen role) and unwittingly enters a world of electronic surveillance, with his entire operation being monitored from the get-go by a range of agencies undertaking covert and illegal operations – the IRS, the FBI, a private detective and so on. So embroiled are they in their own cross-cutting surveillance schemes, none of them second-guess Duke's intended robbery which, inevitably, goes badly wrong.

Connery looked at *The Anderson Tapes* as a chance to propel himself back towards the A-list. Arguably, the role of Duke is another extension of the Bond persona, although Frank Pierson's script is an uneven balance of satire, gangster film, thriller and caper. No manner of electronic infusions to Quincy Jones' jazzy score can disguise the brazen intention to make *The Anderson Tapes* a commentary on a burgeoning surveillance state while at the same time a funky heist picture driven by Connery's charisma. While Duke exudes the same sexual danger, he is a crook with a harder-edged antihero sensibility, abusive to his woman, and a man who characterises the world as 'dog eat dog, and I want the first bite'. No sign of Bond's easy-going charm here. Though Lumet fails to deliver as consistent and hard-hitting a picture as in their first collaboration, *The Hill*, or provide Connery with as powerful or evocative a role, the intention behind Connery's decision to play Duke was driven by the dual desire that would drive his career in the 1970s – both to remain a star *and* defy convention over what audiences might expect to see him in.

The poster for *The Anderson Tapes* displays this muddled approach to his career. We see Connery, suited and booted, arm resting on his knee with a gun in hand, flanked by masked men in staged action poses, and below him Cannon's Ingrid in a state of undress. It is barely a few degrees removed from a James Bond poster, which surely was the point.

*

By the mid-point of the 1970s the fear of stage conspiracy was entrenched, and an economic downturn was to have far-reaching consequences.

The Next Man, one of Connery's least remembered and least critically appreciated pictures, serves up an unusual blend of exotic romance and bold geopolitical commentary which in 1976 – the same year Peter Finch won an Academy Award for screaming to the heavens that he was 'mad as hell' in Sidney Lumet's critically lauded picture *Network* – audiences perhaps were not quite ready for. There is an argument that they may still not be, half a century later.

Set at the time of the Arab oil embargo of 1973/74, Connery portrays Khalil Abdul-Muhsen, the new Saudi Arabian minister of state with a radical political agenda that distinctly rattles the old white cadre of power brokers and politicians in both Washington and Moscow. Seeking to protect Third World nations from the Cold War still looming between the two superpowers, he seeks to recognise the state of Israel, support their membership of OPEC, and sell much-prized Saudi oil to impoverished nations. As he becomes the target of Arab nationalist terrorist groups, a spy in the form of Nicole Scott (played by Cornelia Sharpe) is sent to infiltrate his entourage and seduce him, but, inevitably, the pair fall in love and her mission is compromised.

Though Richard C. Sarafian's film is a rather bland combination of political speeches and romantic assignations, interspersed with the odd moment of action and murder (including the rather gruesome death of Connery's *Thunderball* co-star Adolfo Celi early on), *The Next Man*, known in some territories as *The Arab Conspiracy*, confronts head-on the political consequences of what was known at the time as the 'shock' of an oil crisis – in which a group of Arab states in protest of nations who supported Israel during the Yom Kippur War set an oil embargo on numerous countries in the West and Far East – that sent the price of oil to a sky-high 300% increase and had far-reaching economic consequences.

Connery's casting as a Saudi politician, the second Middle Eastern role in as many years he had portrayed after his turn as the charming rebel leader Raisuli in *The Wind and the Lion*, is inherently problematic, and while Sarafian's film works hard to remove him from traditional Saudi garb as much as possible, thereby often removing many affectations that mark him out as Saudi at all, *The Next Man* works hard to justify his casting in a role that would logically have suited Omar Sharif. At one point it is even suggested that Khalil studied in Edinburgh, hence his pronounced Scottish accent!

Much as with *The Anderson Tapes*, a film asking serious questions about the future yet couching them in a tone and stylistic approach that leans more to escapism, *The Next Man* struggles to ground much of the significant rhetoric, and it drowns somewhat in cheap thrills and melodrama. Connery's Khalil struggles to fully escape the Bond archetype as he romances the beautiful Nicole, even quipping that he knows somewhere that serves an 'excellent Martini'. But when Khalil dies at the end, audiences are, for the first time, shown Connery in a leading role where his character isn't invincible.

Khalil plays to the debonair persona audiences recognised in Connery, yet he exists within a narrative framework that offers greater complexity than many of Connery's more crowd-pleasing, almost frivolous works across the same decade. 'I took the part of Khalil,' Connery reflected, 'based on reasoning that I always use. I thought him to be an interesting character. He is a contemporary man in every sense of the word: sportsman, diplomat, lover, intellectual, a complete man of our times.'

Quite aside from these charismatic attributes, *The Next Man* provides a protagonist who actively seeks to bring the deep reservoirs of bitterness and rancour between Israel and the Arab states to a position of healing and restoration. His agenda was daring enough, even as a piece of fiction, to unsettle the Saudi government to such an extent that they lodged a formal complaint with the film's producer, Martin Bregman. It is a sympathetic, heroic role that to modern eyes, especially with a Western actor in the part, looks impossibly naive and could well be satire, yet *The Next Man* plays it straight. It believes that a Khalil could truly exist.

Roger Ebert, in reviewing the film at the time, seemed confused by *The Next Man*'s bold intention but stubborn refusal to betray the romantic conventions it played to: 'We remember that the film opened with a series of graphic assassinations, and that we never did learn who was being killed, by whom, or for what reasons. We don't know at the end, either; the movie's cheerful unwillingness to explain anything is a little unsettling. Are we supposed to sit entranced by the scenery and Miss Sharpe's cool beauty and Connery's eggplant and witticisms and never expect anything so embarrassing as common sense? I guess so.'

Though Connery sought with such roles to convey complexity, he struggled to emerge from the shadow of the part that defined him. *The Next Man* and *The Anderson Tapes* both disappoint, and in the case of the former underwhelmed to such a degree that it didn't open in the UK for another six years and is now all but forgotten. Both films aspired to bigger ideas, to the conceptual anxieties about technology and geopolitics that framed their decade, but they failed to emerge from the romantic or spry safety nets that underpinned them.

With *Diamonds Are Forever* now in the rear-view mirror, Connery's resolve to be more than Bond would take him to some of the strangest and darkest places in his entire career.

*

In 1968, a play called *This Story of Yours* premiered at the Royal Court in London's West End. Written by John Hopkins, it revolved around police officer Detective Sergeant Johnson, a hard-bitten cop who beats a suspected child molester, Kenneth Baxter, to death.

Hopkins had just a few years earlier co-scripted the adaptation of *Thunderball* alongside regular James Bond writer Richard Maibaum, following a distinguished screenwriting career including writing for *Z-Cars*, one of the most popular crime dramas of 1960s Britain. Though his career was varied, Hopkins seemed to be drawn repeatedly to the idea of morality in not just the police but the security and intelligence services, fascinated as he was by the idea of corrupted icons. 'He's extraordinary,' said Sidney Lumet of Hopkins. 'Unlike [Greek writer Nikos] Kazantzakis, who keeps looking for what's godlike about us, John keeps looking for what's hellish about us.'

This Story of Yours is a play in three acts; DS Johnson interacts with his wife Maureen, his superior DSI Cartwright and, finally, the criminal Baxter himself. He gets under the fingernails of a tainted figure in ways that appealed to Connery, who first saw the play in the late 1960s and struggled to shake it off. It was a role simultaneously in striking contrast to, and in some respects in line with, the Bond persona. Johnson is a wife-beater, and, equally, a man haunted by unspoken predilections.

Connery discussed what drew him to the unconventional role: 'I think Hopkins explored, in that play and in the subsequent screenplay, areas that people just don't get into in films as a rule: the sexuality and the drives that go on in the mind.'

Following his deal with David Picker, Connery looked to option it as a starring vehicle with Hopkins writing the screenplay, changing the title first to *Something Like the Truth* (a line from the play) and finally the simpler *The Offence*. He went back to Lumet, who he had recently worked with on *The Anderson Tapes* and who was emerging as one of his most trusted collaborators. Lumet had his own take on why he felt they continued working together: 'I think one of the reasons we immediately got close was the first thing he felt from me was enormous respect for him as an actor. When you look at the Bond characterisation, everybody says, "Oh, well, he's just charming." Well, shit, that's like saying Cary Grant was just charming. There is more acting skill in playing that kind of character. What he's doing, stylistically, is playing high comedy. And that is extremely difficult to do, which is why there are so few of those actors, so few Cary Grants and Sean Connerys. But it's acting, don't kid yourself. And right away on *The Hill*, the very fact that I cast him in it meant something. And he was so thrilled to be taken that seriously for that kind of a drama. And when he got to produce a picture of his own, *The Offence*, a story he picked out, I was thrilled to be asked by him to direct.'

Connery would continue to explore the darker sides of his relationship with women on screen, not just in *The Offence* but also, in 1968, in the first episode of a three-part drama for ITV, in a rare foray back into television as an established film star, called *Male of the Species* – a show that also starred fellow British star Michael Caine, one of Connery's closest friends and eventual co-star in *The Man Who Would Be King*. Connery played McNeil, described as 'an arrogant master carpenter who treats women as if they were put on earth to please him'. As was standard for the time, tapes of the broadcast, which debuted in early 1969, were later wiped by the channel, so no record of Connery's performance beyond stills exists, which is disappointing as it was likely to have further underscored the determination of the actor to challenge audience preconceptions about the kind of leading man he was on screen.

What we witness with *The Offence* is the closest we ever get to seeing Connery experiencing a psychological breakdown on screen. Before, and in many roles hence, Connery is always in control, whether playing a hero or a *roué* (and usually somewhere in between). As Johnson, he begins to lose his grip on sanity and reality when confronted with a series of child murders, the last of which he manages to prevent. He is transfixed by the image of the rescued girl in a nightmarish combination of protective horror and shameful sexual attraction.

'It was never going to be a film that was going to be a blockbuster,' said Connery. 'It was a very serious subject about a policeman who really can't handle the job any more because he has no other side to his life. He has no home life really, he has no relationship with his wife – so it's just a disintegration and getting into his head. And I don't think you see many films about that particular subject. And it didn't make a penny.'

Johnson takes out his frustrations on a wife (Vivien Merchant) who is deliberately dowdy and downtrodden, an individual who reflects the dark, rain-sodden English setting unlike anything we had seen Connery in before, even during his years as a supporting player in the 1950s. Just a year or two earlier, he was swapping seductive missives opposite the glamorous Dyan Cannon. A year later, he would be the dashing romantic opposite Vanessa Redgrave in *Murder on the Orient Express*. Merchant's Maureen is unlike any actress Connery plays opposite again. She is his psychological punching bag: 'Why aren't you beautiful? You're not even pretty,' he cruelly berates her as he battles his personal demons, unable to cope with the horrors he has seen in his work and trying to reconcile what he did to Baxter.

Though a subject often left unexplored in cinema, British society had reeled in recent years from the shock of the Moors murders, in which Ian Brady and Myra Hindley had kidnapped, sexually assaulted, murdered and buried multiple children on Saddleworth Moor. The serial killer had been explored in ghoulish terms in films such as Hitchcock's *Psycho* and Michael Powell's *Peeping Tom* (both released in 1960), not to mention Richard Fleischer's more recent *10 Rillington Place*, but *The Offence* is a different beast. It avoids the sensationalism of the killer and looks at the interior world of a different kind of victim – the supposedly heroic policeman who brings down the villain.

'Nothing I have done can be one half as bad as the thoughts in your head,' taunts Baxter, played with icy perfection by Ian Bannen, during the interrogation. Connery, giving a remarkable performance in these climactic scenes, breaks down completely as he confesses to thoughts and feelings that terrify him, and asks the killer to help him.

Does *The Offence* stand as Connery's greatest on-screen performance? This debate will continue to rage. It is without doubt the darkest role he ever undertook, combining his desire to explore the range of the performative ability he displayed at points during his engagements in theatre but had rarely been given the opportunity, after Bond, to put on film. Yet, Connery on screen without magnetic charm, without that recalcitrant, almost grumpy, sense of sardonic cool, reduces him on some level to that of the character actor – a perfectly respectable position, inhabited by talented actors such as Bannen and Merchant, but, arguably, at odds with the kind of innate star quality Connery possessed.

'A compelling chronicle of the crack up of a British police detective hunting a child molester,' wrote the *New York Times* reviewer, '*The Offence* makes no concessions to the audience or the studio executives – no gags, no sensational thrills, no romantic interest, no facile, convenient explanation for the horrors we are asked to contemplate. This film, in other words, has integrity – the hardest commodity to market these days.'

The Offence may have been critically lauded but commercially it was unsuccessful, perhaps inevitably, given the subject matter, even with Connery's presence. It took almost a decade to enter the black in terms of profit. Connery was understandably less than sanguine about this, certainly from a marketing perspective: 'When it came to *The Offence*, well, there's a right way and a wrong way to sell a film. Now, my favourite director is Ingmar Bergman. And his *Cries and Whispers* – Jesus, it's a marvellous film. The test of a film for me is if I go into the cinema to see it, and while I'm there I'm completely unaware of time, then it has succeeded for me . . . Now *Cries and Whispers* played in London at the Curzon, which caters for a certain kind of audience. So the film has a start – a foothold on its own kind of public, which you can do if you've got a small enough cinema. I think in our case with *The Offence*, putting it into the Odeon Leicester Square, the place was just too big. If you take the figures for our first three weeks there, well, if we'd only got half that number in three weeks at the Curzon, the place would have been full. And a series of full houses can create a kind of impetus.'

As a result of this financial failure, United Artists backed out of the second film they agreed Connery could make if he played 007 one last time. It would put paid to Connery's attempt to rebrand himself through his own producing efforts and see him edge, as the 1970s continued, into a push-pull between commercially viable projects that relied on his natural charisma and attempts to push the envelope as to what audiences were prepared to see him become.

And almost nobody, to an even greater degree than *The Offence*, was quite prepared for the world Connery would enter alongside his next director: John Boorman.

*

Following the success of his Lee Marvin-starring modern noir *Point Blank* in 1967 and the uncompromising *Deliverance* (1972), Boorman set about a project that would not see fruition in live action for almost thirty years – adapting Tolkien's magisterial *The*

Lord of the Rings for a 1970s audience. Though it turned out to be biting off more than he could chew, Boorman's fascination with the Grail legend and Judaeo-Christian myth combined to form the seeds of what would become *Zardoz*, his original screenplay.

In Boorman's film, set in a fictional 2293, Connery plays Zed, known as a 'Brutal Exterminator', who in a world divided between the immortal 'Eternals' and the mortal 'Brutals', who live in an irradiated wasteland, sets about terrorising and killing Brutals on behalf of Zardoz, a huge, flying stone head that provides them with food. When Zed breaks free of his role, entering Zardoz and killing its Eternal-operator Arthur Frayn, he enters the world of the Eternals, a bored race descending into immortal madness. And as Zed learns about their world, and about the manner of his creation, he begins to kickstart a revolution that will forever change the future.

Connery discussed his first impressions of a script unlike anything else he had previously grappled with: 'I'd only seen one film that John had made, which was *Deliverance*, and I thought it was superb. I heard that he wanted me to act in *Zardoz* because he'd not been able to finalise arrangements to have Burt Reynolds in it. And he needed a quick decision from me. I was in Spain at the time and the script was delivered to my flat in London so that I could read it when I flew back on the Sunday night. Well, after about twenty pages I was absolutely caught by its originality, and I read it through twice and telephoned John the following morning. It was one of the best ideas I'd come across for ages.'

Going down in cinematic history as a cult curio, certainly in the context of both Boorman and Connery's work, *Zardoz* is a deeply strange examination of fundamental religious and philosophical concepts that is perhaps best remembered, half a century on, for the sight of Connery sporting long, plaited hair, a giant bushy moustache, and a costume that resembles a man-sized red nappy. It is almost comically exploiting his rugged middle-aged masculinity at a time when Connery, emerging from *The Offence*'s commercial failure and lingering audience expectations of him as 007, was struggling to find work in the way he once did.

Zed is a powerful sexual symbol in an asexual future, humanity having separated between numbed immortals and savage beasts – a bridge between the present and future. Burt Reynolds, first in line for the part, pulled out due to illness, and as perhaps the closest American equivalent to Connery at that time, Reynolds would have made sense in such a knowing role. Boorman nonetheless felt that Connery understood what they were making from the outset: 'He is a very intelligent actor. He understood it from the very beginning and his performance was a revelation . . . there was something mystical about him which was just waiting to be brought to the surface. He is very instinctive in everything he does and one of his strong points as an actor is that he had a very direct approach to every scene.'

Zardoz, in some sense, adopts a similar position to that of *Barbarella* in 1960s fiction, in which Jane Fonda brought her beauty and presense as a screen icon to a deliberately artificial future. It was a period before *Star Wars* in which science fiction was characterised as much through sexual charisma as it was fantasy or horror, which we would see later in *Star Wars*, *Alien* and beyond. Connery discussed how he preferred the path *Zardoz* was taking in relation to such content: 'What gripped me especially was the direction the people in it were taking in this future existence, as opposed to spaceships and rockets and all that. I'm not a science-fiction buff. The idea of going to the moon is kind of interesting in itself, of course, but I'm not interested to go there personally. What does interest me is the possible development of society in centuries to come. The way different levels and types evolve in the script is intriguing and refreshing, and could well be true. The fact that people would not die, for example.'

An easy-to-laugh-off aberration in Connery's experimental phase, *Zardoz* sees the actor engaging in the kind of lyrical text he would later profess a lack of understanding for. Though he agreed in 1975 after making *Zardoz* to play King Arthur for Boorman in his long-gestating take on Arthurian myth in *Excalibur*, he eventually changed his mind when the film enters production at the beginning of the 1980s (only to produce a very different take on the role a decade and a half later in Jerry Zucker's *First Knight*). Whether Connery was burned by *Zardoz*'s commercial and critical failure – the film faced a phalanx of terrible reviews – or its weirdness, it is hard to say. Even when experimenting with styles and directors, he never again made a movie quite as 'out there' as *Zardoz*, and as time passed he seemed to run from the challenge.

Ironically, in the case of both *The Offence* and *Zardoz*, their stock has significantly risen over time, the latter having gained a cult following. They are perhaps two of Connery's better examples of what he was capable of, the range he could display and his admirable openness to unusual or challenging material.

As the 1970s rolled on, he instead slipped into roles plenty of other actors could have played, reliant as they were on the traditional representation of him in the face of existential threats to a dark, desperate decade.

*

While the 1970s was coloured not only by corrupt government actions and anxieties about the growing influence of technology and science in human life, not to mention economic strife as Keynesian economics steadily gave way to coming globalisation, it was also a decade filled with numerous existential concerns about both territorial and broader global security.

Halfway through the decade, and towards its end, Connery would appear in two films that rank among his least remembered but both of which, in different facets, see him taking on serious-minded professional roles of men drafted in to, in their limited capacity, save the nation state and nothing less than the entire world.

Ransom, also known as *The Terrorists* when released in the United States, arrived in the spring of 1974 and saw Connery, as he would frequently across the decade, adopt a role from an entirely different nationality, in this case Colonel Nils Tahlvik, head of security for a fictionalised nation state simply referred to as 'Scandinavia'. Tahlvik is called in when a group of terrorists seize the British ambassador in his residence, after which a second group hijack a plane at the airport which they intend to be the terrorist group's transportation after their demands have been met. Tahlvik subsequently comes to learn he is part of a British secret service plot to capture the leader of the terrorist group and is further drawn into espionage and subterfuge.

Sporting a heavy moustache in line with his middle-aged look in *The Offence*, released the same year, Connery continued in *Ransom* to edge away from his suave signature role towards the humourless and taciturn, with Tahlvik a long way from being a charming and flighty secret agent – Ian McShane's terrorist Petrie serves more of that function. Tahlvik is a serious man resolved to finding his way through an increasingly delicate political situation, though *Ransom* struggles to reconcile the allegorical intentions behind the story with a pulp reality – as indicated by the action-based American alternate title – of attempting to attract modern audiences by way of action and thrills, neither of which is evident.

One intriguing aspect from the production of the film, which speaks to the murky waters of corruption that could even embroil film crews during this period, involves the plane rented by the production team for filming at Oslo airport in Norway. It was a Boeing 737-200 displaying the livery of Mey-Air, a Norwegian charter airline in operation between 1970 and 1974, owned by one Hans Otto Meyer, who invited the cast – including Connery and McShane – to his villa for a party during filming and gave the actors a tour of what was, in fact, a secret weapons cache for the Norwegian Stay Behind army, part of a post-war plan to establish a covert army who could operate behind enemy lines in the event of a Soviet invasion. The chances of this were remote by 1973, when *Ransom* was filmed, but there existed during the Cold War a perpetual state of national anxiety across Scandinavia should the geopolitical map suddenly change. Meyer was eventually arrested and the cache recovered by the government.

Terrorism, the central element of the film, had not been consistently portrayed in cinema to the degree that audiences would later see in the post-9/11 era, even though Paul Wheeler's script for *Ransom* was inspired by a growing number of attacks, kidnappings and hijackings across the late 1960s and into the 1970s by a range of emerging terrorist groups that were making national and international news. *Ransom* remained rather anaemically neutral – consider how the country central to the attack is named after an entire European sub-region, without expressly being tethered to individual nations. The film does, however, attempt to evoke actions that could fall under the remit of well-publicised groups such as the Irish Republican Army or violent left-wing militant revolutionary groups such as the PKK or the Red Army Faction.

Ransom courted controversy at the time, with some alleging the film was seeking to cash in on such terrorist activity and exploit dangerous, volatile situations in which innocent people died for entertainment purposes. The film's director, Caspar Wrede, presides over a film which is ultimately toothless in depicting the growing threat of terrorist activity, descending as it does into a conspiratorial story whereby Tahlvik turns detective as much as negotiator and smokes out British intelligence seeking to control Scandinavian security forces by secretly working to capture Martin Shepherd, the leader of the terrorist group.

Connery was perhaps attracted to the role because of Wrede's earlier film, *One Day in the Life of Ivan Denisovich* – starring one of Connery's compatriots from the British New Wave, Tom Courtenay – which likely impressed him, as would Wrede's cinematographer, Sven Nykvist, who was a frequent collaborator with Swedish auteur Ingmar Bergman (and later worked with Andrei Tarkovsky, Nora Ephron and Woody Allen). But the fact that Tahlvik is the kind of protagonist who draws a professional line in the sand in the face of terrorist activity and a government seemingly willing, scared, to accede to their demands may also have appealed. 'National security becomes a farce if we throw away the rule of law,' Tahlvik declares, thereby cementing him as the moral centre of a story in which both the terrorists and the governments involved have an absence of morality. Though much less evocative or successful, *Ransom*'s depiction of terrorism, while lacking anything in the way of the true impassioned radicalism later films will cover, certainly feeds into the 1970s cinematic perpetuation of societal and structural breakdown by agents of chaos who were deeply feared by citizens and governments.

Tahlvik is a character working to protect and defend the system, the security of the nation state, and is prepared to do what he can – even if it means defying orders – to do the right thing. This is perhaps why, when we later see Connery in the role of a revolutionary in *The Wind and the Lion*, his is a romantic construction. Connery certainly didn't believe in anarchy, yet in his roles, he was clearly attracted to rejections of authority.

As *Ransom* faded almost immediately into obscurity, so too would a film towards the end of the decade where Connery would play another character drafted in by an anxious government to tackle a threat greater than any the actor had previously faced.

*

On 27 June 1949, German astronomer Walter Baade discovered what was subsequently classified as a potentially hazardous asteroid orbiting the solar system, the first in 1968 to be observed by radar and detected as flying closer to the sun than many other similar objects. It was, perhaps inevitably, named Icarus.

Meteor, one of Connery's final films of the 1970s, was born out of the so-called 'Project Icarus', a student project at Massachusetts Institute of Technology in 1968 which devised a plan to detect and destroy Icarus should its flight path place it on a direct collision course with Earth, one that involved using missiles to deflect the asteroid off course and prevent devastation.

In the film, directed by Ronald Neame, an asteroid called Orpheus is shunted onto a collision course that could trigger an extinction-level event and wipe out all life on Earth should it strike. Connery plays Dr Paul Bradley, a scientist who devised *Hercules*, a secret orbital missile platform operated by the United States and designed to ward off asteroid threats, but which has since been commandeered by the military who aim it at the Soviet Union, aware they have developed their own platform. As fragments begin to cause chaos on Earth, Bradley convinces the Americans that they must combine both US and Soviet missile power as the only means of stopping Orpheus, and so begins a collaboration between both countries to stop the meteor before it's too late.

Though naturally a different existential threat to the spectre of terrorism, which in 1979 continued to rear its head in the form of events such as the assassination of Lord Mountbatten by the IRA, global and especially Western world anxiety about the possibility of an asteroid hitting Earth has been an endemic part of life since science developed the tools to understand the many extinction-events that have shaped prehistory, including the one all children are taught from a very young age: the extinction of the dinosaurs.

Meteor nonetheless ventured into cinematic territory nobody had previously trod. Long since eclipsed by the two most culturally recognisable humans vs asteroid pictures, *Armageddon* and *Deep Impact* – both of which were released, coincidentally, in short succession in 1998 at the tail end of the 1990s blockbuster era, in which Connery would later play a key role – *Meteor* emerged as part of a succession of pictures across the 1970s that foregrounded disasters of various means.

It also, by nature of the narrative, sees an early example of forced cinematic *perestroika*, as American and Soviet forces work to put their ideological differences aside to face a bigger existential threat, putting the Cold War into sobering context. Connery's Bradley, aside from throwing out the kind of caustic one-liners the actor clearly relished, has absolutely no time for the kind of political skulduggery that pits nations against each other. He is a scientist with a clear-eyed objective, again drawing another line in the sand – as he does with Tahlvik – about the correct course of action. In these kinds of roles, he rejects the political complexity of pictures such as *The Next Man*.

Connery himself was aware that Bradley, given his technical expertise, was not the kind of character he could precisely relate to, but he found a Scottish connection as a means of finding the character, as he related in an interview with journalist Bobbie Wygant: 'What I used was a chap that I knew in Scotland who worked as a – just outside Edinburgh there's an American company, Honeywell – and this chap, he's not dissimilar to that; a rather short fuse and kind of disguises a lot of things, and you have to sort of dig around to find out what he's really about.'

Though Connery was happy with a script rewrite by screenwriter Stanley Mann, a friend he had known since his pre-Bond days in cinema, a level of genre authenticity came from initial screenwriter Edmund H. North, who, in 1951, had penned the screenplay for Robert Wise's signature science-fiction picture *The Day the Earth Stood Still*. *Meteor* was therefore designed to show co-operation between the two superpowers, continuing the vein of other franchises – even Bond – where in *The Spy Who Loved Me*, 007 worked with a Russian agent to stop the machinations of a madman with no geopolitical affiliation. *Meteor* attempted to presage the Reagan–Gorbachev era of co-operation that would ultimately contribute to the end of the USSR itself, suggesting a cultural thawing of relations between such enemies.

Ultimately, though, *Meteor* is designed as big-budget entertainment for audiences thirsty for high-concept storytelling and escapism, at the end of a dark and difficult decade. Connery is afforded a fair dose of laconic charm, despite Bradley's determination, and is paired opposite a classic screen star in

Natalie Wood (just a couple of years away from her tragic, endlessly mysterious demise), which frames *Meteor* in line with earlier roles. It is a sign that he is edging closer to the kind of roles he would take in the next decade, ones that would, in many ways, turn him into a bigger star than he ever had been before.

A hellish shoot, a bland script and, even for the era, some rather terrible special effects put paid to any danger of *Meteor* standing out on Connery's CV. This and *Ransom* stand as two of his worst films overall, but they share his commitment to play traditional, heroic professionals fighting back against existential threats with a dangerous edge. What we also witness across the 1970s is Connery's determination to take on roles that would allow him to play with the aspects of his acting style that brought him to fame. He would not simply be the tortured detective or the professional problem-solver. He could also be the lover, the fighter, even sometimes the rogue – and, as in the 1980s to come, the rest of the 1970s saw Connery seek to be a man of adventure.

SIX

MAN OF ADVENTURE

WHETHER CONNERY FAILED in his aspirations after *Diamonds Are Forever* to reinvent himself is open to debate. Creatively, he certainly tried, but commercially, it was a different story: for the majority of the 1970s he was box-office poison and was plagued by numerous private and public difficulties.

His father Joe, having finally moved out of the Fountainbridge tenement where he grew up, passed away from cancer while Sean was making *The Offence*. Soon after, Connery's divorce from Diane Cilento – lengthy, bitter and complicated – was finally settled. Then came ire from the British press after, following the second term of Harold Wilson's Labour government, a huge tax squeeze on the wealthy saw Connery become a tax exile in Spain.

'It got to the point where I anticipated being asked for 98 per cent of my earnings in tax,' said Connery of his personal crusade against Denis Healey, then Chancellor of the Exchequer. 'And I still hadn't paid my agent his 10 per cent.'

These significant changes to his life saw him distance himself from British cinema, and as the 1970s rolled on, he pivoted increasingly towards Hollywood. He could never be described as simpatico with the American New Wave, where directors and writers were becoming as famous as actors and flexing their muscles within the studio system. Yet he was not making the Bond-style blockbusters, either.

What he sought in the latter half of the 1970s was to move beyond Bond; to be free of the character was simply not enough for him or, to an extent, for audiences. A trio of pictures served as a turning point. *The Wind and the Lion*, *The Man Who Would Be King* and *Robin and Marian* featured Connery in classic adventure stories which showed that there was a greater depth to his abilities than many might have perceived. These are not pictures that necessarily sit at the top of Connery's greatest commercial hits, but they demonstrate how durable he was in retaining both star power and critical respect.

*

The trend in Hollywood was shifting towards big-budget disaster movies as cinema looked to attract audiences through escapist entertainment. Aside from films such as *Earthquake* or *The Towering Inferno* featuring apocalyptic scenarios, they also frequently deployed another audience-grabbing tactic: the ensemble cast.

Although the first example of ensemble films can be traced back to the birth of large-scale pictures in the 1910s with D. W. Griffith's epic (albeit controversial) works such as *The Birth of a Nation* or *Intolerance*, from the 1930s through to the 1960s the Hollywood studio system was built on star names, contract players who were a safe bet for studios to build pictures around with assigned directors. This began to change as the studio system began to break down in the 1960s and films such as 1963's *It's a Mad, Mad, Mad, Mad World* brought together an array of stars, past and present (and indeed future, such as a pre-*Columbo* Peter Falk), all of whom had roughly equal screen time.

Connery, not used to being part of ensemble pieces, was approached by Sidney Lumet, seeking their third collaboration after *The Hill* and *The Anderson Tapes*, to appear in his adaptation of Agatha Christie's *Murder on the Orient Express* – perhaps Christie's most famous novel featuring legendary Belgian sleuth Hercule Poirot. Outside the Bond franchise, this was the closest Connery had come to entertaining, mass-market fare, as Lumet asked him to play not Poirot, but rather Colonel Arbuthnot, a British military officer on the train with his mistress, Ms Debenham (played by Vanessa Redgrave), who he plans to marry when he divorces his philandering wife.

Christie's novels had been adapted for the screen since the 1920s, but she was unhappy with certain adaptations of her work during the 1960s and only came around because she liked several of the producers' previous movies and the rumoured encouragement of Lord Mountbatten. Lumet's cachet as a director and the galaxy of stars recruited would arguably not have hindered proceedings. He assembled a cast that, even to this day, is to die for: Connery, Albert Finney, Lauren Bacall, John Gielgud, Martin Balsam (another Lumet favourite who also joined Connery for *The Anderson Tapes*), Anthony Perkins, Jacqueline Bisset, Richard Widmark and Ingrid Bergman, amongst others. Kenneth Branagh's 2017 remake aside, with modern legends such as Judi Dench and Johnny Depp aboard, it remains the most remarkable cast for a Christie adaptation ever seen on screen.

Remarkably, such an array of famous players does not seem to have caused issues during filming. 'Were there any divas?' said producer Richard Goodwin. 'No, they were well behaved, although Lauren Bacall insisted on having her shoes made in Paris, Albert Finney got paid more because his Hercule Poirot had most of the lines, and Sean Connery got a percentage because he was such a big star. The rest all got paid the same: $100,000 each. Vanessa Redgrave would spend all her lunchtimes converting the workers, making speeches about politics in the canteen, while the rest of the actors would sit and listen to John Gielgud telling his amazing stories.'

Connery, in particular, was flattered at being considered the biggest star of them all by Lumet, thanks to the popularity of Bond. Lumet courted Connery's involvement early as a means of galvanising the other stars to join the project. His role is, even within the collegiate structure of Lumet's film, rather small. Anyone who knows the denouement of Christie's story, an unexpected and imaginative solution, is aware of the role Colonel Arbuthnot plays as a character in the murder, but Connery's character is a stolid, stiff-backed veteran of a bygone colonial era (the story is set in the 1930s). However, it is telling that he plays what could be construed as the film's most romantic role – the dashing officer who courts Redgrave's Mary Debenham, the beautiful attaché to Bergman's Swedish missionary.

Featuring a well-known character by England's best-loved mystery author, and a story that millions would have read over the decades, *Murder on the Orient Express* is the kind of lavish production that bridges the Golden Age of Hollywood – the tail end of which Connery passed through and in which many of his co-stars here played signature roles – and the coming blockbuster era Connery would find resurgent fame within.

Vincent Canby in *The New York Times* perhaps best summed up the importance of such a film being made at the time it was released: 'Had Dame Agatha Christie's *Murder on the Orient Express* been made into a movie 40 years ago (when it was published here as *Murder on the Calais Coach*), it would have been photographed in black-and-white on a back lot in Burbank or Culver City, with one or two stars and a dozen character actors and studio contract players. Its running time would have been around 67 minutes and it could have been a very respectable B-picture. *Murder on the Orient Express* wasn't made into a movie 40 years ago, and after you see the Sidney Lumet production that opened yesterday at the Coronet, you may be both surprised and glad it wasn't. An earlier adaptation could have interfered with plans to produce this terrifically entertaining super-valentine to a kind of whodunnit that may well be one of the last fixed points in our inflationary universe.'

Connery would understand the value of being part of such an ensemble cast, repeating the trick in just three years' time for a very different movie. Though, in one sense, he had been where he was going next before.

*

Back in 1962, within the same month as the release of *Dr. No* that sent his career stratospheric, Connery had appeared as Private Flanagan in *The Longest Day*, 20th Century Fox's epic retelling of the Normandy landings that kickstarted the Allied victory in the Second World War.

His part in the film is slim: he engages in witty banter with Norman Rossington's fellow officer as they're about to make the landing, which lasts a mere few minutes and does little to establish Connery as more than the likeable comic foil seen around the same time in *On the Fiddle* before Bond entirely transformed his reputation.

A Bridge Too Far was based on a book by the same writer, Cornelius Ryan, who had developed *The Longest Day*, but unlike that film, where Fox deployed three directorial teams from three different nations to lens the picture, this adaptation was driven by two film titans: screenwriter William Goldman and actor/director Richard Attenborough, both in the prime of a career that, to a degree, Connery, in 1977, when the film emerged, was not.

Much like *The Longest Day*, the film focuses on a wartime event rather than specific characters, in this case Operation Market Garden, a military plan hatched in the Netherlands in 1944 to create a 64-mile salient (a battlefield advance) into German territory, which included establishing a bridgehead over the Rhine to allow the Allies an invasion route into the northern tip of Germany. *A Bridge Too Far* concentrates on the overreach by

Sean Connery joined the Navy when he was seventeen. After two years as a Royal Naval Volunteer he became an able seaman on the battleship HMS *King George V* before being invalided out with ulcers. *Alamy*

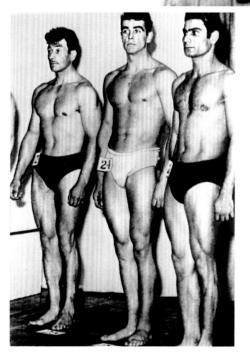

Connery competes in Mr Universe, where he finished third in the tall man's class. It was while in London for this contest that he saw an advert for a casting for *South Pacific*. His decision to audition launched his acting career. *Alamy*

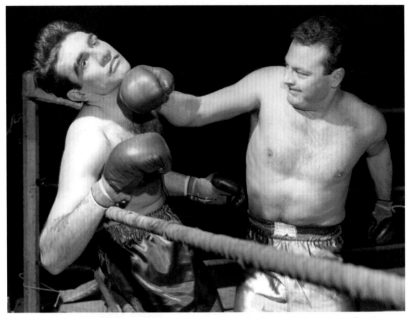

Connery plays Harlan 'Mountain' McClintock alongside Larry Hoodkoff as Charles 'Bo Bo' Gibbons in *Blood Money* in 1957. *BBC Archive*

As Johnny Kates in *Hell Divers*, 1957. *Alamy*

Connery plays Mike opposite Martine Carol (Tracy Malvoisie) and Van Johnson (Carson) in his first involvement with Terence Young in *Action of the Tiger*. *Alamy*

Connery with Glynis Johns in *Another Time, Another Place*, 1958. *BFI*

Singing his heart out with Janet Munro in
Disney's *Darby O'Gill and the Little People*. *Alamy*

As Pedlar Pascoe in *On the
Fiddle*, 1961. *BFI*

Playing Count Alexis Vronsky in the BBC's
adaptation of *Anna Karenina, 1961. BBC Archive*

Private Flanagan prepares to storm the beach in Normandy in *The Longest Day. Alamy*

'Bond. James Bond.' And with those three words, Connery introduced audiences around the world to an icon in *Dr. N* *Alamy*

Connery and Ian Fleming share notes on the set of *Dr No. Alamy*

Terence Young directs Connery and Daniela Bianchi (Tatiana) in *From Russia With Love*. *Alamy*

Alfred Hitchcock takes a moment to talk with Connery and Tippi Hedren on the set of *Marnie*, 1964. *Alamy*

In one of the most famous scenes in the Bond franchise, Auric Goldfinger (Gert Fröbe) questions Bond while a laser closes in on his groin. *Alamy*

Connery drew on his experiences in the navy for his performance in *The Hill*, one of his favourite films. *Alamy*

The Bowler and the Bunnet was a one-hour documentary that examined the so-called 'Fairfield Experiment' which had been carried out a year earlier at the Fairfield Shipbuilding and Engineering Company in Glasgow, which was presented, narrated and directed by Connery. It aired on Scottish television in July 1967. *BFI*

Led by Connery's Jack Kehoe, the 'Molly Maguires' were a secret society of Irish-American miners fighting back against the exploitation by the wealthy mine owners where they work. *Alamy*

Connery returned to play Bond for a big pay day in *Diamonds Are Forever*, but he looked both tired and bored throughout. *Alamy*

The Offence is the closest we ever get to see Connery experiencing a psychological breakdown on screen as his character (Johnson) is confronted with a series of child murders. *Alamy*

Zed, a 'Brutal Exterminator' with a brutal fashion
sense, in John Boorman's *Zardoz* in 1974. *Alamy*

Peachy Carnehan (Michael Caine) and Daniel Dravot (Connery) in John Houston's *The
Man Who Would Be King*, a film that both actors had a wonderful time making. *Alamy*

Connery starred alongside Audrey Hepburn in *Robin and Marian*, which approached the legend of Robin Hood in the latter days of the great hero's life. *Alamy*

Connery (pictured with co-star Kim Basinger) made a surprise return to the role he had long try to escape, playing Bond one final time in Kevin McClory's *Never Say Never Again* in 1983. *Alamy*

The Scotsman Connery plays an immortal Egyptian with a Spanish name, Juan Sanchez-Villalobos Ramirez, opposite Frenchman Christopher Lambert playing Scotsman Connor MacLeod, in 1986's *Highlander*. *Alamy*

Connery won a BAFTA for his role as William of Baskerville in the medieval whodunnit *The Name of the Rose* (1986) alongside a fresh-faced Christian Slater (Adso) in his first role. *Alamy*

1987's *The Untouchables* saw Connery turn in a performance as Jim Malone that would win him a Best Supporting Actor Oscar. *Alamy*

Connery was at his humorous and charismatic best in *Indiana Jones and the Last Crusade* playing Henry Jones Sr., the father of the eponymous hero (Harrison Ford). *Alamy*

Connery as Marko Ramius, the commander of a Soviet ballistic missile submarine in *The Hunt for Red October*, the hugely successful adaptation of the best-selling novel by Tom Clancy. *Alamy*

Michael Bay's *The Rock* arrived during a golden age for the star-driven action picture and saw John Patrick Mason (Connery) recruited by the US government to break into Alcatraz, the island prison he had escaped from decades earlier. *Alamy*

One of the last films Connery made, *Finding Forrester* sees him turn in one of his finest performances as the reclusive author, William Forrester, opposite Rob Brown (Jamal Wallace). *Alamy*

In his final on-screen role, Connery plays Allan Quatermain in the helter-skelter adaptation of comic book series, *The League of Extraordinary Gentlemen. Alamy*

desperate Allied forces seeking to end the war. The success of the operation remains debated to this day but was largely considered a failure; the title itself reputedly came from the mouth of General Browning, played here by Dirk Bogarde, who voiced such anxieties before the operation.

Connery was part of a large ensemble of actors for Attenborough's revival of what, even by 1977, was an increasingly outdated style of war picture, flanked by stars as varied as Bogarde, Michael Caine, James Caan, Edward Fox, Gene Hackman, Robert Redford, Maximilian Schell, Anthony Hopkins, Elliott Gould and Laurence Olivier. Unlike *Murder on the Orient Express*, Connery takes a bigger chunk of screen time as Major-General Roy Urquhart, who is leading the British division to land near Arnhem as part of Market Garden. Here, unlike in *The Longest Day* or *The Hill*, he portrays a real-life wartime figure, still alive at the time the film was made. Amusingly, Urquhart had no idea who Connery was: his excited daughters had to explain why it was such a coup to be portrayed by one of the best-known actors in the world.

In truth, Connery's star had continued to wane throughout the 1970s as he delved into more personal, dramatic projects, many of which did not set the box office or critics alight. However, during a period that saw him eschew traditional leading-man roles while seeking to retain a position within popular culture, some of these endeavours stand as his most intriguing and colourful. In *A Bridge Too Far*, a film made with the rather functional and stolid attention to detail of war pictures from earlier decades, Connery lacks the elegant *joie de vivre* that *Murder on the Orient Express* allowed him. His role within an ensemble suggests he could suppress his ego (although he was incensed that Redford was earning more for a much smaller role) but equally suggests Connery needed to appear in an 'event' picture that would make him accessible to a broader variety of cinemagoers.

Although the war film as a cinematic franchise was on the wane, Connery's gamble paid off. *A Bridge Too Far* did well, and indeed served as the actor's biggest hit (in box-office terms) of the decade.

He would only appear in two more ensemble films, both wildly different in tone and structure – 1981's *Time Bandits* and 1998's *Playing by Heart* – and in some ways, *A Bridge Too Far* is one of Connery's final cinematic paeans to the movie landscape that existed earlier in his career.

*

What was the name of the Robin Hood film that first featured Sean Connery? It might be a good question for a pub quizmaster . . .

Many might answer that it was 1991's monster hit *Robin Hood: Prince of Thieves*. But, in fact, *Prince of Thieves* was Connery's second appearance in a Robin Hood movie after 1976's *Robin and Marian*, a picture about the daring medieval thief in danger of being forgotten by modern audiences.

Helmed by Richard Lester, a flavour of the moment after his hugely successful adaptation of Alexandre Dumas' *The Three Musketeers*, which injected a sense of escapist brio into downtrodden 1970s cinema, *Robin and Marian* approaches the legend of Robin Hood differently from the sprightly depictions audiences had been used to from Errol Flynn's *The Adventures of Robin Hood* in 1938 through to Disney's popular animated version in 1973. Connery's Robin is older, his adventuring years behind him, and the career he enjoyed robbing from the rich to feed the poor is now consigned to his youthful legend. In Lester's film, a carefree Robin returns to England, back to Sherwood Forest, after decades of fighting, romancing and voyaging through the Crusades, to reconnect with his roots. Lester's film takes a steady look at Connery's Robin bedding back into a life he left behind, his narrative inverting the well-worn story of Robin Hood for an elegiac examination of lost youth.

Connery was originally courted for the role of Little John, with the slightly younger Albert Finney as Robin, but this would have given the film an entirely different complexion. It works on the basis of Connery engaging with his own advancing years.

The difference here to something like *Diamonds Are Forever*, where he looks bored, heavy-set, and washed-out, is that Connery is having fun with *Robin and Marian*. Playing the cheery troubadour allows him to utilise the kind of boyish charm we saw in the early 007 movies when Connery was engaged in the part, as he partners up with Nicol Williamson's sidekick in combating Richard Harris's maniacal Richard the Lionheart (the same role Connery would end up playing 15 years later) and later Robert Shaw's aged Sheriff of Nottingham. Harris had agreed to appear in the small role as a favour after appearing with Connery in *The Molly Maguires*.

The other draw as to why *Robin and Marian* works is the return of Audrey Hepburn, herself middle-aged and playing off her own status as an icon of the 1960s. Before this, she had not appeared in a picture for eight years, since *Wait Until Dark*, as she devoted her time to family. Hepburn, as the aged Maid Marian who has since become a pious abbess and turned to God to fill the void left by Robin, is a great foil for Connery's charming portrayal. Quiet yet forceful, strong yet sensitive, it is entirely easy to believe Marian being awakened from her duty to the Lord in the face of the human love that returns, suddenly, into her life. Their romance anchors the picture and contains a sweetness that is never cloying, filled rather with a poignant regret.

Lester wisely allows these two cinematic titans to dominate the screen, though in doing so Robert Shaw gets somewhat left behind, making nowhere near the impression other sheriffs (most memorably Alan Rickman a decade and a half later) would. Shaw would die of a heart attack only a couple of years later and was immensely competitive with Connery, career-wise, after their sparring during the signature Bond movie *From Russia with Love* over a decade earlier. The difference is that while Connery looks energised, Shaw looks, understandably, tired.

The fatigue is, to an extent, part of the point. *Robin and Marian* could only have been made in a decade like the 1970s, where cinema before the dawn of *Star Wars* was imbued with a level of cynicism, certainly when it came to adventure, which marks Lester's film out as a refreshing alternative. The script still lingers with tinges of regret, as Robin returns to find little has changed, with the Sheriff of Nottingham, however jaded, still ruling – and still coveting Marian. The land remains oppressed. And Robin has seen the darkness of fighting for unjust rulers in foreign lands for little return, as he recounts Richard's dark deeds in the Holy Land. 'King Richard spared the rich for ransoms, took the strong for slaves, then he took the children – *all* the children – and had them chopped apart. Then he had their mothers killed. When they were all dead, three thousand bodies on the plain, he had them all opened up so their guts could be explored for gold and precious stones. Our churchmen on the scene – and there were many – took it for a triumph! One bishop put on his mitre and led us all in prayer.'

The fact that Marian turns from God to love Robin at the end is pointed, a conclusion designed to reinforce the secular nature of a story which throws suspicion on mindless adherence to religious ritual and traditional practice. To underscore this disillusionment, neither Robin nor Marian or the Sheriff are at the peak of their powers or their lives. Their best years are behind them, and, throughout the picture, as they rediscover their love, Robin and Marian rediscover who they once were. Robin reforms his merry men and again becomes a folk hero as the Sheriff and the cruel King John (a nice cameo from Ian Holm) oppress the populace. Robin sums this feeling up: 'It's so beautiful, this place . . . the woods just now . . . full of noises . . . everything so alive. I kept thinking of all the death I've seen. I've hardly lost a battle, and I don't know what I've won. "The day is ours, Robin," you used to say, and then it was tomorrow. But where did the day go?'

Yet that adventure, that revival, is destined to be bittersweet. Set to John Barry's sumptuous score (which Lester, inexplicably, disliked), we are delivered a conclusion whereby Connery engages his desire to avoid marquee, Bond-like characters by playing Robin to his Shakespearean end alongside Marian. The film was originally titled *The Death of Robin Hood*, which rather gave the game away; it was changed to better reflect the importance of Hepburn's Marian to proceedings, giving these two megastars equal billing in a picture as much about one as the other. It is about their rebirth and, ultimately, their peaceful demise.

As Connery said about the title, perhaps aptly summing up a difference between American and British filmmaking: '*Robin and Marian* was supposed to be called *The Death of Robin Hood*, but Americans don't like heroes who die or anything that might not smack of being a victory.

'I think *Robin and Marian* is on a par with *The Man Who Would Be King* as a complete script. James Goldman captured everything about the story. It's rather sad that the picture was not a success at all when it came out, but fortunately it was resurrected as a kind of semi-cult movie quite quickly – certainly quicker than any of the others. *The Hill*, for example, took much longer for that to happen. I think they made one fatal flaw when promoting the film [*Robin and Marian*] by trying to make it a romantic story. As I say, the film was written by Goldman as *The Death of Robin Hood* and should have been left as that because that was what he was examining – the death of a hero and revealing really that he's not too intelligent; in fact the smart one is the Sheriff. To explore it in that way, it starts off rather jolly but then eventually the reality of the tale prevails and you realise, my God, it's about someone who is really over-the-hill, he's not too smart, he's a boy at heart, albeit with some kind of charisma, and shows that's how it was – and makes heroes.'

One wonders if, to an extent, *Robin and Marian* is an attempt by Connery to exorcise his own heroic demons, as he plays a classic hero and is perfectly happy to let him die. If so, this is among his more pleasing and poignant epitaphs as, like Robin, he too enters middle age.

*

John Milius, writer and director of the film Connery made a year earlier, *The Wind and the Lion*, sought to make a film rooted in adventure. In his case, the inspirations for his early 20th-century story came from the stories of 19th-century imperialist Rudyard Kipling and British adventure serial *Boy's Own*, not to mention 1930s adventure films such as *Gunga Din* and *The Four Feathers*. He was also influenced by one of the signature American Westerns in 1956's *The Searchers* and foreign epics such as Akira Kurosawa's 1958 film *The Hidden Fortress*. Though pressed by the studio to make his characters younger and increase the romantic interests, some of which Milius acceded to, he sought to stay true to the historical events he was depicting. Here, Connery would play a genuine romantic adventure figure from history, rather than an ageing mythical legend.

The Wind and the Lion is set in 1904 and takes inspiration from the story of Ion Pedecaris, a Greek-American activist, writer and playboy, who, along with his stepson, was kidnapped by rebel Berber tribesmen of Morocco, led by Mulai Ahmed er Raisuni (known as Raisuli to English speakers), as a means of forcing the Sultan not to make accessions to the imperialist powers of Britain, France and Germany, which were looking to make inroads into the country. Milius turns Ion into a beautiful woman, Eden Pedecaris (played by Candice Bergen), who is captured and comes to care for the charming zealot Raisuli (here played by Connery), while in the United States, a bullish President Roosevelt seeks to utilise the kidnapping as propaganda to aid his re-election chances.

Though not ostensibly a role tailor-made for Connery – Omar Sharif was the first choice (he turned it down, as did Anthony Quinn) – Raisuli serves as a counterpoint in many respects to his Robin; the man can be cruel, mercurial and brutal, although Milius always paints him as a noble hero seeking to protect his people. Connery appears to understand his place in such a role, even if – much like his role in *The Next Man* around the same time

– it is a shameless example of cultural appropriation that would not stand today.

Connery nonetheless believed that such concerns did not detract from his ability to play this or any other role: 'My strength as an actor is that I've stayed close to the core of myself, which has something to do with a voice, a music, a tune that's very much tied up with my background experience.

'What I wanted to explore was the character in terms of his pleasures and temptations, attitude and decisions, and what have you, rather than go for a detailed reality of him as a Middle Eastern man.

'It's a very ambitious film in terms of what you can do today and [to] move an entire unit to all these places [eleven in total] around the world.'

Connery's involvement worked as part of his 1970s career balance between striking out as a serious actor and simultaneously trading on his charismatic persona. While Raisuli is by no means an out-and-out hero – he is a brutal insurrectionist – he nonetheless has the kind of principles that Connery rarely shied away from in the characters he played. Arguably to appease the studio machine Milius repeatedly proved he had no real interest in, he was minded to sand down the edges of the real Raisuli in order to ensure *The Wind and the Lion* had a broad appeal. Backed by striking visuals and a sweeping and melodic Jerry Goldsmith score, Milius's film seeks to recapture a heat-blasted sense of colonial adventure from an earlier age.

'The writing of something is what always grabs me,' said Connery. 'And I think John Milius is an exceptional writer. A better writer than he is a director. I think the film is very, very good and would have been a fantastic movie with a different director. But the appeal of *The Wind and the Lion* for me was that it was such a great story and about a great character who was also a real person. To put him in that setting against Hoover in America was just a terrific combination.'

Though Milius never gained the cultural recognition or the critical approbation of his New Wave peers – Francis Ford Coppola for *The Godfather* or George Lucas for *Star Wars* – he, like those directors, sought with films such as *The Wind and the Lion* and, later in the early 1980s, *Conan the Barbarian* (one of the breakout films for a certain Arnold Schwarzenegger) to revive classic storytelling trends in the manner that Lucas combined science fiction and fantasy and Steven Spielberg with *Raiders of the Lost Ark* recaptured 1930s adventure serials on a modern canvas. Milius was looking back further, to 19th-century literature, to Kipling and H. Rider Haggard, which also likely appealed to Connery's sensibilities. (In his final screen role, he portrayed Haggard's famous hero Allan Quatermain in *The League of Extraordinary Gentlemen*.)

In that sense, Milius seeks in *The Wind and the Lion* to buck the trend of the 1970s in giving modern heroes a postmodern complexity. This served as a reintroduction to Connery after years in the cinematic wilderness after *Diamonds Are Forever*, moving from one eccentric or darkly dramatic project to the other. *The Wind and the Lion*, while not achieving the great success of John Huston's broadly similar *The Man Who Would Be King*, in which Connery would star at the end of 1975, nonetheless reminded audiences that the Connery whose cinematic appeal helped define the 1960s was still in evidence, even as he was ageing out of the dynamic, sexual roles that had defined his career.

At the tail end of the 1970s, he would make one last film, another of his barely remembered ventures, that established the pattern that would carry him into his fifties and a new decade in which he would achieve the balance that had eluded him across the 1970s.

*

Cuba could well be the most James Bond-esque film Connery ever performed in that had nothing remotely to do with his signature cinematic creation.

Released in 1979, and in a rare instance of the actor teaming up again with a director whose name was not Sidney Lumet (in this case *Robin and Marian*'s Richard Lester), *Cuba* is set twenty years earlier and sees Connery play former British Army major and now mercenary, Robert Dapes, who is hired to train forces loyal to General Batista as they prepare for Fidel Castro's Communist revolution. While in Cuba, Robert encounters an old flame, Alexandra (Brooke Adams), now married to a selfish cigar-factory owner, and they rekindle their affair as Cuban workers begin to strike and Robert, increasingly growing to loathe Batista's government forces, joins up with the rebellion to fight back, all the while trying to convince Alex to flee the country and start a new life with him away from Cuba.

As is clear in the plot, Robert Dapes is a classic romantic hero, the debonair, sharp-suited, noble Brit abroad, who Connery by this stage could conjure in his sleep. *Cuba* is also the first example of Connery romancing on screen a woman half his age, a trend that would reach its apogee in 1999's *Entrapment*, and indeed Lester's film draws the unsavoury conclusion that Robert first slept with Alex in North Africa years before when she was 15 and he was 30. Cinematic and cultural attitudes to the seduction of the beautiful ingénue by the dashing older man have now thankfully evolved, though *Cuba* never once attempts to portray Connery as anything other than a less deadly, less flippant 007.

Film critic Neil Sinyard, in discussing Lester's work, draws out the overt intended similarities to one of Hollywood's best known romance stories set in exotic climes: '[The film] developed originally out of an idea of Lester's own, inspired by a conversation with a friend about great modern leaders. From there, Lester's thoughts began to formulate in complex ways around Castro and *Casablanca* (1942), and out of that audaciously bizarre combination comes *Cuba*.'

The ending, whereby Robert encourages Alex to join him on a plane leaving Cuba as the Communist regime comes to power, deliberately evokes the bittersweet ending to Michael Curtiz's masterpiece, although nowhere near as successfully. Whereas in *Casablanca* Humphrey Bogart's Rick forces Ingrid Bergman's Ilsa onto the plane for her own good, here Alex gets to the airport too late, having seemingly decided to join Robert, where she sadly watches him fly away and contemplates life in a radically different Cuba.

There are also clear visual and aesthetic similarities with *Never Say Never Again*, Connery's return as 007 which he would make just four short years after *Cuba*. Robert Dapes in another life, with better dialogue, could easily be a middle-aged 007 dabbling in political intrigue and espionage within troubled foreign climes, and given Ian Fleming's portrayal of Bond lined up with the suave, hard-drinking, Bogart-esque figures of masculinity from a bygone age, it is not hard to see the mould in which Dapes was fashioned. Connery was, perhaps without realising, slipping back into the kind of natural role he was best suited for with *Cuba*, and he approached the role with optimism despite some misgivings: 'When they brought me the *Cuba* script, it wasn't completely worked out and was too long. But I was convinced that it was a fascinating story with political intrigue, adventure, a clash of cultures and a love story.'

In all the films discussed in this chapter, where Connery portrays an ageing man of adventure or the charming rogue, there is a consistent theme of rebellion and revolution. *Robin and Marian* sees the elderly Robin returning to find the despotic Sheriff of Nottingham still in charge; Raisuli in *The Wind and the Lion* battles against imperialist aggression in an attempt to preserve his culture and way of life; while Dapes begins in *Cuba* as an example of colonial detachment and privilege, and through the love of a beautiful native woman comes to support the cultural and political revolution of a nation that seeks egalitarian principles. Indeed, the love, or in Raisuli's case the respect, of a woman is central to all of Connery's twilight men of adventure, be it long-lost Marian, captured Eden or passionate Alex. They all work to ground

Connery's larger-than-life characters under threat of control and domination as either saviours or tragic heroes.

Yet there is one last exploration of Connery's cinematic output in the 1970s, when looking at films trading on his natural charisma, that differ from either his ensemble roles or the portrayals of dashing heroic figures. There are two films specifically in which Connery plays less the romantic rogue, but rather the devilish crook.

*

There is a reason why Michael Crichton's adapted 1975 novel, *The Great Train Robbery*, was given the title *The First Great Train Robbery* when it arrived in cinemas in 1978. Audiences at that time, and for decades beyond, associated the 'Great Train Robbery' with a very different and much more contemporary crime.

Ronnie Biggs became the infamous face of the 1963 robbery of a train travelling from Glasgow to London in which a gang of thieves stole £2.6 million, many of whom were arrested and sentenced to lengthy jail terms. The crime featured heavily in popular culture from the 1960s onwards – including in Connery's fourth Bond adventure *Thunderball*, where criminal organisation SPECTRE claim they received £250,000 as a consultation fee for the robbery – and the British public associated the high-stakes robbery of a train with the real-life incident rather than a much earlier event Crichton used as the basis for his story, the 'Great Gold Robbery' of 1854.

In that heist, three boxes of gold bullion were stolen from a guard's van while being shipped from London to Paris, by four men who stole the equivalent of almost £1.5 million in modern money. One of those men was William Pierce (renamed Edward Pierce by Crichton when adapting his tale). Connery plays the Victorian-era high-society figure who plans to steal the bullion destined to pay British soldiers fighting the Crimean War, recruiting a team including Robert Agar (Donald Sutherland, affecting a horrid Irish accent) and his mistress Miriam (Lesley-Anne Down).

What Crichton presented was, at the time, a rather innovative take on a heist movie. Deliberately eschewing the forensic, serious-minded structure of the novel he was adapting, the director set out to make a colourful, crowd-pleasing romp, filled with lavish 19th-century production design and a rip-roaring score from the musical maestro, Jerry Goldsmith (who had previously reaped dividends for John Milius on *The Wind and the Lion*). Crichton had previous form for combining genres and styles – for instance his 1973 film *Westworld* fused the classic American Western with science fiction. Here, Crichton takes an era we have largely experienced through period drama and injects adventure and crime into the mix, providing an anachronistic blend he never seeks to take all that seriously.

Connery is, of course, playing a crook, which when we consider many of his previous roles (notwithstanding *The Anderson Tapes*) is a change of pace. Granted, he had played controlling sexual predators (*Marnie*, *A Fine Madness*) and damaged, abusive husbands (*The Offence*, *Male of the Species*), but the amoral gentleman thief feels like a natural extension from his ethically questionable role as the British assassin with a licence to kill.

Swaggering and seductive, Edward Pierce is openly crooked to a degree we hadn't see Connery play before, even as 'Duke' Anderson. In Lumet's contemporary heist film, Duke is embroiled in surveillance and technological espionage that adds a level of paranoia to proceedings, but none of that anxiety is in evidence here. While we are meant to enjoy Pierce's larceny via Connery's charismatic performance, he is rotten through and through. He constantly lies, is concerned only with what he can gain, and at his trial when a judge asks why he executed his crime, Pierce simply responds: 'I wanted the money.' But what comes of his admission? Support from the common folk, who cheer him on as Miriam helps him escape justice and flee into the night.

This jollity in the face of a terrible crime and how Crichton has him loved for it, is perhaps what attracted an initially weary Connery to a role that, much like Robert Dapes in *Cuba*, would appeal to the side of his persona that audiences often turned out for (and often didn't when he tried to explore other facets). Pierce is a rebellious character taking on an entrenched system that is considered corrupt by the populace, even if he is only seeking personal material gain.

There was also a Bond-esque flavour, even down to Connery performing one or two of his own death-defying stunts in Crichton's set pieces. His second wife Micheline Roquebrune was unhappy to learn that he, not a stunt double, had run across the roof of a train and almost fallen between carriages in doing so. This stunt was performed on top of what he had been assured was an antique carriage from the Irish Railway Preservation Society, which could not go above 35mph. It turned out to be capable of up to 60mph and, following filming, Connery learned that the vehicle had no speedometer. 'How do you know what speed you're doing, then?' he asked the driver.

'Oh, that's easy. I just count the trees!' was the jovial and slightly alarming response.

At the end of a decade riddled with state corruption and recession in the West, Connery perhaps understood with *The First Great Train Robbery* that what audiences wanted to see were antiheroes taking on the system and getting away with it. After all, what was Ronnie Biggs but a modern folk hero?

*

By the mid-1970s, John Huston, one of Hollywood's most consistent and eclectic auteurs, had spent twenty years attempting to put Rudyard Kipling's *The Man Who Would Be King* on screen. It is the story of Peachy Carnehan and Daniel Dravot, two ex-British Army officers in India who had travelled to the remote land of

Kafiristan, now part of Afghanistan, in the early 1880s, seeking to bring arms to a people who had barely been visited by Europeans since the time of Alexander the Great. When Dravot is wounded and he survives, the people of Kafiristan take him to be a god, and while Peachy seeks to rob them of the riches Dravot is given access to, Dravot comes to enjoy his status as a god, falls in love with a local woman, and seeks to rule as god and king of the province. Inevitably, it all ends in tragedy and death.

'It's a morality tale,' explained Connery. 'You know, you mess around with the gods and they fix you! I think it's an amazing story. It's only twenty-two pages as [a] short story by Rudyard Kipling.'

Huston originally sought Humphrey Bogart and Clark Gable for the two central roles, later considering Burt Lancaster and Kirk Douglas, and subsequently Richard Burton and Peter O'Toole. After their breakout success as a double act in *Butch Cassidy and the Sundance Kid* cemented them as cast-iron 1960s movie stars, Huston considered the duo of Robert Redford and Paul Newman for the roles, but Newman convinced him that British actors should be cast in such colonially British roles and suggested Connery and Caine. When Huston was finally able to mount the production, he would believe he had, ultimately, found the perfect duo to cast after his long search: 'I believe Connery and Caine gave better performances than either Bogart or Gable could have, because they are the real thing. They are those characters.'

'It was a great pleasure to do that movie. And that doesn't happen a lot,' mused Connery. 'John Huston waited 39 years to make the movie. Talk about patience! We had a lot of fun, Michael Caine and myself – although John had originally wanted Clark Gable and Humphrey Bogart. For an actor – and Michael would agree with this – it was a dream. But it was also quite difficult as well because you couldn't miss a couple of words and paraphrase because of the way it's structured. It's only if you read the text will you see what I mean.

'We had the most marvellous locations on the picture and we

had a very, very good art director, Alex Trauner, so you couldn't go anywhere without finding something interesting to do or react to.'

Connery was, Pauline Kael of *The New Yorker* wrote upon the film's release, 'a far better Danny than Gable would ever have been. With the glorious exceptions of Brando and Olivier, there's no screen actor I'd rather watch than Sean Connery. His vitality may make him the most richly masculine of all English-speaking actors.' Few actors, she added, 'are as un-self-consciously silly as Connery is willing to be – as he *enjoys* being.'

Though Caine's Peachy bookends the film, setting up the narrative with a fictionalised version of Kipling himself (played by Christopher Plummer), Connery is afforded the role of the man-made king in Dravot, who succumbs entirely to the native allure of the foreign land he initially seeks to plunder, not to mention potentially conquer with the zeal of a true colonial Englishman. 'In any place where they fight,' says Danny to Kipling, 'a man who knows how to drill men can always be a king. We shall go to those parts and say to any king we find – "D'you want to vanquish your foes?" And we will show him how to drill men; for that we know better than anything else. Then we will subvert that king and seize his throne and establish a dynasty.'

There is a sense of manifest destiny about Connery's character and his performance. Though his partnership with Caine allows for a requisite amount of sparring and derring-do, with Huston's film ultimately as much of an adventure movie as many of those previously discussed, Connery's Dravot is adhering to a falsehood when it comes to Kafiristan.

At the same time, Connery also plays Dravot with an unusual sense of comedic charm that he did not – apart from the droll wit of Bond – have the opportunity in many pictures to display. He actively avoided comedies during the 1970s in the main, but when he was given the opportunity, such as at points in lighter fare like *Robin and Marian*, he excelled. *The Man Who Would Be King*, especially when having fun working opposite Caine, sees Connery somewhat off the leash. It displays his versatility and how, with the right sparring partner such as Caine, he could serve as part of an engaging double act. He would repeat that trick very effectively alongside Nicolas Cage two decades on in Michael Bay's very different film, *The Rock*.

By all accounts, the shoot was an enjoyable experience for Connery, starring opposite his friend and working for Huston. He was at one point told that he must appease a local sheik by eating sheep's eyes only to later discover the said sheik was his comedian friend Eric Sykes in disguise. And as Caine recalled, aware of Connery's fear of heights and uncertainty about filming a climactic moment on a rope bridge: 'There was a day when we were shooting on the rope bridge and Sean turned to John and said, "Do you think the bridge looks safe?" John lowered his eyes and said, "Sean, the bridge looks the way it always has. The only difference is that today, you're going to be standing in the middle of it."'

It is fascinating to consider *The Man Who Would Be King* as more than just an adventure story with Connery playing a morally dubious colonialist Englishman who attempts to fake divinity to achieve the ultimate delusion of grandeur with the actor's own troubled relationship with fame across the 1970s. The roles he chose, the blend of personal projects alongside populist-driven excursions into ageing troubadours and charming folk heroes, suggest the schism in the kind of film star Connery wanted to be in the wake of James Bond. Many of his choices skew towards exploring political and cultural reflections of a complex decade of economic strife and paranoia-driven hardship.

Dravot does not survive the end of *The Man Who Would Be King*. Peachy returns home, begging and in some disgrace, and presents Kipling – one of the signature authors at the height of the British Empire – with the still-crowned skull of Dravot. The message is clear: beware hubris. Beware hero worship. For Connery, perhaps, beware buying into one's own hype. As the decade progressed, and the roles he took on became even more varied and, in some senses, more self-deprecating, and driven by his own sense of what he was capable of, the door began to open for Connery's career transformation in the 1980s, a decade in which the movie star was reborn in the blockbuster era.

It is a world Connery, with and without James Bond, would find his place within. At the same time, it would challenge him to undertake some of his most eccentric and unusual screen roles yet. For, while he would become the man who would be Bond (again), he would also venture into territory easily defined in three words: nothing like Bond.

SEVEN

MAN OF SUBSTANCE

CONNERY'S CAREER WAS in the doldrums as the 1980s arrived. A decade earlier, while still working to throw off the shackles of Bond and take on roles that steered away from the escapism of those films, he remained a bankable entity. Life and cinema had changed in the years since. Stars had ceased to drive cinematic success to the same degree as when he rose to prominence, even if it wasn't his name directly that had made the Bond franchise such a triumph.

Nevertheless, Connery remained determined to blaze his own trail. He would, especially in the first half of the 1980s, dabble in science fiction and fantasy, with films such as *Outland* and *Time Bandits*. He would work for directorial legends, men touched by greatness but long past their time, crafting uniquely defiant pictures audiences would immediately forget such as *Wrong Is Right* or *Five Days One Summer*.

It was the most under-the-radar period, perhaps, of Connery's career – post-Bond, pre-Bond return, and just ahead of a 1980s renaissance as a star and icon once more. In fiercely seeking to make films that were nothing like Bond, Connery steadfastly refused to give the people what they wanted. The result: some of the most unusual and creatively divisive pictures he ever made.

*

At the tail end of the 1970s, Peter Hyams wrote and directed *Capricorn One*, a film which took seriously a possibility that *Diamonds Are Forever* had lampooned at the beginning of the same decade: what if the *Apollo 11* moon landings in 1969 had been faked?

One of the most pervasive conspiracy theories to emerge in the 1970s, public opinion on whether the moon landings were faked has ranged anywhere from 9% saying they were, in a 1994 *Washington Post* poll, to 20% in 2001 after the airing of a Fox documentary which once again brought these theories into the light. Both polls emerged during a decade in which conspiracy theories were rife, and populated in mainstream fiction such as *The X-Files*. Today, almost 11% of millennials believe it could be true, despite widespread evidence to the contrary.

Connery's first principal starring role of the 1980s was in Hyams' second film to explore conspiracy and science fiction: *Outland*. Despite mixed reviews, *Capricorn One* ended up being the most successful independently made film of 1978; audiences responded to what was in the mass discourse a fringe idea. And although *Outland* is a very different film, Hyams sought out Connery to play a deliberate outsider. 'I wanted to do a Western,' recalled Hyams. 'Everybody said, "You can't do a Western; Westerns are dead; nobody will do a Western." I remember thinking it was weird that this genre that had endured for so long was just gone. But then I woke up and came to the conclusion – obviously after other people – that it was actually alive and well, but in outer space. I wanted to make a film about the frontier. Not the wonder of it or the glamour of it: I wanted to do something about Dodge City and how hard life was.'

Many have drawn a clear link between *Outland* and Fred Zinnemann's classic 1952 picture *High Noon*, starring Gary Cooper and Grace Kelly, which still stands as one of the high points in the American Western genre. *Outland*'s central plot clearly takes inspiration from Zinnemann's work as Connery plays Federal Marshal William O'Niel, despatched to a titanium ore mining colony in orbit of Io, one of Jupiter's moons, on a tour of duty with his family. Once there, O'Niel uncovers a corporate conspiracy in which illegal performance-enhancing drugs are given to employees to improve work efficiency; the side effects lead some to suffer psychotic episodes and kill themselves. O'Niel refuses to be bought off by the corporation behind this and finds himself in a last stand against hired killers sent to silence him for good.

Connery was well aware of the comparisons to Zinnemann's classic, as he told Tony Crawley for *Starburst Magazine*: 'What was clever, I think, was the idea of setting it in space – a frontier town. That's what appealed to me in the first place . . . I liked his mixture of Western, science fiction, adventure and the sort of thriller where one was using computers, surveillance instruments that visually told the story.'

It sees Connery, unusually, as a devoted husband and father, a portrayal he had often avoided even in the wake of James Bond. Connery's typical leading men in recent years were charming rogues, romantic heroes or experts in their field drafted in to solve a key problem. O'Niel is an everyman and a different beast from Shalako, Connery's more conventional protagonist in the Western genre. Connery's hero is the last man standing: the honourable, moral family man who, unlike Cooper's sheriff in *High Noon* who faces down a vicious gang of outlaws, must contend with an entire corporate structure in a dark, cold future where human rights are secondary to financial gain.

Outland therefore owes more of a debt to Ridley Scott's *Alien*, released in 1979, a film which from a visual and storytelling aesthetic could share universes. *Alien* edges into body horror and haunted-house terror rather than overt conspiracy, but they both share ideas of a future for humanity very different from the luxurious galaxy-exploring cruise ships of *Star Trek* or the derring-do space fantasy of *Star Wars*. In Hyams and Scott's worlds, humans are in a desperate fight for survival, and in both movies the conclusion comes down to one solo figure against a corrupted external force. For *Alien*, it is the female Ripley against the terrifying xenomorph. In *Outland*, O'Niel draws a line in the sand in a world where the sanctity of life means nothing.

At first, Connery wasn't entirely sold on the script, despite wanting to play O'Niel. 'My initial complaint was that it was too black and white,' he remarked. 'Too . . . certain. Therefore, not quite as truthful as I would have liked. The character, O'Niel, was suddenly able to handle the whole problem. I wanted more kinda doubt in the part. Hyams, I think, is a technical and first-rate director. I don't think he's in the same class as a writer. But the actual dramatic impulse and story are sufficiently dramatic to take the thrust through to the end.'

Yet, as perhaps fits Connery and the echo of the 1970s in which *Outland* rests, his hero does not precisely fit either the Gary Cooper analogy or the traditional family-man hero. His wife is continually frustrated by the career he has chosen, which routinely drags them to the backwater of civilisation, in distant and remote working colonies, to the point that there are hints the marriage could even be in trouble. And, as film writer Tim Pelan notes: 'O'Niel isn't a hearts-and-minds kind of guy. He's a plodder. He's promised himself one last case, because it's his job, then he's out, with his family. He feels a compulsion to know if his principles are really worth fighting for in this roughneck hellhole that most likely will brush over his investigation and move on, driven as ever by the almighty dollar. He opens up to Lazarus: "I want to find out if . . .

well, if they're right. There's a whole machine that works because everybody does what they are supposed to. And I found out . . . I was supposed to be something I didn't like. That's what's in the program. That's my rotten little part in the rotten machine. I don't like it. So I'm going to find out if they're right."'

Connery is both the outsider in *Outland* as regards his work, his job, but also, to an extent, his family. As he couldn't play a traditional husband in *The Offence*, a role darkened by internal demons and personal moral corruption, as O'Niel he is a noble man fighting for a world he may not believe in. Unlike many of the blockbuster films the 1980s would present, with big-name stars saving cities, worlds and universes, O'Niel is less an antihero than a reverse-hero, begotten of a cinematic landscape that was rapidly about to change.

Perhaps due to the dour, mechanical and conspiratorial air coupled with Connery's intense performance, *Outland* has not lived on in the same vein as *Alien*. This is in part down to Hyams not being as skilled a filmmaker as Ridley Scott, but *Alien* also appealed to the burgeoning combination in the 1980s of science fiction and horror – a natural evolution from 1950s B-movies – that would take flight in remakes such as John Carpenter's *The Thing*, David Cronenberg's *The Fly*, and even Stuart Gordon's schlocky adaptations of H. P. Lovecraft. *Outland* is part of no such revisionist moment for the Western, or even the combination of that genre with science fiction, and as such it appropriately serves as an outlier for Connery as an actor.

Five years later, in a very different but perhaps equally alien world, Connery would again play an outsider looking in, a man of moral fortitude embroiled in intrigue.

*

Umberto Eco, the author of *The Name of the Rose*, believed in the ephemeral nature of conspiracy, of secret knowledge and a hidden world, one that goes far beyond that of a mere government hoax as witnessed in *Capricorn One*, for example.

Eco was not thrilled at the idea of his book being adapted by Jean-Jacques Annaud, a French filmmaker who believed passionately in bringing the story to the screen. Connery portrays William of Baskerville, a fictitious Franciscan friar in the year 1327, who with his young protégé Adso of Melk (played by a fresh-faced Christian Slater in his screen debut), investigates the apparent suicide of Adelmo of Otranto, a gifted, youthful monk and manuscript illuminator, which leads both men into the challenge of proving he did not die by the assumed demonic means as believed by the Church. For William, it is a problem-solving exercise and for Adso, narrating events as a much older man in the future, it is a coming-of-age tale.

In creating his medieval sleuth, Eco drew on two famous individuals: one real – the medieval friar, philosopher and theologian William of Ockham, who lived in the same era and is the origin of the premise of 'Occam's razor'; the other fictional – Victorian amateur detective Sherlock Holmes. William of Baskerville is a man out of his own time – an intellectual outsider who challenges the doctrine of the self-imposed truths of the Church during a time when superstition, pagan ritual, black magic and the power of heresy frequently gave way to anything from torture to genocide. The conspiracy he exposes in *The Name of the Rose* is one designed to hide truth and knowledge itself.

The Name of the Rose presages, therefore, the resurgent fascination in occult conspiracy we would see as the 1990s beckoned, with Eco a forerunner of writers and creatives such as Dan Brown, who would, on a far simpler and mass-market level, promote the idea of sacred, mystical lost history, and of powerful extremist forces seeking to uphold doctrine. It is the first time Connery as an actor will clash with F. Murray Abraham, who plays Inquisition leader Bernardo Gui (a real character from history): they will find themselves cast in a similar fashion, albeit in a very different context, in the contemporary literary drama *Finding Forrester* over a decade later.

Though not a picture in which religious worship is necessarily front and centre, it is almost a surprise to witness Connery take on the role of a man of faith, given his personal views on religion: 'I'm not a religious man at all, but I remember that at that time I got deeply interested in religion and thought I'd like to become a Catholic. I visited the priest in every town we played and took religious instruction. But I never became a Catholic. I think the celibacy of the priests and nuns made me nervous. Asexuality disturbs me.'

Andrew Birkin, one of the writers of *The Name of the Rose*'s eventual screenplay, has discussed Connery's involvement in the film – a film, it is worth noting, that Arnaud resisted casting Connery in and Columbia Pictures pulled funding for given Connery's lacklustre career at the time. Birkin suggests Connery was focused on reining in any tendencies to make William more of a conventional character. He read Eco. He even read Aristotle. He sought a philosophical approach where others baulked at it. 'He gave [Baskerville] a dour, rather Scots sense of humour,' said Birkin. 'He brought pensiveness and thoughtfulness to the part. Things he wasn't able to play in Bond. Bond is a man of action. Here, Sean played a man of words.'

Such films gave Connery, at the turn of the 1980s, space to play with words, to play with characters who defied the convention of what to expect from him as an actor, and he would soon find himself edging towards an unconventional genre that would connect to the new kind of actor that Connery was becoming.

*

During the 1970s, Connery had made unusual career choices that occasionally veered into the realm of escapism and fantasy, notably John Boorman's *Zardoz*, although he turned down Boorman's

Excalibur several years later, deferring one of the ultimate mythic roles as King Arthur till later in his career.

When he wasn't playing more serious, political and dramatic roles, perhaps determined to detach from the high camp and fantasy that his last James Bond film, *Diamonds Are Forever*, had employed, he stuck to adventure. Though he didn't move to pull any swords from stones in 1981 and team up with Boorman again, that same year he did choose to work for a director who would outdo Boorman for surrealism and would develop a subgenre and style all his own.

Terry Gilliam first came to fame as part of Monty Python's Flying Circus, the signature British comedy troupe who brought absurdity and surrealism into the homes of millions during the 1960s and 1970s with several series of their BBC TV sketch show. Gilliam was first animator of the series' cartoonish comic sketches and later appeared alongside his cohorts John Cleese, Michael Palin, Eric Idle, Graham Chapman and Terry Jones in writing and delivering some of the most iconic moments in British comic history.

As *Monty Python* rocketed into the stratosphere and became a key foundation of what would become an 'alternative comedy' scene in Britain at the end of the 1970s into the 1980s, Gilliam worked with Jones on taking the troupe to the big screen – first in 1975's *Monty Python and the Holy Grail*, then in 1979's *Life of Brian*, and finally 1983's *The Meaning of Life* – but amidst these outings Gilliam firmly established his own directorial style, voice and unique visual approach with *Time Bandits* (written with Palin and co-starring he and Cleese amongst a galaxy of thespians). The noun 'Gilliamesque' would soon follow.

Time Bandits takes a comic, fantastical approach to the world experienced through imaginative young English schoolboy Kevin (Craig Warnock) who is dragged into a serious of escapades across time from Ancient Greece through to the sinking of the *Titanic* alongside a band of dwarves with a map being pursued by a Godlike figure, the Supreme Being. It is episodic, bizarre and exuberant in the manner of *Python* while moving to the beat of its own drum. Gilliam is ostensibly making a film for children but it is told through the twisted prism of adulthood.

Parenthood turns out to be key to Connery's role in *Time Bandits*. He plays Agamemnon, the king of Mycenae in Ancient Greece, who encounters Kevin after he is separated from the dwarves. He adopts the boy as his own. Connery's role is brief, appearing only at the very end for a time-bending dual appearance as a modern-day fireman who gives a *Never Say Never Again*-esque wink to an audience who clearly appreciate Connery is the biggest star in the film. Gilliam never expected to cast him; he simply used him in the script as shorthand for an A-list actor he would love to cast. Yet, as it turned out, Denis O'Brien – manager of ex-Beatle George Harrison, who had formed the recently minted HandMade Films who were producing *Time Bandits* – happened to play a round of golf with Connery. 'He mentioned the possibility of being in this film,' recounted Gilliam. 'And Sean liked the idea. I guess he was a *Python* fan. I'm convinced the reason he said yes was that he was having some guilt feelings about having been an absent father. And here was a chance to be a surrogate father.'

I have left Connery's personal life – his various relationships and marriages, the issues around tax and other financial problems – aside in this book; they have been covered elsewhere. But it does feel relevant, and perhaps not coincidental, that in 1981 he would play two roles as a father figure – in *Time Bandits* and *Outland* – in a manner we rarely saw Connery portray before or subsequently. He had one son from his marriage to Diane Cilento, Jason, who like Connery's brother Neil would later dabble in acting – memorably performing a role Connery himself played twice, Robin Hood, in 1980s TV series *Robin of Sherwood* – but his marriage to Cilento, after a honeymoon period, was often distant and fractious. Cilento was a successful actor herself, and the couple were frequently apart, shooting film projects.

Did he see Jason in Kevin? Did he see the father he wanted to be in *Outland's* O'Niel, or rather the father he was? These are questions that will remain unanswered, but Connery perhaps found in these fantastical realms – be they gregarious mythical Greek kings or space marshals on a dark corporate frontier – a way to play the kind of wise, protective paternal figure that he otherwise struggled to realise. Perhaps this is why Connery, just a couple of years later in downtime while shooting *Never Say Never Again*, took a walk-on part in Stephen Weeks' little known 1984 fantasy film, *Sword of the Valiant*, a telling of the late 14th-century poem 'Sir Gawain and the Green Knight' – recently brought to life in vivid fashion by David Lowery with Dev Patel in the lead role.

The Green Knight, played by Connery, gives Gawain a year to solve a riddle; if Gawain fails, the Green Knight will claim his head. So begins a quest narrative bookended by Connery, in a small role (although prominent on the poster), which concludes in much more of a 1980s fantastical heroic way than Lowery's version almost forty years later. After *Time Bandits'* critical and commercial success, Connery found a new seam of fantastical worlds opening themselves up: *Highlander* and a signature role in the world of Indiana Jones were right around the corner, in both of which Connery would continue to develop his position as mentor/father figure.

'The reason Burt Lancaster had a longer, more varied career than Kirk Douglas was that he refused to allow himself to be limited,' Connery told *The New York Times* in 1987. 'He was more ready to play less romantic parts, and was more experimental in his choice of roles. And that's the way I've tried to be. I don't mind being older or looking stupid or whatever. I've tried to be guided by what was different, what was refreshing, stimulating to me.'

Connery would lean towards directors and scripts that actively defied a conventional career move. The year 1982 was an especially strange one for Connery, thanks to two highly unusual films.

'If you start thinking of your image, or what the mysterious "they" out there are thinking of you, you're in a trap,' he continued in the *New York Times* interview. 'What's important is that you're doing the work that's best for you. What matters is just to be a serious actor.'

*

In 1979, an author named Charles McCarry released a thriller called *The Better Angels*. Set in a future version of 1992, the novel revolved around political intrigue in Washington, the White House and a fictional Middle Eastern nation state called Hagreb. It is remembered for only two reasons.

The first is that it featured Arab terrorists flying passenger planes into buildings, giving the book a brief but questionable resurgence in the wake of 9/11. The second is that it was adapted only three years after publication by filmmaker Richard Brooks as *Wrong Is Right* (internationally as *The Man with the Deadly Lens*) and starred Sean Connery during what is possibly the most unusual year of his career: 1982.

In many ways, it should have gone down as one of his most profound or eclectic years, given that he was working with two Oscar-winning directors. Richard Brooks was never recognised as a directorial name for the masses but he was the man behind celebrated classic Hollywood pictures such as *Blackboard Jungle* and *Cat on a Hot Tin Roof*, and he aided the birth of Hollywood's edgy New Wave in the late 1960s through his adaptation of Truman Capote's searing true crime novel, *In Cold Blood*.

Like Connery himself, Brooks was something of a chameleon, able to move between a variety of unique projects, and the two of them had a long association.

What Brooks might have intended as a *Dr. Strangelove* for a decade that was embracing fast food, fast TV and fast technology struggled to evoke the satirical absurdity that Stanley Kubrick's film offered in the wake of the nuclear crisis. The tagline on the poster for *Wrong Is Right*, above Connery's grinning news anchor and a nuclear mushroom cloud, conveys a similar tone: 'In a moment World War III . . . but first a word from our sponsor.' But *Wrong Is Right* pulls its punches.

This is despite Connery, arguably somewhat miscast in such an irony-driven piece, as Patrick Hale, giving bravura monologues that unpick the facile nature of televised news and what journalism was transforming into. 'What kind of journalism was it when television paid half a million for an exclusive on the Bay of Pigs?' cries Hale. 'A million dollars for Nixon to apologise coast to coast? CBS paid Haldeman, Eisenhower and Johnson. NBC paid John Dean and Robert Kennedy's assassin. ABC paid Lieutenant Calley and for breakfast served up the My Lai massacre. And what about the killer I put on television? From death row to the electric chair, fried meat on prime time. You paid one hundred thousand dollars for that! Paid it to the killer! Do you call that journalism? We're in show business, baby. Make them laugh, make them cry, make them buy, by and by. Get that guy on camera.'

Connery himself, years later, in the wake of the first Iraq War, was more pragmatic. When asked whether Saddam Hussein should have been toppled, he told journalist Elisa Leonetti: 'You saw what Saddam did, burning all those wells and polluting the place, I mean, they'll never get over the damage this maniac has done. So, if he'd gone on with any more power than he had, he would have damaged everything. The only unsatisfactory aspect of it is that he's still there; but it's difficult to blame Bush on that respect, for pulling back after arriving at the walls of Baghdad, because you have to be careful, otherwise you dilute the potency of something like the United Nations, when you're attempting to make a war without breaching sovereignty in other countries. The criteria for everything is democracy, and that's the one strength the United States have in most issues, the combination of the Congress and the Bill of Rights make for events to take a pace that dictatorships and totalitarian countries don't have.'

Despite the talent of Brooks, *Wrong Is Right* died a swift death at the box office. It was proof that even when looking to capitalise on current affairs and future political trends, and working with a Hollywood legend, audiences would not automatically turn up for Connery.

*

The second Oscar-winning director Connery worked for in 1982 was Fred Zinnemann, perhaps best known for *High Noon* in 1952 (the inspiration behind *Outland* just a year earlier). Arguably a director with greater commercial and critical success than Brooks, Zinnemann was, by the time he made *Five Days One Summer* with Connery, a cinematic giant spanning decades. It would be the last picture he made before his death in 1997.

Based on the short story 'Maiden, Maiden' by Kay Boyle, *Five Days One Summer* is set in 1932. Connery plays Douglas Meredith, a Scottish doctor on holiday in the Alps with his much younger wife Kate (Betsy Brantley). They befriend a local guide, Johann (Lambert Wilson), who agrees to prepare them for a hike up the Maiden mountain, but as Kate grows close to Johann and Douglas's jealousy begins to intensify, the incestuous truth about their relationship is revealed through flashbacks: Kate is in fact Douglas's niece.

For a film that was a failure on all fronts and could well be Connery's least well-known picture, there is a great deal to unpick with *Five Days One Summer*, to explain what is otherwise an odd career choice.

For a start, this is the first time Connery played both his actual age (with his actual receded hairline) and a dyed-in-the-wool Scot on screen, outside his fleeting appearances in *The Bowler and the Bunnet*. He was deeply committed to working with Zinnemann, whose work he had long admired, and he was prepared to work hard for the director. 'His physical courage and his gruff, sarcastic sense of humour made him enormously popular with the crew,' recalled Zinnemann. 'He would much rather have played golf than muck about in mountains but he didn't grumble when asked to drop, suspended on a rope, into a 200-foot deep crevasse. He projected an air of complete authority.'

Connery was utterly confident in a story which, to put it mildly, would be regarded by modern eyes with concern. The film projects itself as a romantic melodrama and trades on Connery's charisma to help us believe that Kate would move from teenage infatuation, in the wake of her father's death, with an uncle who in 1920s Edinburgh as a self-made businessman at the tail end of the Industrial Revolution radiated not just authority but security, into a sexual awakening with the man in middle age. Does Douglas groom Kate? Or is it a 'natural' evolution as Kate enters womanhood and there is merely the taboo of an unseemly age gap?

The idea that Connery would have actively chosen, in his early fifties, to portray a borderline paedophile is bizarre. Although *The Offence* (arguably a much better film) had taken him into dark, psychosexual areas, Connery always had one canny eye on his broader appeal, even when he was experimenting with off-the-beaten-track fare.

Though incest has long been taboo in Western Christian society, in the early 1980s and beyond, audiences have proven to be forgiving of questionable age gaps and what would now be considered as sexually manipulative, coercive relationships. David Schwimmer's Ross Geller in the popular TV comedy *Friends* seducing his student is one such accepted relationship being re-evaluated in the modern day, in a #MeToo cultural landscape where activism and awareness of consent and female agency is much more in the public consciousness.

Just as Connery's own remarks and actions regarding violence towards women were again brought to light, in the wake of his death, and had long been questioned by audiences, so too is it hard to view *Five Days One Summer* as Zinnemann intended: a haunting, beautiful paean to the mountain, on which the director set a doomed love story with Connery cast less as a groomer, or predator, and rather as a distinguished gentleman who loses his heart to a girl who came of age with him, unable to accept the reality of not being able to retain her for long.

It would be the first, but far from the last, time that Connery enjoyed a significant age gap between himself and his leading lady, and it was not something he considered problematic, even as late in the day as 1999's *Entrapment*, one of his final films. By all accounts, given Zinnemann's skill and the richness of the text, Connery was quite bemused by *Five Days One Summer*'s abject failure. He might well have felt the same about why *Wrong Is Right* failed to connect with audiences that same year.

What he missed about his 1982 output was that audiences were not as ready for Connery's move into ironic satire or arthouse fare as he was. This was the continuing battle, throughout his career, that by the end of the 1980s he finally began to realise he had lost: that the perception of Connery as a heroic symbol of cinematic culture could never be altered. He might wish to play roles that were nothing like Bond, but he wasn't doing what Patrick Hale believed mass media was now all about: giving the people what they want.

So, in 1983, that is exactly what Sean Connery did next.

EIGHT

HIS CHARLEMAGNE

THE RETURN OF Connery as James Bond in 1983's *Never Say Never Again* was thanks to a curious, unprecedented loophole that tied Eon Productions and the established Bond franchise up in litigation that wasn't fully resolved for half a century.

A name briefly mentioned earlier when discussing *Thunderball*, Kevin McClory, is infamous in the annals of James Bond mythology. Although *Thunderball* ended up as the fourth released James Bond picture, and Fleming's ninth novel of the series in 1961, the origins of his story existed in meetings Fleming undertook with his friend Ivar Bryce and McClory in 1958 over the possibility of bringing 007 to the big screen, where many of the details of the story – including the creation of a character named Fatima Blush – were thrashed out. McClory brought in Jack Whittingham, an experienced screenwriter, to help pull together the plot for a film variously known as *SPECTRE* and *James Bond of the Secret Service*.

By 1961, Fleming had changed the name of the story to *Thunderball* and taken many of the constituent elements within the screenplay for his eventual novel, at which point McClory and Whittingham sued for plagiarism. They lost, and the novel was published, but Fleming, suffering from heart disease (and just a few years from his death), was convinced by Bryce to settle out of court. Fleming agreed to provide McClory with the literary and film rights to the content within *Thunderball*, while he retained control of the novel. Consequently, when *Thunderball* entered film production after Fleming's death, Eon had to involve McClory as a producer, even though he was already making noises about creating a rival 007 film to the established franchise.

The court case had provided McClory with the 'exclusive right to use James Bond as a character in any such scripts or film of *Thunderball*' and 'the exclusive right to reproduce any part of the novel in films and for the purpose of making such films to make scripts'. The case did, however, enforce a ten-year gap between *Thunderball* and McClory being able to produce his own, non-Eon version of the material. When the period elapsed in 1975 it was long after Connery had departed from the series in *Diamonds Are Forever* with the seemingly concrete decision 'never again' to play Bond. Roger Moore was now the established James Bond successor, a greater success than George Lazenby, and looking at the third outing that would define his 007 – 1977's hugely successful *The Spy Who Loved Me*.

In 1975, with Connery's star power on the wane, McClory – who had remained a good friend since the Bond days – came calling with the intention to not only make a new version of *Thunderball* for the 1970s, but for Connery to return – again – as James Bond. At first Connery gave him an expected and unequivocal no. But McClory kept at it and offered Connery the chance to collaborate on the script, which he knew might be the bait that could change Connery's mind. It worked. Connery's penchant for offering script contributions to directors and screenwriters recurred throughout his career, but he had never received a screen credit. What McClory was offering with his new, rival Bond film was the kind of opportunity Connery would never have been granted working with Eon, especially given the fractious relationship he maintained with Broccoli and Saltzman – the latter of whom had walked away from the Bond universe after 1974's *The Man with the Golden Gun*, leaving Broccoli the sole producing force for most of the Moore era.

Work began between Connery, McClory and Len Deighton – the esteemed spy novelist behind Michael Caine's rival espionage character Harry Palmer – on a film they gave the working title of *James Bond of the Secret Service*.

'I was in Almeria finishing *The Wind and Lion*,' remembered Connery, 'and Kevin McClory came to see me. And he said that after ten years the rights [for *Thunderball*] reverted back to him; he knew I wasn't interested in playing the part, but would I be interested in writing the screenplay with Len Deighton? And that appealed to me, so I said, "Sure." I worked with Len over a period of, I dunno, four months . . . six months nearly.'

'It was really a tremendous experience working with Sean as a writer,' recalled McClory, 'because he did not contribute just throwaway lines, he also got involved in the construction of the plot. And he's a very good storyteller. Therefore he's a very good story writer, and he writes visually. He made enormous contributions and we all got along very well.'

Due to objections about the title from Eon, justifiably frustrated that the film was a going concern, McClory agreed to change the title first to *Hammerhead* (Deighton's preferred suggestion) and then the more simplistic *Warhead*. Connery discussed the content of the story that he had had a hand in: 'Those airplanes that were disappearing over the Bermuda Triangle? We had SPECTRE doing that. There was this fantastic fleet of planes under the sea – a whole world of stuff had been brought down. They [SPECTRE] were going to attack the financial nerve centre of the United States by going in through the sewers of New York – which you can do – right into Wall Street. They'd have mechanical sharks in the bay and take over the Statue of Liberty, which is quite easy, and have the main line of troops on Ellis Island.'

Warhead once again saw SPECTRE led by Ernst Stavro Blofeld (with McClory hoping to cast Orson Welles, who had already played a Bond villain in the 1967 curiosity that was *Casino Royale*). Emilio Largo served again as the chief villain, flanked by seductive hench-woman Fatima Blush, who, in this version, turned out to be the twin sister of Bond girl Domino Petachi (affording whatever actress cast to play both villain and heroine), and much of the early part of the story saw Bond stumble upon the villainous plot at Shrublands – here recast as a Bahamian aquatic training facility. Yet the *Warhead* narrative also allowed for lots of unique affectations, some of which would be retained for *Never Say Never Again*, others perhaps wisely jettisoned.

McClory, Connery and Deighton's script elected to have Bond attacked at home by a cleaning-lady called Effie – perhaps a nod to Bond's maid May, who had never featured in the cinematic series, but more overtly a reference to Connery's mother of the same name – who tries to kill him before being crushed under the weight of Bond and Fatima's athletic sexual escapades on his bed. The Freudian symbolism of such a scene is stark.

Warhead would have ended in a similar fashion perhaps to *The Spy Who Loved Me*, with Bond and Domino in a clinch inside a mini sub, floating away on the Hudson to the strains of 'Rule Britannia'. Moore's third film in the Eon series also delivered such a sop to patriotism with Bond's Union Jack parachute and the distinctly British, jovial strings of 'Nobody Does It Better' which kick in at the end of that film before being replaced by Carly Simon's smooth vocals. In that sense, while McClory's film was being proposed as a Bond movie with the kind of grandiosity not seen since *You Only Live Twice*, it was cleaving to many of the established components of the 007 franchise that fans had come to expect from both Connery and Moore.

Whether *Warhead* would have resulted in the same kind of overt patriotism is open to question, given the specific American elements of the script and story. It is possible we would have seen, as we do in *Never Say Never Again*, a hybridisation of the particularly Americanised 007 of the early 1970s and the more European and British flavour of the later Moore era. Though McClory sought Welles, a titan of American filmmaking, he also hoped for Trevor Howard – a grand figure of British theatre and cinema (and Connery's co-star on *The Offence*) as M – and Richard Attenborough as director was considered.

'The script was coming along rather well,' recalled Connery, 'and I was discussing it with my wife and she said, "Well, if it's going so well, why don't you play the part?" And coming from her I gave it more thought than I would normally have done, I suppose. And it seemed quite a good idea after all these years.'

McClory likened the moment to 'Muhammad Ali, when he's at his most fit, when someone else is champion of the world, throwing his hat into the ring.' Though these allusions to prize fighting only serve to reinforce the masculine mythology around Connery, it was all enough to convince the actor that maybe 'never again' was too strong. He signed up, later admitting, 'There was a certain amount of curiosity in me about the role, having been away for so long.'

What followed, however, was years of legal acrimony as Broccoli – incensed at the changes he had been forced to make to *The Spy Who Loved Me*, a film he had intended as a major 'relaunch' after Saltzman acceded full creative control to a series he was concerned was losing box-office appeal – launched whatever legal action he could to thwart the intended production of *Warhead*.

'The moment I said, "Yeah, okay, I'll do it," there was a terrific furore with lawyers,' said Connery, 'because obviously there was a great deal of money involved. And that always attracts lawyers.'

McClory railed publicly and privately, but Broccoli's injunctions caused everyone from bankrollers Paramount, studio United Artists and even Connery to get the jitters. By 1980, Connery decided to back out of the project, perhaps frustrated at the delays and concerned that too much time had passed. Moore was increasingly becoming the definitive Bond for a new generation and although he would never quite eclipse Connery's iconic status, he was coming close. *The Spy Who Loved Me* had been a huge hit and *Moonraker* leaned, smartly, into the fervour for *Star Wars* and science fiction.

Enter one Jack Schwartzman, a former high-ranking studio executive and the husband of Talia Shire. Shire is the sister of Francis Ford Coppola, for whom she would co-star in *The Godfather* trilogy – although her biggest claim to fame came as Rocky Balboa's wife Adrian in Sylvester Stallone's successful boxing saga. Schwartzman had created a production company with Shire and approached McClory with an offer to get the project up and running again, but the *Warhead* script had to go – mired as it was in litigation and likely to be too ambitious and expensive to shoot in the way envisaged. The plan was to start again at first principles. Connery agreed to rejoin the project, with the stipulation that he would have complete creative control over script, direction and casting. Along with a hefty pay day, Schwartzman gave him everything he asked for.

Cynics were wondering at the time why Connery once again was returning to a role he had said no to on multiple occasions. 'I don't think any role changes a man quite so much as Bond,' said Connery. 'It's a cross, a privilege, a joke, a challenge. And as bloody intrusive as a nightmare.'

The revived Bond project, which would be named *Never Say Never Again* after a quip by Micheline about playing the character (a title Connery immediately liked), went into production in 1982 at the same time as Moore's sixth and penultimate turn as 007 for Eon in *Octopussy*. Both pictures were set to arrive in 1983. Despite Connery and Moore having been good friends for years, the British press crafted antagonism and headlines such as 'Battle of the Bonds', given that this was the first and only time that rival Bond movies would be filming at the same time. Though Moore was well-established and well-loved in the role, Connery back as Bond was equivalent to the return of a messiah in entertainment quarters. He had risen.

'I made it quite clear from the outset that I wasn't going to get involved in any silly race or any hype in terms of rivalry,' said Connery. 'I'd known Roger 20 years or so. We started around the same time and I bumped into Roger around St James's and he asked where I was off to and I said, "The Bahamas," and he said he was off to India, and we chatted about it. And I said to him, "They're going to try and play us off in a hype business but we shouldn't really pay any attention to it." And we didn't. In fact, we saw quite a bit of each other because we were both filming in London at the same time and we had one of the best parties in town together, all the boys were in town – Michael Caine was there as well. And we didn't talk very much about the filming.

'There's a different appetite for the character between us. I played Bond with a reality, credibility – and albeit with the stunts and everything – but everything that happens is possible. And I feel that Roger, I think he may have inherited in part from *Diamonds Are Forever* where they were already getting into that area of too much hardware, that that was more important, and his sort of parody of the character as it were, in that situation, so that you will go for the laugh or the humour at whatever the cost of the credibility or the reality, I think that's basically the difference. I think he took another direction with it and acquired an entirely different audience.'

One of the key differences about *Never Say Never Again*, quite apart from the metatextual nature of the title and the very creation of the film, is that it embraces the idea of an older 007 to a degree we would only see matched in the Daniel Craig era, where *Skyfall* puts him through his physical paces as a man approaching 50. Connery had been a lithe 31-year-old when he made *Dr. No*, and would be 52 when making *Never Say Never Again* (still managing to look younger somehow than in *Diamonds Are Forever*), while Moore was 46 when he debuted in *Live and Let Die* (though he looked to be in his early thirties) and would be 57 when he made his final film in 1984, *A View to a Kill*. Though audiences could almost hear him creaking if he broke into a run, Moore's films never reconciled the character as being older or wrote him accordingly.

There is at least an attempt in *Never Say Never Again* to do that with Connery, as director Irvin Kershner, who first worked with Connery back in 1966's *A Fine Madness*, attests to: 'They asked me how I wanted to do the film and I said, "I want to use Sean as the person he is, at the age he is. He shouldn't be a duplicate of what he was 13 years before." He'd gotten older. I didn't want him hanging by one finger from a helicopter while it's moving along at 200mph. And it took weeks before finally they said okay and I said okay.'

As a result, *Never Say Never Again* sees Connery's Bond fail at a training exercise in North Africa, at which point he is sent to Shrublands and ordered by a particularly officious M (played by Edward Fox) to cut out what he terms the 'free radicals' he consistently consumes. 'Toxins that destroy the body and the brain, caused by eating too much red meat and white bread. Too many dry Martinis!' 'Then I shall cut out the white bread, sir,' is Bond's wonderfully pithy response. There is a deliberate attempt in Lorenzo Semple Jr's script (which Connery had comedy duo Dick Clement and Ian La Frenais brought in to polish, to the point they even reprised their best gag from Ronnie Barker-starring British comedy hit *Porridge*) to examine the very deliberate 'Bondian' indulgences audiences had grown used to – the fine dining, hard drinking, casual sex and tearing the body apart in the pursuit of villainy.

'I thought *From Russia with Love* contained the best of Fleming with the marvellous locations, interesting ambience, good stories, interesting characters [. . .] like a detective story with espionage, and exotic settings and nice women and what have you,' said Connery. 'And I felt that they also had not been cast as heavily as they could have been. So that was what I was more interested in and to push for when we came back to do the film [*Never Say Never Again*]. For example, to get somebody like Klaus Maria Brandauer – in my opinion, one of the best ten actors around – to play Largo was one of my first choices. We got him. And it was the same across the board. I wanted Edward Fox for M and I wanted Alec McCowen for Q, Max von Sydow for Blofeld, and when you've got these sort of actors – and then the actresses, I had met Barbara Carrera in Los Angeles and discussed it at length with her and Kim Basinger, the essence of what the films were about. And once I had Barbara you wanted somebody quite different like Kim, who is a marvellous and rather interesting actress.'

Schwartzman for one believed they were depicting the character appropriately for the age and time he was in: 'The best way to describe how our film will look is rich, grand, even magnificent, but totally realistic. It has a definite 1980s feel, and if Bond were being written about in the Secret Service of now, we reckon that this is roughly how he would behave. He is getting on a bit, and to some extent he's a maverick in that he relies mainly on his wits in a computer age. I think Sean is rather enjoying that side of it. It's funny and a little cynical, but totally believable.'

There is more than a little magnanimity in Schwartzman's statement. *Never Say Never Again* is no more realistic than *Octopussy* or any of the Eon Bond films of the same era; indeed, it is arguably less gritty and stripped-back than 1981's *For Your Eyes Only*. This Bond still relies on gadgets, he still performs outlandish stunts (take the bizarre beat of the horse going over a cliff), and the message of the film is certainly not one of Puritan tolerance and treating the body like a temple. The look on nurse Patricia Fearing's face as Connery seduces her with caviar from a secret stash of rich food he's smuggled into Shrublands says it all. Unlike the aggressive sexual advances Connery's Bond in 1965 forces onto the same character, in 1983 Connery's Bond seduces Patricia with temptation and taste. He leads her into forbidden territory.

Connery's elder Bond is laconic but incorrigible, and the actor glides through the film with a different confidence than witnessed in *Diamonds Are Forever* and a renewed interest – perhaps given the wittier lines and more cohesive story he is given. But he is also demonstrably unable to perform the kind of stunts he would have done as a man in his thirties, despite still being 'in pretty good shape'. Bond looks positively ancient in what turns out to be a rather comedic fight at Shrublands against Pat Roach's towering SPECTRE henchman – Roach reprising the same kind of role he performed opposite Harrison Ford's Indiana Jones a couple of years earlier in *Raiders of the Lost Ark*.

There are nonetheless reminders to the audience that Connery is the same 007 of old, even if he starts the picture as a teacher dragged out of retirement. Connery rejected the idea that he was playing the role as an older man, and *Never Say Never Again* still pairs him with a much younger leading lady, as Moore's films were doing, in a pre-stardom Kim Basinger as Domino (who, a couple of years later, would help define the erotic thriller in Adrian Lyne's steamy *9½ Weeks*); indeed, one scene, where Bond poses as a masseur to get information from Domino, borders on sexual assault. When Domino realises this, she just smiles. It is a moment that has not aged well. Perhaps it leans towards the film's attempt at more realism, which Schwartzman sought as producer, and what Alec McCowen's pleasantly shabby Q – far more convivial to Bond's presence than Desmond Llewelyn's Eon counterpart – says to 007: 'Things have been awfully dull around here. Bureaucrats running the whole place. Everything done by the book. Can't make a decision unless the computer gives you the go ahead. Now you're on this, I hope we're going to have some gratuitous sex and violence!' 'I certainly hope so, too,' is Bond's cheeky response.

Kirshner's film takes him to the South of France, to the Bahamas, to North Africa and under the ocean in a travelogue to beat many of his previous adventures. *Never Say Never Again* cannot match Connery's greatest pictures from the 1960s – it is too encased within the era it is set – but it does immortalise Connery as a particular type of Bond. He is no longer superhuman, but he defies age to remain tethered to an iconic role that wasn't written for him but one he made his own in a manner few other actors have ever achieved – even the successful Bonds such as Moore, Brosnan and Craig who came after him.

'One of the key questions of the current film season can now be answered,' said Janet Maslin in her review of the film in *The New York Times*. 'This is the better Bond, and by a wide margin. It's not a matter of casting – though Sean Connery makes a welcome return in *Never Say Never Again*, Roger Moore has certainly done nicely with the role – but rather one of creaks. Last summer's *Octopussy* reworked the same old Bond formula in all its anachronistic glory, with 007 winking his way through the usual intrigue, a figure of devilish charm and inexhaustible vigour. In *Never Say Never Again*, however, the material has been successfully updated. Here, time has caught up with Bond – and he's very much the better for wear.'

Connery signs off with a playful audacity in the final scene. Bond, ensconced with Domino after foiling SPECTRE, is visited by Rowan Atkinson's bumbling British official Small-Fawcett, who declares that M has sent him 'only to plead for your return, sir. M says that without you in the Service, he fears for the security of the civilised world.' Bond – or should that be Connery? – saunters off with a gruff, 'Never again,' to which Domino responds, 'Never?' Cue Lani Hall's theme song as Connery turns to the camera, winks and disappears inside a gun barrel that fades to an emblazoned 007. It is the ultimate cinematic wink to the audience, who longed for Connery back as 007 for years and wanted him to forever play a role he forever wished to avoid being solely known for.

For now, he would head into a decade that would renew his career as a leading man. Never saying never had proved to be a great decision.

*

Beyond returning as Bond in *Never Say Never Again*, and his rousing, decade-ending appearance in *Indiana Jones and the Last*

Crusade, there are two films that mark Sean Connery's presence in the 1980s: *Highlander* and *The Untouchables*.

Both made around the same time, both incredibly different films made by altogether different filmmakers, yet both sharing one aspect in common – both films present Connery in the vaunted 'and' credit, which by the mid-1980s had become a staple of significance and presence. One of the first examples goes as far back as 1944's *Thirty Seconds Over Tokyo* which gives Spencer Tracy the 'and' credit over Van Johnson in the main starring role. In these instances, it marked Connery as an emeritus player; the films' protagonists might have been Christopher Lambert and Kevin Costner respectively, but such a credit of importance was reserved for an actor who remained a big enough star to command his own features but would lend his talents, however briefly, to other movies, big or small.

Though a relatively throwaway example of 1980s mullet-haired excess, *Highlander* turned out to be quite a key moment in Connery's career and part of the broader transformation in the 1980s of popular cinema. Although the film was a box-office failure and at the time would not have been considered a blockbuster in the conventional sense of the term, it has developed a cult following over the decades and is now considered one of the greats of 1980s popular cinema. Russell Mulcahy's film contains one of the performances audiences most remember of Connery in Juan Sánchez-Villalobos Ramírez, an immortal adventurer who has walked the earth for 2,500 years since his birth in Ancient Egypt. It is the first true epitome of the running joke that Connery does the same, quasi-Scottish accent no matter what the role, something that became a personal affectation but was particularly apparent when playing an Egyptian who trained in Japan but spent most of his life in Spain!

'I think you have to march to your own drum,' said Connery on the issue. 'I can be less Scottish-sounding than I am, but there's a certain music for me in words, which is one of the reasons I always work on a script with the director or writer in terms of speech patterns. Emotions are international anyway. I always felt that whenever I was attempting to go too far away from my speech pattern, I lost the picture of what I was trying to do, so I made an early decision not to do that.'

Written initially by Gregory Widen while in college as a paean to Ridley Scott's late-1970s period picture *The Duellists*, and directed by MTV music video impresario Mulcahy, *Highlander* is the story of Connor MacLeod, an antique dealer in 1986 New York who is also an immortal, born in the 16th-century Scottish Highlands and part of a contest that has spanned throughout history between immortals for the Prize, the power of all immortals across time, which can only be gained by being the last immortal standing. Connor is trained by Ramírez and drawn into a battle with the sinister Kurgan, who wants the Prize for himself.

Mulcahy commented on the film's reception: 'The US release was a disaster. It had one of the worst posters ever: a black-and-white close-up of Christopher. It looked like he had acne. You thought: "What the fuck's this about?" But at the premiere in France, there were 30-foot cut-outs of Sean and Christopher all the way down the Champs-Élysées. The audience went apeshit. It became an enormous hit in Europe.'

Yet *Highlander* feels, in so many ways, a definably American product and construction, in how it presents a rock'n'roll aesthetic with special effects, fantastical ideas and classic adventure set pieces. Connery takes it both seriously and with the kind of raised eyebrow 007 would have been proud of, intoning gravitas into the opening voiceover (recorded in the bathroom of his Spanish villa, no less) and chewing what became iconic lines such as 'there can be only one' with relish. He enjoyed shooting scenes in the Scottish Highlands, a chance rarely afforded him given his globetrotting pictures. And as Ramírez, he is the archetypal mentor, re-established in 1977 by Alec Guinness as Obi-Wan Kenobi, only with an added sense of brio and flourish.

Crucially, and importantly given his 'and' credit, Connery does something in both *Highlander* and *The Untouchables* which is rare in the annals of his work: he dies. In *Highlander*, where he is just having fun for a million dollars and a week's work, it means less. In *The Untouchables*, where he will walk away with the biggest accolade of his career, it will mean so much more.

*

'You wanna know how to get Capone? They pull a knife, you pull a gun. He sends one of yours to the hospital, you send one of his to the morgue. *That's* the Chicago way! And that's how you get Capone.'

Surely these were the lines that landed Sean Connery his Best Supporting Actor Oscar at the 1988 Academy Awards? Beyond even the *Highlander* catchphrase that helped, with the deepest of ironies, to spawn numerous sequels, spin-off TV series and a rumoured modern-day reboot, these lines, voiced by Jim Malone, the hard-bitten Irish cop in 1930s Chicago to Kevin Costner's embattled Eliot Ness, have gone down in history as classic. And they were uttered in what must rival *The Offence* as Connery's greatest performance in, easily, one of the finest pictures he ever put his name to.

The Untouchables both adapts the memoir by Ness written before his death in 1957, recounting his battle during Prohibition to bring down legendary gangster Al Capone with his team of Chicago cops and law enforcers known as the 'untouchables', and serves another Hollywood trend in reviving a popular TV series of the 1960s. *The Untouchables* had run on TV, with Robert Stack in the Costner lead role, from 1959 to 1963, spawned over 100 episodes and was a hit with viewers. Brian De Palma, directing the big-screen retelling of the Ness legend via a script from skilled playwright David Mamet, would repeat the same revival trick when, a decade later, he successfully brought to cinemas a slick new version of *Mission Impossible* with Tom Cruise, a franchise going stronger than ever in the 2020s.

The Untouchables provides us with heroes deep-rooted in moral truth. Capone might live like a Corleone in *The Godfather*, luxuriating in wealth and flanked by ostensibly lawful glamour, with his tentacles deep inside corrupt law enforcement and business, but he has none of the Corleones' corporate, familial class. He is a thug who got lucky, a gangster of the kind Hollywood presented in the 1930s in *Public Enemy* and the original *Scarface*, as pugnacious a villain as Paul Muni or James Cagney. Robert De Niro, who portrayed Michael Corleone in the *Godfather* trilogy, expertly conveys sleaze and violence, while Costner's Ness and Connery's Malone, in particular, stand as bulwarks against widespread national corruption. Vito Corleone might intone 'I believe in America' but the 'untouchables' really *do* – and they mean it.

Connery knew the original television series well, but what really attracted him to the movie version, he said, was the quality of David Mamet's script and the chance to work with director De Palma. 'It's a long time since De Palma had a film in which the characters are so complete,' said Connery in 1987. 'And getting Mamet was a brilliant stroke, not only because he was born in Chicago and is very knowledgeable about the ethnic problems in the city, the police, the corruption and all that. He was able to go back to basics and made the story almost biblical. It's about justice. There are times when the law is enough, and times when it isn't, times when it falls over backward to be fair and favours people like Capone, and so times when you have almost to overstep it.'

Malone exists right on the line, which is why Connery makes sense as the choice of actor to depict this amalgamation of real-world figures from the time. In describing 'the Chicago way', he reflects a pragmatism that contrasts nicely with Ness's idealism and the belief that the law will protect them as they root out and bring down Capone.

'Malone is a guy who's worldly-wise, streetwise, knows the score with the crooks, is frightened for his life and had just planned on staying alive, until he met Ness,' reflected Connery. 'Jimmy

Malone was so cynical about Al Capone, and no one [in the police or government] really understood how to deal with such venom as the Capone regime. Malone understood how it could be done, but he wasn't in a position to be able to do anything about it. Then he gets the chance, near retirement, to be a main feature player in turning it around.'

'The purity and truthfulness of the character stood out to me,' Connery told *Entertainment Weekly*, recalling *The Untouchables* just a few years before his death. Malone stands as one of his finest character portrayals thanks to its fusion of an array of traits Connery had employed across his career. 'I like contrast,' he told *The New York Times* in 1987. 'Marlon Brando was one of the best examples. He was very powerful and dynamic in *On the Waterfront* and *A Streetcar Named Desire*, yet there were touches which showed he had sensitivity, too. I like it when an actor looks one thing and conveys something else, perhaps something diametrically opposite. With Malone, I tried to show at the beginning he could be a real pain in the ass, so that you wouldn't think he could be concerned with such things as Ness's feelings or Ness's family, and then show he was someone else underneath, capable of real relationships.'

Writing in *The New Yorker* in 1987, Pauline Kael was not bowled over by the film itself but was enamoured by Connery's portrayal: 'At fifty-six, this grizzled Scots actor has an impudent authority that's very like Olivier's, except that Connery is so much brawnier. His performance here is probably his most sheerly likeable turn since *The Man Who Would Be King*; it's a far less imaginative role, but he gives it a similar straightforward bravura. Mamet has provided him with lines that have a Biblical simplicity, and Connery delivers them with a resonant underlayer – Malone is always thinking and feeling much more than he's saying.'

Such nuance, such a sense that Connery played Malone with layers that represented the dichotomy in Mamet's script between moral virtue and the necessity of surviving the streets, is what made his performance stand out. *The Untouchables* is a film about heroism, bravery and virtue, and a fight to protect citizens from the dark side of American corruption, but Connery couldn't – and wouldn't – have played Ness in his younger days. He never played a heroic character without some level of taint or corrupted value. James Bond was certainly such an antihero, in that sense. Even Henry Jones Sr, who he would soon depict, for all his bumbling righteousness was a poor and even psychologically abusive father.

So, when Malone dies in *The Untouchables*, it could be Connery's most meaningful screen death. In *Robin and Marian*, he is the venerable troubadour who passes away having rekindled the fire in his heart and home. In *Highlander*, he is Obi-Wan struck down by Vader, whose legend will become more powerful than could possibly be imagined (and he comes back for the sequel anyway). In *The Untouchables*, Malone the mentor is struck down during the hero's desperate hour, when all hope seems lost. His death graces him with the movie's central heroic moment.

De Palma was determined to have an initially reticent Connery in the film because 'If I kill Sean Connery, no one will believe it!', which itself speaks to the power of Connery as a larger-than-life figure. Perhaps he never saw him die in *Robin and Marian* or *Highlander*, or he understood Malone's demise would carry greater weight. Either way, the Academy rewarded Connery and the 'and' credit served to underline the continued evolution across the 1980s of his career.

Both films, especially *The Untouchables*, helped fix Connery's position as principally a star of American films set in the United States, which, barring a few notable outliers, would be a trend he continued for the remainder of his career. Jim Malone wasn't just Irish; he made Connery an American man.

'At the point of *Untouchables*, he really became untouchable,' reflected Kevin Costner in the wake of Connery's Oscar triumph. 'Everybody realised what a fantastic film actor he was. But he also had great humanity. There's a scene on a bridge in *Untouchables* where his character is schooling my character, and it could have been Sean talking to me. That scene was an older man talking to a younger man, seeing his hurt and understanding that. That's why Sean is so successful – because he has great humanity. Here's this mega-star, but there's humanity in everything he does.'

'I was very pleased to get it,' reflected Connery of his Academy Award. 'I'd never really been a member of that club. I wasn't even eligible to win because I wasn't a member of the Academy. I didn't know anything about the Academy until my agent put me onto it. I was under the impression that the Academy was for people that had been nominated for Academy Awards or people who'd won Academy Awards. I must say that I wasn't convinced that I would get the Oscar. It didn't seem that important to me, but I have to admit that when I *did* receive it, it did seem very important. And I was caught with it [emotion], which came out at the end of my acceptance speech.'

*

Towards the end of the 1980s, Connery appeared in three films that positioned him as alternative versions of the elder, experienced father who, in varying degrees, seems ready to pass the torch to the next generation.

The Presidio casts him as the decorated military officer; *Family Business*, the head of a modern crime family; and *Indiana Jones and the Last Crusade* as the bookish emeritus professor at a distinguished university – the latter role key in Connery's twilight years as a performer.

Connery enjoys a reunion on two fronts with *The Presidio*. It was written by Larry Ferguson, who worked on the shooting draft of *Highlander*, and directed by Peter Hyams, who he had worked with on *Outland*. They must have been simpatico as it was rare for Connery to work with the same director twice, and only Sidney Lumet – who he would join for a final time on *Family Business* – was granted the honour more times than that.

Following Academy success, and after years in the box-office wilderness, Connery was considered a bankable star once more and, in this period, he turned down a variety of fascinating projects that would have turned out very differently had he taken starring roles.

In *The Presidio*, Connery plays Lieutenant Colonel Alan Caldwell, the provost marshal of the Presidio army base in San Francisco where a military police officer is shot and killed. Jay Austin (Mark Harmon in a role originally earmarked for *Miami Vice*'s Don Johnson, and then Kevin Costner), an SFPD detective and former 'MP' himself, who once worked for Caldwell and left the army after his boss refused to support him in a case against an individual who is now his new chief suspect in the murder, is drafted in to investigate. Although he initially clashes with Caldwell – not helping matters by romancing his daughter Donna (a pre-*When Harry Met Sally* stardom Meg Ryan) – Austin ends up recruiting his old boss as they uncover a deeper murderous conspiracy.

There is little about *The Presidio* that stands out either on a visual or narrative level. The film reaches an entertainment zenith when, in a clear metatextual audience understanding of Connery's physical presence as an action star, he beats up a goon in a bar using just his thumb. 'My right thumb. Left one's much too powerful for you,' Caldwell playfully warns his incumbent victim.

Yet this amusing line suggests *The Presidio* is more fun, more mischievous, than the film actually is. Connery's role was written with Lee Marvin in mind (he died the same year the film was made), but Caldwell is definably a patriarchal figure that moves Connery out of the space of plucky, dashing hero and into the role of the cranky elder statesman who doesn't, at one point, know who The Grateful Dead are. Harmon fills the Richard Gere-esque void of the handsome protagonist (he was voted *People*'s Sexiest Man of the Year late in 1987) who gets the girl. Connery is now the irascible father who disapproves of the young buck he himself once was, albeit one less clean-cut than Harmon's slick police officer.

Though *The Presidio* struggles to convey the idea that Harmon's youthful investigator is ready to take on the mantle, the core idea of the older generation growing slack and even corrupt over time is underscored by Caldwell's realisation that his old friend and sparring partner, Sergeant Major Ross Maclure (Jack Warden, in a role written initially for Marlon Brando), was complicit in a diamond-smuggling venture. It forces Caldwell to accept that Jay's intuition might hold water and to reconsider the rather brutish way he chastises Donna, in a patriarchal sense, from seeing him. There is an ugliness about Caldwell that Connery doesn't always disguise.

Certainly not one of Connery's better or more interesting roles, taking on *The Presidio* makes sense when you consider the transitional point Connery was undertaking, and how interested he appeared in his relationship to younger stars making their mark on a changing Hollywood landscape.

He demonstrated awareness of his own star power when he appeared, in his *Presidio* costume, as himself in a film for the first and only time in Henry Winkler's saccharine but tender, now largely forgotten comedy drama *Memories of Me*, which was being filmed simultaneously on the same lot. It is somewhat in-jokey: Connery stops and notices Alan King's charming, ailing long-term film extra Abe and recognises him, much to the amazement of Abe's son (played by Billy Crystal) and his girlfriend Lisa (JoBeth Williams), asking him how he is before sauntering away. He is on screen for less than 20 seconds.

And while this might seem even frivolous to mention, the point of the scene is both to casually establish how Abe has friends who are stars, but also to underline how big a star Connery, even in the late 1980s, still is. (Connery starred with King in *The Anderson Tapes* and would have known him for a long time.) His mere presence sends Lisa into paroxysms of excitement once he's gone. 'That was Sean Connery! You *know* Sean Connery?!' A forgotten cameo it might be, one in which Connery seems a genial enough leading man to remember the extras he worked with, but it is a telling moment for his stardom and where it remained in American cinema.

*

Where in *The Untouchables* we saw Connery play an Irish-American who believed in the law and fought dirty to protect it, *Family Business* sees him invert that persona in the role of Jessie McMullen.

'There's a new emphasis on father–son relationships in films,' said Connery, talking around the time he teamed up with Lumet again, for the first time since 1974's *Murder on the Orient Express* and their fifth and final collaboration in total, for the multi-generational story of a New York crime family. 'Look at Kevin's [Costner] baseball picture [*Field of Dreams*]. I think right now we're all looking for a guide, for a big daddy, because life just gets more and more difficult.'

Jessie is a Scottish (rather than Irish, more appropriately) American émigré who came with his Sicilian wife (now deceased) just after the Second World War and set up a crime empire, which his son Vito (Dustin Hoffman, just seven years Connery's junior) rejected when he was 21 and set up a respectable business. He has raised his own son Adam (Matthew Broderick) to know as little about Jessie and his criminality as possible, but despite having a college scholarship, he lionises his mysterious grandfather and comes to him with the idea for a robbery. A reluctant Vito then becomes embroiled in planning one last big score.

There is naturally a touch of humour about *Family Business* in naming Hoffman's character Vito, after Corleone, given he is the one generation out of the three who truly wants to go straight, and Lumet's film positions Connery as both a criminal godfather type and the Scottish-born street fighter who came to New York seeking a new life with his glamorous wife. Producer Lawrence Gordon claimed that Connery's role as the head of this dysfunctional family was crucial to the film: 'Sean was the key. We knew the story turned on the charm and appeal of the grandfather. Face it, a man who is encouraging his grandson to take up a life of crime is not, on the surface, an easy guy to like. We needed someone irresistibly charismatic, so the audience would believe that a very bright young man might perceive him as a romantic role model.'

The Presidio presented Connery as one of the old guard and out of touch with the modern American man, but *Family Business* presented Jessie, a hardened criminal, as not just a loveable old rogue but also someone to be learned from. Adam is a bright young man who has a scholarship in the sciences and the opportunity to excel in academia, but he is entranced by the glamour of Jessie's world, perhaps one he would have imagined through cinema or legendary stories from a different age. Connery here might, technically, be the grandfather figure in *Family Business* but he is unquestionably the 'father' to Broderick, with Hoffman squeezed in elsewhere as the difficult other child.

Family Business seems to consolidate not just Connery's interest in familial relationships between siblings, or his position within American-centred cinematic worlds, but also his appeal to younger audiences who were increasingly focused on franchise fare and pop culture icons. This was the decade of Luke Skywalker, the Terminator, RoboCop, John Rambo and so on. Although the fresh-faced Timothy Dalton was now at the helm of the Bond movies, Connery was still popular across a spectrum of ages. His role in *Highlander* added to his appeal to a more youthful audience, and *Family Business*, though unsuccessful at the box office, was an example of how Connery would operate in the decade to come.

There is one final 1980s performance to examine, the last and most enduring of his three roles as a father figure to the younger generation. Connery's performance as Dr Henry Jones Sr is among the greatest he ever gave and would cement him as a legend beyond James Bond for generations to come.

*

We hear Sean Connery in *Indiana Jones and the Last Crusade* before we see him . . .

Steven Spielberg's conclusion to what was initially a trilogy of films featuring Harrison Ford's intrepid archaeologist in the 1930s begins with an extended prologue, set in the 1910s, when Indy is an impetuous youth. After splitting from his scout group and witnessing a group of grave robbers raiding a Utah cave for a golden crucifix called the Cross of Coronado, Indy steals the treasure and is pursued in a bravura sequence through a passing circus train before escaping back to his family home, where he intends to excitedly present the find to his father, Henry Jones. The boy is stopped in his tracks as we meet a father immersed in his work, sketching what we will come to learn is the Holy Grail and purring in his inimitable tones: 'Let he who illuminated this . . . illuminate me . . .'

It is an enigmatic introduction to a character who will disappear from the screen for at least forty minutes, probably the latest Connery ever appears in a film that is not a broad ensemble piece, and around whose rescue and recovery the narrative will initially concern. Spielberg understands that we do not need to see Connery to visualise what Indiana Jones' father might look like; he knows that the voice is enough, and audiences will recognise that relationship – of a stern, authoritarian father in pre-war America and his dutiful son.

'The dad thing was my idea,' said Spielberg. 'The Grail doesn't offer a lot of special effects and doesn't promise a huge physical climax. I just thought that the Grail that everybody seeks could be a metaphor for a son seeking reconciliation with a father and a father seeking reconciliation with a son. It also gave me a chance to suggest Sean Connery. Who else but Bond could have been worthy enough to play Indiana Jones's dad?'

'I wasn't crazy to have Sean,' confessed George Lucas, the co-writer and executive producer. 'Steve is the one that pushed for Sean very hard.'

'People said, "What are you making? Is this Indiana Jones meets James Bond?"' said Spielberg. 'And I said, "No, it's nothing of the sort. It's Indiana Jones meets the strongest father alive." Who else could possibly play Indiana Jones's father except someone with the charisma and the strong presence [of] Sean Connery?'

Spielberg's comment there is crucial on several levels, not just to the Indiana Jones franchise but also the continuing evolution of Connery's career. 'That's one of those where he actually had the right instinct,' said Lucas. 'And it turned out spectacularly.'

Though beloved of audiences for over forty years, Indiana Jones broke out of his initial conception in ways that belied the origins of the character and the film, recognised with time as a classic of modern American filmmaking, *Raiders of the Lost Ark*, that birthed him. Originally named Indiana Smith and devised by Lucas in the early 1970s before the sensational blockbuster success of *Star Wars*, the original concept was to make an updated version of the movie serials popular in the 1930s and 1940s that Lucas, and indeed Spielberg, as children coming of age in the 1950s would have enjoyed: *Buck Rogers*, *Zorro's Fighting Legion*, *Spy Smasher* and so on. Serials were aired weekly in movie theatres, built around impossible scenarios that heroes would struggle to escape and end on cliff-hangers to draw audiences back in for the next one. They were a building block in modern serialised storytelling, on television and film.

Ultimately, Spielberg lobbied to fashion Indy as an American version of Bond, despite the differences in their character. While Bond's tuxedo is merely a glamorous trapping of the ruthless assassin he is inside (Daniel Craig's version has reinterpreted this to suggest the tuxedo is his 'armour', as Vesper Lynd notes in 2006's *Casino Royale*), Indy does wear what would now be considered a 'costume', perhaps akin to Bruce Wayne. By day he is Dr Jones, a bookish, tweed-clad 1930s professor at Barnett College in New York, being mooned at by lovelorn female students while discussing dry old archaeological sites and proclaiming, as he does in *Last*

Crusade, that 'X never, ever, marks the spot'. Until, of course, it does. But by night, Indiana is a whip-lashing, tomb-raiding, gung-ho adventurer and, as we see in the opening sequence of the second film, *Indiana Jones and the Temple of Doom*, a playboy. The Shanghai sequence is Spielberg's most overt nod to Indy's origin as, in the manner Lucas confidently put it: 'James Bond but better'.

Spielberg's trilogy evokes a formula established in the 1960s through the Connery-era Bond movies that by the 1980s, the Roger Moore and Timothy Dalton eras of the franchise, was becoming stale. Box-office profits remained in place, and there was no dimming of 007's popularity, but on a critical level the latter-day Moore films, released around Spielberg's movies, offered nothing new and fresh. The Indiana Jones trilogy, fusing together Bond-originated stylistics with a populist, family-friendly charm (although there is a significant amount of visual content unsuitable for small children) and a nostalgic flavour of an earlier age created in Indy a hero to rival the ageing 007 for modern, blockbuster-friendly audiences.

Indy, meanwhile, did get beaten up. Regularly. It was almost a stock-in-trade aspect of Spielberg's films that Harrison Ford would be dusted and cut up, dragged along the ground by a truck, almost plunged into molten hot lava and variously squashed, drowned or cut into pieces by any number of booby traps. Indiana Jones was suave, intelligent and sophisticated, but he was physically destructible, lacked any gadgets (beyond his whip) to help him, and often only escaped by the skin of his teeth. He was a new kind of Bond – slightly less amoral, perhaps, and not as urbane, but every bit as capable of saving the day and getting the girl, which he does in two out of his three movies.

Last Crusade, where Connery finally enters the picture, is different. The girl turns out to be a Nazi who, despite a moment of possible redemption, dies thanks to her own zealotry and hubris. In much the same way that, decades on, *Skyfall* subverts the formula of Bond's female sidekick being his love interest by placing Judi

Dench's M in that role for the climax, *Last Crusade* challenges the same preconceptions by placing Connery's Henry Jones Sr in a similar supportive role. At first one of the 'MacGuffins' of the film, the prize Indy needs to attain, Henry is revealed in a German castle as a prisoner, in wonderfully expressionistic fashion by Spielberg: his shadow cast on the wall as he creeps up behind his son, thinking him a Nazi goon, and bashes him over the head with a vase. Connery steps into the light and realises who it is, saying, 'Junior?' His son immediately stands upright, back to being the young boy from the prologue, with a salute and a 'yes, sir!'

Almost immediately, Spielberg subverts our expectations of Connery. We are not greeted with the powerful, dashing and dignified Henry we might have expected following his voiced introduction at the start of the film. Henry is immediately played for laughs; he's much more interested in proving the Ming dynasty vase he clocked his son with was a fake than in Indy's wellbeing, and he is revealed to be a bumbling sidekick. Dressed as Indy would be at Barnett, every inch the bookish professor who rarely leaves his desk, and boasting a comical trilby hat, briefcase and umbrella, he is precisely the opposite to the swaggering, confident man of action Connery typically presents. His performance is, in that sense, a revelation.

'Sean was much funnier than I expected him to be,' said Lucas. 'He was great as an old man, and the chemistry between them was fantastic. He'll be remembered as one of the great actors of our time.'

'I wanted to play Henry Jones as a kind of Sir Richard Burton,' said Connery. 'There was so much behind him and so many hidden elements in his life. I was bound to have fun with the role of a gruff, Victorian Scottish father. And have fun I did – so much so that I told Harrison, "If you give me all the jokes, you'll really have to work for your scenes."'

Connery refers here not to his contemporary, the Welsh actor, but the 19th-century explorer, writer and soldier of the same name, though he perhaps has more directly in common with Allan Quatermain, H. Rider Haggard's famed 19th-century hero, who Connery would play in his final role in *The League of Extraordinary Gentlemen*. Henry does, arguably, evolve from the sarcastic, recalcitrant father figure into the Burton-esque dashing hero across the course of the film; indeed it could be argued that, come the final scene, where the comic buffoonery is fully transferred to Henry's old friend, Marcus Brody (played by Denholm Elliott), Connery is on horseback looking every inch an elder Bond, or perhaps Raisuli, or maybe even Shalako. He transforms back into the archetype we are used to.

The enjoyment nonetheless of *Last Crusade* lies in the dynamic between Indy and Henry – and the chemistry between the two characters – that drives their search to find the Holy Grail before Donovan and his Nazi backers can reach it and discover the power of eternal life. It is rare to see Connery as such an ebullient and nerdy character, such as when we see Henry 'giddy as a schoolboy' after Indy has pieced together clues from his Grail diary after Henry's capture, or when he first meets Marcus, and they instantly break into a ridiculous schoolboy rhyme and coded greeting. Yet it contrasts with moments where, despite Henry constantly needing to be saved and rescued by Indy, he shows schoolmaster fire and righteousness towards a son he still considers 'junior'. He tells him off for bringing the diary – 'I should have mailed it to the Marx Brothers' – and later slaps him when Indy blasphemes. Connery manages to balance those clear character juxtapositions with conviction.

There is also the deeper undercurrent of masculinity and sexuality that someone like Gregory Peck would have found impossible to bring to Henry in the same way. Elsa Schneider describes Henry as a charming man, and later, in a throwaway exchange, Henry tells Indy he knew she was a Nazi because 'she talks in her sleep' (a line improvised by Connery which the crew loved so much it stayed in). This reveals that Henry slept with Elsa before Indy does while in Venice, and Indy's look of undisguised horror that he has slept with the same woman as his father is hilarious. Were it not Connery, it would be very hard to believe a character like Henry could, or would, have romanced the half-his-age, drop-dead-gorgeous Alison Doody (whose film debut was as a Bond girl in *A View to a Kill*). Yet we as an audience can, and do, buy this, both for laughs and with an understanding that Henry is played by a man still being voted amongst the sexiest men in the world at nearly 60 years old, who in his next film *The Russia House* will romance Michelle Pfeiffer and, a decade later, Catherine Zeta-Jones in *Entrapment*.

The most acute aspect of the dynamic, however, is the one Spielberg fought for – the metaphor of what the Grail represents. A young widower who buried his grief in his work, at the expense of the relationship with his son, Henry has spent his life searching for the literal Grail. 'This is an obsession, Dad. I never understood it. Never,' Indy claims. This search – so beautifully conveyed in Tom Stoppard's screenplay, developed from Lucas's story – is for approval and acceptance from a father he, in some way, modelled himself on. The underlying commentary is even clear in casting Connery – Indy fashioned himself after James Bond in more ways than one.

In a revealing scene on a Zeppelin, escaping Germany after having recovered the diary in Berlin – and a close encounter with Adolf Hitler himself – Indy and Henry have a conversation that underpins the psychological dynamic between the two men. 'It was just the two of us, Dad. It was a lonely way to grow up. For you, too. If you had been an ordinary, average father like the other guys' dads, you'd have understood that,' Indy says, confessing what he wanted was a father who took an interest. But Henry rejects the idea that he failed in his paternal duties. 'Did I ever tell you to eat up? Go to bed? Wash your ears? Do your homework? No. I respected your privacy and I taught you self-reliance.' Of course, the space and maturity he thought he gave his son was not for Indy's sake but his own. In these scenes, Connery throws away Henry's comic sensibility and doubles down on his ignorance about what fatherhood truly means.

These scenes provide Connery with some of the richest content of his career, allowing him to craft one of his most flawed, complicated and yet still charming on-screen characters. He gamely spends most of the film allowing himself to be the 'damsel in distress', constantly rescued by Ford's younger hero, and in an incredibly touching moment, allows for melancholy towards the climax when he believes Indy has plunged to his death over a ravine. 'I've lost him . . . and I never told him anything . . .' It is a poignant moment of realisation and regret from a man who held to a traditional masculine identity and was unable to communicate to his child how he really felt. Having built a career on all-powerful male figures not inclined to show vulnerability, the admission means even more from an actor like Connery: Henry is, undoubtedly, his most vulnerable character.

Last Crusade toys with what in Connery's Bond days would have been unthinkable: the idea of him dying on screen after Henry is shot by Donovan to force Indy to undertake the challenge to reach the Grail and find the elixir to save him, but spares us the rousing heroic deaths in *Robin and Marian*, *Highlander* or the tragic punctuation mark in *The Untouchables*. Henry is saved and attains wisdom enough to value what is important. When Indy is prepared to plunge into a canyon to retrieve the Grail, Henry – clinging onto his son – calmly tells him to do what he has by this point already done: 'Indiana . . . let it go.' It completes Henry's transformation to caring father, free of his own psychological burdens, and Connery's deliverance back towards a hero we recognise – yet at the same time quite unlike anyone he had played before. A charming, dashing Bond figure but also a sensitive father figure. Maybe even the father we all might secretly wish for.

When Indiana Jones unexpectedly returned, almost 20 years later, Connery had long since retired and turned down the opportunity to make a cameo appearance as Henry in the 1950s-set *Kingdom of the Crystal Skull*, a film that saw Indy evolve into the figurative (and literal) father figure, which Connery discussed in 2007: 'I spoke with Spielberg, but it didn't work out. It was not that generous a part, worth getting back into the harness and go for. And they had taken the story in a different line anyway, so the father of Indy was kind of really not that important. I had suggested they kill him in the movie, it would have taken care of it better.'

Indeed, that is what *Kingdom* ended up doing, providing Connery a cameo in a still image of Henry – looking as he did in *Last Crusade* – on Indy's desk at home as he mentions that Henry has recently passed away. While it would have been joyous for cinemagoers and Indiana Jones fans to see Connery come out of retirement to reprise Henry, it is equally a special thing that Henry is preserved in amber as a wonderfully written and performed creation in *Last Crusade*, as everything that could have been said about the character and his relationship with Indy had been said already in that film. The parts Connery turned down would not always be wise decisions, but this perhaps was. Now that Connery himself has passed on, the eulogised image of him as Henry in *Kingdom* carries an extra sadness and resonance as a tribute almost to Connery himself.

In 1989, however, fully in middle age, Connery showed no signs yet of retirement. After seeing Indy has survived the ravine crash towards the climax, Henry excitedly asks: 'Why are you sitting there resting when we're so near the end?' Connery delivers it with an energy that would propel him into the 1990s, the last full decade he would consistently make movies, and one in which he glances towards old age, having learned the lessons of a decade where cinema morphed swiftly around him, but he grew in stature and legend.

He might never say Bond again (on screena anyway), but he would grow more content at the end of his career to embrace the echo of his signature cinematic creation.

NINE

TO RUSSIA AND BACK AGAIN

ON 9 NOVEMBER 1989, the Berlin Wall came down, allowing for the first time in almost thirty years East German citizens, who had lived under the yoke of the Soviet Union ever since the division of Germany, to cross over to the American-influenced, democratic West Germany. It was the first step towards the collapse of the USSR in just two years' time.

Between these monumental events for Western democratic society, Sean Connery made two pictures, in 1990, that concerned Russian politics and the intersection between West and East. Both were espionage thrillers, adapted from works by radically different writers: one, the techno-American naval thrills of Tom Clancy, and the other, the moral intricacies of grubby spy work from John le Carré. One of these pictures was a major box-office and cultural success, still appreciated decades on. The other, putting it kindly, wasn't.

The Hunt for Red October, first released as a Clancy novel in 1984, sees Connery portray Marko Ramius, the commander of a Soviet ballistic missile submarine who disobeys his orders and begins sailing for the United States. As the Americans fear it could be the beginnings of a Soviet nuclear attack, CIA analyst Jack Ryan (Alec Baldwin) comes to believe that Ramius is attempting to defect to the United States and bring advanced Soviet technology with him. This leads to a race against time as Ryan tries to prove his theory and Ramius staves off his fellow countrymen, determined to stop him.

Crucially, having replaced his *Never Say Never Again* co-star Klaus Maria Brandauer as Ramius at the last minute, Connery almost turned down the part in John McTiernan's film – he claimed the script 'didn't make any sense' – until he learned the story was set before the advent of Mikhail Gorbachev's term in office, which began the era of *glasnost* and *perestroika*. Connery struggled to believe such a defection could happen in the dying days of a conflict that, by the time *The Hunt for Red October* was being filmed, many were starting to believe was coming to an end. In contrast, in September 1983, when Clancy would have been writing the novel, there was a false-alarm incident involving Soviet early-warning radar which stated that the United States had launched four intercontinental ballistic missiles at the Soviet Union. Only the steadfast refusal of Stanislav Petrov, an officer on duty at the time, to send a warning up the chain of command to the Kremlin prevented a Soviet response that could have triggered a full-scale nuclear war.

Come the filming of the movie, tensions between America and the Soviet Union had eased, but there remained a deep-rooted generational anxiety about the possibility of nuclear Armageddon. Connery had come of age at the height of the Cold War and found the paradox of Ramius, a dignified commander who had lost faith in Soviet ideals, a fascinating example of Communist disillusionment. Ramius also chooses a significant date to defect – the anniversary of his wife's death – and again Connery leans towards a character both haunted and driven by personal loss – as was Henry Jones Sr – as a motivator for what in this case is a geopolitical quest. 'Forty years I've been at sea,' says Ramius. 'A war at sea. A war with no battles, no monuments . . . only casualties. I widowed her the day I married her. My wife died while I was at sea, you know.'

McTiernan's film does, of course, present Ramius as a liar, certainly to his crew, to whom he pretends the *Red October* is undertaking a secret mission against America, and it ramps up the notion of Soviet propaganda and strength, likening their new technology to a silent drive to past glories. 'It reminds me of the heady days of Sputnik and Yuri Gagarin when the world trembled at the sound of our rockets. Now they will tremble again – at the sound of our silence.' Ramius becomes an avatar through Connery's powerful delivery of the West's anxiety about Russian stealth and infiltration, which cinema and television would explore in more relaxed terms in later years, in series such as *Alias* or *The Americans*. In 1990, the palpable fear of nuclear conflict and the power of what lay in the hands of commanders in silent, lurking submarines lingered, and Hollywood would later explore it in more exuberant, American-focused terms with Tony Scott's *Crimson Tide*. 'We will pass through the American patrols, past their sonar nets, and lay off their largest city, and listen to their rock and roll . . . while we conduct missile drills,' Ramius declares to his crew, and we believe it, even if he doesn't.

This was not the first time Connery had portrayed an 'outsider' in the context of a broader system who stands up to tyranny, but in this case Ramius is a renegade with the force of will and personality to bring people – such as Sam Neill's Captain Vasily Borodin – into his circle of trust. Connery brought in John Milius, his writer-director on 1975's *The Wind and the Lion*, to 'punch up' the dialogue for Ramius. He considered Clancy's characterisation paper-thin, and added monologues and the rather romantic idea of Ramius perhaps as an Ahab figure, his white whale being defection to the West and a democratic end to his life. 'Make it about me,' Connery told his old colleague, and Milius obliged.

Hopeful of turning McTiernan's film into a *Top Gun* for submarines, much more of a gung-ho, pro-American action affair, the director was pressured by the studio into making Ryan much more patriotic and commanding – an early draft of the script began with Ryan sailing down the Potomac with a cigar in his mouth. This wouldn't have worked with Baldwin, or Harrison Ford (who turned it down before accepting the Ryan role for 1992's *Patriot Games*), or even Kevin Costner (forgoing a reunion with his *Untouchables* co-star Connery to make *Dances with Wolves*). McTiernan resisted, in part because the movie is the story of Ramius as opposed to Ryan, and because he regarded Clancy's tale in clear terms: 'It's *Treasure Island*. The story of a boy who has to go off and find the scariest man of the sea on Earth, who turns out to be a sweet old bastard. Once I had that, I had the movie.'

'I was just beginning to work in the movies and I was kind of conscious about being on screen with people,' remembers Alec Baldwin. 'And I thought, "Sean Connery. Huh. Well, you know, he's got no hair, he's kind of old now, maybe I'll have a chance when I'm on screen with this guy." Well, he showed up the first day of shooting and he had this incredible steel-coloured hair piece and this beard and this uniform, and I thought, "I'm dead. The guy is still the best-looking guy you've ever seen in your life." Of course, I just became a piece of furniture whenever he was around after that.'

'You should get better all the time in everything you do,' reflected Connery. 'That's the impetus, that's the stimulus, that's the enjoyment for me. Never to stop learning. And if you do, that's the time to change direction again or find something else that will replace that.'

Ryan's final line to Ramius – 'Welcome to the New World, Captain' – is both a reference to Columbus's original conception of the Americas as an untapped land, but also very clearly to the impending collapse of Soviet Communism and the end of an entrenched geopolitical conflict that had framed the lives of Connery, Baldwin, McTiernan and much of the post-Second

World War audience watching at that moment. It was no doubt why *The Hunt for Red October* was such a success, the sixth most profitable movie of 1990, because everyone knew a man like Ramius was ahead of his time.

The so-called 'end of history', as Francis Fukuyama famously called it, was in reach.

*

The Russia House, which Connery made next, is famed less for the content of the film and more for the fact that it was only the second Hollywood picture (after Walter Hill's Arnold Schwarzenegger-starring *Red Heat* in 1988) to be filmed in the Soviet Union before the collapse of the state.

There was distinct pedigree behind Fred Schepisi's film. The story was based on a 1989 novel by John le Carré, who formerly worked as an intelligence officer before turning his hand to writing and who became, in the wake of Ian Fleming and alongside contemporaries such as Len Deighton and Frederick Forsyth, the pre-eminent British writer of complex espionage fiction for almost sixty years. The adapted screenplay was penned by playwright Tom Stoppard, whose work on *Indiana Jones and the Last Crusade* a year earlier had received universal acclaim. Aside from Connery, the film was chock-a-block with outstanding British and American talent – Roy Scheider, James Fox, John Mahoney, J. T. Walsh, David Threlfall and even eccentric film director Ken Russell.

Second billing went to Michelle Pfeiffer, who portrays Soviet contact Katya. In le Carré's story, she reaches out to give Connery's publishing company director, Bartholomew 'Barley' Blair, a manuscript secreted from a Russian physicist codenamed 'Dante' which contains details of the Russians' ability – or rather inability – to wage nuclear war. Barley becomes embroiled in a game of espionage between British and American security forces who seek to use him as a conduit to Dante. However, they don't account for Barley falling in love with Katya and deciding to play his own game between East and West to prevent her death by suspicious Soviet forces.

Schepisi's film therefore presents *The Russia House* less as a murkier Bond movie and more of an elegant romance set against the stark bleakness of Soviet-era Russia. Pfeiffer, though miscast here, was arguably one of the biggest female stars in Hollywood, thanks to several successful movies – *Dangerous Liaisons*, *The Witches of Eastwick*, *Tequila Sunrise* and, further back, *Grease 2* and De Palma's *Scarface*. More recently her unforgettable sultry turn on a piano in *The Fabulous Baker Boys* had wooed audiences, and her memorable portrayal of Catwoman in Tim Burton's *Batman Returns* lay ahead. In her early thirties, Pfeiffer was a generation removed from Connery, and given that he has rarely looked shabbier in his role as the alcoholic Barley, at least as the film begins, this was an early example of Connery's unconvincing romances on screen with much younger actors. (He was not alone in this trend, granted.)

The last time we had seen Connery's Englishman romance a Russian woman on screen was almost thirty years earlier, in a very different age, in his second Bond movie *From Russia with Love*, as 007 charms KGB agent Tatiana Romanova. There are echoes of that here, with Barley working to try and protect Katya from the monolithic state forces who would shut down her treacherous efforts, but the tone is very different. For one thing, Bond never actually went to Russia in that story. Bond considered Tatiana a means to an end in Fleming's spy story whereas Barley genuinely cares for Katya and wants to rescue her. 'I love you. All my failings were preparation for me to you. It's like nothing I have ever known: it's unselfish love, grown-up love. You know it is. It's mature, absolute, thrilling love.'

It is unusual to hear a Connery character be so openly effusive about his feelings and in many ways it is one of Connery's finest emotional performances.

'A film I adored was *The Russia House*,' he would later reflect. 'It meandered a bit in the third act, but I liked the movie, I liked the whole John le Carré story and what it was trying to do and I found it very moving. Le Carré was very enthusiastic about it, too. But it didn't do well at all.'

Few actors beyond Connery would have been able, in the same year, to make characters like Ramius and Barley – both hugely distinct creations yet both caught up in the same shifting political context – work so adroitly, but while *The Hunt for Red October*'s more direct message about the crumbling Soviet apparatus was one that audiences were more receptive to, *The Russia House* perhaps presents the more authentic reality (as you would expect from le Carré's source material). A Soviet nuclear commander defecting is political fantasy. A British publisher compromised by Western security agencies still looking for a profitable advantage from the end of Communism is, even in the context of Hollywood storytelling, the more realistic scenario.

'I'm always intrigued by how other people see the film and what their response is,' remarked Connery, 'but in general it seems to be, everyone's more interested in the political situation. And their response is, in many cases, they would like to go to Russia. Which isn't quite what one had expected.'

A new world was beckoning, indeed, for Western democracy and cinema generally. By 1995, James Bond would be in Moscow for the first time in *GoldenEye*, as Pierce Brosnan worked to take the 'sexist, misogynist dinosaur' into the post-Cold War paradigm and rehabilitate Connery's template. It is interesting that Connery's explorations of Cold War realpolitik and the characters he played in *The Russia House* and *The Hunt for Red October* further established, as his penchant for the father figure and mentor in the late 1980s had done, the kind of roles he would take on in the last decade of his career.

First, however, Connery would head back into worlds he had previously inhabited for a rarity, outside the Bond franchise, in his career. The sequel.

*

By the early 1990s, the Hollywood sequel had firmly established itself in the cinematic lexicon. Throughout the previous decade, the sequel had become ubiquitous. If a film was a success, from a profit-driven perspective, studios would, in most circumstances, look to repeat the trick, while audiences came to expect more from characters and storylines they loved. In fact the *Star Trek* and *Superman* franchises delivered more than three films apiece across the 1980s. Carrying on into the 1990s, the *Star Wars* and *Indiana Jones* trilogies gave way to a plethora of examples – *Lethal Weapon*, *The Terminator*, *Die Hard* and so on. If a film was financially or culturally successful, a sequel or trilogy was almost a guarantee.

As a result, what became *Highlander II: The Quickening* was commissioned, and Connery, after a great deal of wrangling through agents and financial negotiation agreed to return to play the immortal Juan Sánchez-Villalobos Ramírez again, only the second character (as it would turn out in his entire career) he would play more than once on screen. Though he earned millions for three weeks' work on what, according to director Russell Mulcahy, was a much more genial, post-*Untouchables* Connery than during the original *Highlander*, his only sequel is, regrettably, the worst film he ever put his name to.

Conceptually, sequels are designed to take the building blocks of what the initial film established and construct new layers, often calling back to the characters' or their universes' backstories to help the audience reach a deeper understanding. If we compare *Highlander* to *Star Wars* briefly, in both films the young hero – Connor MacLeod and Luke Skywalker – is taught the ways of mystical power, be it the Prize or the Force, by a mentor – Ramírez and Obi-Wan Kenobi – who sacrifices his life to the ultimate villain – the Kurgan and Darth Vader – which gives the hero their motivation to reach his destiny. It is an archetypal story which both films shared. George Lucas used two subsequent *Star Wars* films to build Luke into that hero; *Highlander* bizarrely decided to ground the series for the sequel in a completely redundant backstory that entirely changes the fabric of what audiences thought they understood about Connor, Ramírez, the immortals, and their battle for the Prize.

Crucially, *Star Wars* never entirely brought Obi-Wan back. Alec Guinness appeared in sequels in spectral form to offer guidance, but he was never resurrected. Ramírez is literally resurrected – after it is revealed he, like Connor, is an extraterrestrial from a planet called Zeist with a history that evokes the fate of Krypton in *Superman* mythology – only to die once again to save Connor as they battle to destroy fellow Zeistian immortal alien General Katana. As if to underscore the grand theatre of Ramírez's return the film sought to find, he reappears amid a performance of Shakespeare's *Hamlet*, only to be given such woeful lines as: 'Enough of this useless banter, I will be on my way and leave you to converse with your skull. Farewell, dear shithead, farewell.'

Connery would end up featuring in around 20 minutes of the eventual screen time, with Mulcahy – who despised the final product so much that he refused to attend the premiere – aware that to secure financing and get the film produced, they would need the star power of Connery. The critical response was scathing. Film critic Roger Ebert gave it a half-star rating, saying, 'This movie has to be seen to be believed. On the other hand, maybe that's too high a price to pay. *Highlander II: The Quickening* is the most hilariously incomprehensible movie I've seen in many a long day – a movie almost awesome in its badness.' *Empire* magazine, meanwhile, stated simply: 'No plot, no real story, no point really.'

Though it would be a guess to say *Highlander II* soured Connery from reprising roles, the failure of the one sequel he agreed to participate in could well have prevented him from repeating the trick in future, which is perhaps why he turned down the chance to play Henry Jones Sr once more. While ongoing series and franchises would be a trend throughout the final years of Connery's career, he remained resolutely a banner film star who moved between singular projects with very different tones and styles.

The power of his name fuelled the only other film franchise he appeared in twice that wasn't James Bond, although in this case it wasn't quite a sequel.

*

Connery and Hepburn's *Robin and Marian*, released in 1976, is one of the forgotten Robin Hood pictures, but even today, despite the classic animated Disney version, a Ridley Scott gritty take starring Russell Crowe, and a Taron Egerton-headlined punk reboot, one Robin Hood film still stands tall in the cultural consciousness decades after its release.

Robin Hood: Prince of Thieves was, apart from James Cameron's *Terminator 2: Judgment Day*, the biggest film of 1991. It saw Kevin Costner at the height of his fame as a film star, on a roll after the success of *Field of Dreams* and *Dances with Wolves*, and before the catastrophe of *Waterworld*. Alan Rickman gave the most iconic performance of his varied career as the Sheriff of Nottingham, the soundtrack featured Bryan Adams' pop hit, '(Everything I Do) I Do It For You', which complemented Michael Kamen's love theme for Robin and Maid Marian, and the film was a roaring success across the world.

The film tells the story of Robin Hood returning from the Crusades to find the Sheriff ruling England under a cruel yoke, forming his band of merry men (as well as falling in love with his childhood friend Marian) and striving to rid the land of their oppressor. The climax sees King Richard the Lionheart return after years fighting in France in order to preside over the marriage of Robin and Marian. Obviously, it was a key moment at the end of the film, and writer Pen Densham wanted it to have gravitas. He was, understandably, horrified to learn that the studio sought John

Cleese in the role of Richard: 'I couldn't stomach that because I felt all of the care, all of the investment, all the love, all the effort that the characters were playing all came down to a joke.'

Such a joke would have referenced Cleese's previous roles in *Monty Python and the Holy Grail*, in which he played a range of medieval characters, and especially his 1981 cameo in Terry Gilliam's *Time Bandits* where he played a comical version of Robin Hood himself. The mood of the scene would have been radically different from the moment portrayed by Connery as the king. He was given a quarter of a million dollars for a day's work, which he donated to a Scottish hospital. Densham described to Connery's agent that his appearance would be a 'part of film history' and it is hard to argue against that.

In the scene, Friar Tuck is marrying Robin and Marian, and asking the guests to speak up if they object when we hear Connery's familiar voice shout, 'Hold! I shall speak.' The guests at the wedding gasp – they know that voice. For a moment the camera disguises the man on horseback, then, as he dismounts, Kamen's score provides a brief fanfare as King Richard is revealed. The astonishment from all involved – the guests at the wedding on screen and the audience who would have had no idea Connery was appearing when the film first debuted (he went uncredited) – is not that Richard the Lionheart has arrived. It is that Richard is Sean Connery. This climactic appearance remains one of the great talking points of *Prince of Thieves* and has rightly gone down in film history as one of the best cameos of all time.

Although not a sequel, and not a case of Connery playing the same role twice, in a sense his appearance in *Prince of Thieves* is another example of Connery giving way to the younger generation. Richard thanks Robin – Lord Locksley – for saving his kingdom and happily stands as the father figure to Marian, giving her away. Though Connery played a middle-aged Robin, who never married a young Marian and enjoyed more of a bittersweet end to their romance, by taking this role in *Prince of Thieves* he is establishing himself as the elder statesman allowing a new actor – in this case Costner – to step into the role of a hero he could no longer conventionally portray.

Would his final role, as Allan Quatermain, have led to sequels had *The League of Extraordinary Gentlemen* been a greater success? We will never know. It was perhaps for the best that we never found out. For every Richard, a Ramírez could be lurking around the corner.

*

It was perhaps inevitable that, as Connery entered his sixties, the roles he would take on leaned more to either grizzled old veterans or wise figures of esteem and renown, and between 1992 and 1994 he portrayed men of science – a doctor and a pioneering researcher – stationed in foreign climes.

Medicine Man saw him collaborate with John McTiernan, his director on *The Hunt for Red October*, again. McTiernan was still at the height of a career that would be ignominiously cut short a decade later by a spell in prison for tax evasion.

Connery plays the irascible Dr Robert Campbell, a researcher in the Amazon who claims to have found a cure for cancer but has lost the compound. When his wife and research partner abandon him, the pharmaceutical company backing him send Dr Rae Crane (Lorraine Bracco) to judge whether his funding should continue. A spiky relationship between them soon develops into one of mutual respect, and perhaps more, as Campbell and Rae must gain the trust of the local natives and their 'medicine man' in a race to synthesise the compound before a logging company destroys the local flora needed for their work and displaces the community.

Though filmed in Mexico, in what Connery and Bracco would describe as humid and difficult conditions, and despite script contributions once again from the reliable Tom Stoppard, there remains a sense about *Medicine Man* that it applies a 'white saviour' narrative to the sensitive subject of Amazonian logging and the protection of tribespeople, while also trying to frame a story of a grumpy old scientist and his younger, attractive, able sidekick as a screwball romance. McTiernan's film wants to be *The African Queen*, but Bracco, on a career high after her Oscar-nominated turn in Martin Scorsese's *Goodfellas* and before her critically acclaimed role in *The Sopranos*, is sadly no Katharine Hepburn. Nor here, in truth, is Connery much of a Bogart.

Connery seemed more interested in the broader ecological themes within the picture when discussing it in interviews: '*Medicine Man* is set in the jungle in Brazil, where they have this slash-and-burn policy, and it has some ecological aspects. Héctor Babenco was saying there is nothing that gets more media coverage than the rainforest with so little action in response. Sting is certainly bringing it to the attention of everybody, he's spending his energy and time raising money for it. The next step obviously will be for this to become an issue in the United Nations, and then, in this new international order they're attempting to establish, they'll do something about it.'

It is hard to come away from *Medicine Man*, which takes Connery from being a pompous researcher replete with ponytail (Connery insisted on adopting it after he met celebrated composer Jerry Goldsmith – whose work is perhaps the best aspect of the movie – and saw that he had one) through to being the hero of the moment, believing it is little more than a poor imitation of recent exotic adventure fare such as *Romancing the Stone*, where Michael Douglas and Kathleen Turner lit up the screen. Little of that is in evidence here between Connery and Bracco.

McTiernan believed the ultimate failure of the film came down to misjudged marketing: 'It was a little art movie with Sean Connery that cost only $27 million. If the press hadn't defined it as an action movie, it probably wouldn't have been considered a disappointment.'

Owen Gleiberman, one of the critics who savaged the film, summed up the overarching sentiment of how the movie attempted to fuse the political and melodramatic: 'In the end, there's something opportunistic and glib about the way that *Medicine Man* yokes together medical wish-fulfilment and save-the-rain-forest agitprop into a neat, messagey package. Nothing takes the fun out of romance quite like liberal earnestness.'

Connery would never play a scientist again. But he would play a doctor, on a different continent but with a similar view towards a latent colonial earnestness that was rapidly becoming passé in a liberal decade.

*

A Good Man in Africa arrived in the middle of 1994, a decade in which the blockbuster was now king – be it driven by the action tentpole star (more on that later), revived classic franchise (more on that later, too) or broad lowbrow comedy – none of which Connery had started the decade participating in, his *Highlander* sojourn aside.

Bruce Beresford's film was a smaller affair in which, unlike *Medicine Man*, Connery was one of the key supporting players around the primary star, Colin Friels, a Scottish actor who in the adaptation of William Boyd's novel (penned by Boyd himself), plays Morgan Leafy, a British diplomat living in Kinjanja, a fictional Central African nation recently independent of British colonial rule. After he sleeps with the wife of the corrupt presidential candidate, Morgan is forced to bribe officials who are holding out on an oil reserve project that will make him rich. Dr Alex Murray, a moralistic local doctor (Connery), is the one 'good man' who refuses to be bought.

It is an oddity, to say the least, awkwardly marrying rather broad middle-class comedy with outdated colonial views on cultural appropriation, while Friels tries to hold his own alongside acting heavyweights such as John Lithgow, Joanne Whalley-Kilmer, Louis Gossett Jr and Diana Rigg (who in another universe could well have starred opposite Connery many years before in *On Her Majesty's Secret Service*). Critics were not kind.

Although Connery was more than capable of still commanding leading roles in the mid-1990s, *A Good Man in Africa* saw him play in the ensemble, despite arguably being the biggest star in the film. As Scottish expat Dr Murray, he is the titular 'good man' of Boyd's source material, but there is an irascible refusal to conform in Connery's performance that matches McTiernan's earlier film. He finds little patience for Morgan's deferential attempt to make his acquaintance and barks lines such as: 'Show me the man who is completely content, and I'll show you the lobotomy scar.'

What would have appealed to Connery about Murray, apart from his grouchiness and Scottish origins, was the fact that he retained a moral core inside a story populated by racist, hard-drinking or just plain corrupt officials – especially within the British government – who want to capitalise on Africa's natural abundance of untapped riches. If Connery is the 'good man', then Boyd's tale assumes he is the outlier, the outsider, in a continent filled with bad men (and, indeed, women), many of them latent colonialists. Murray might be grumpy, as Dr Campbell was in South America, but both are old men of science who refuse to be corrupted.

Connery's instinctive enjoyment of rejecting the establishment is also clear here in the short shrift he gives Morgan, who is entitled enough to jump the queue to Murray's surgery over a hundred African people. Though we are meant, as an audience, to find Morgan's antics amusing, he is such a loathsome character that enjoying Friels' performance is largely impossible. The film fails on that level. Boyd said of his debut novel (that closely aligns to the eventual film) that 'there is an autobiographical element in that the character of Dr Murray is very much a two-dimensional portrait of my father. He had died the year before I wrote the novel so he was very much present in my mind. The clash in the novel is between a dissolute, overweight diplomat and the rectitude and solidity of somebody rather like my father. It may echo the clash which he and I had.'

Is this another example of Connery choosing to play the reluctant father? *Medicine Man* saw him portray the reluctant quasi-mentor and potential lover opposite Lorraine Bracco; *A Good Man in Africa* has Connery wrestling with questions of whether a man like Morgan Leafy, the kind of fool one suspects Connery would have struggled to tolerate in real life, can be guided and shaped. In these films, featuring men abroad in less developed nations whose ecosystems and natural resources are under threat, Connery portrays old-fashioned Scottish curmudgeons with a strong moral core who refuse to budge. It suggests a growing exasperation with a capitalist world, especially following the neoliberalism of the 1980s and the increasing divide between the northern and southern hemispheres, that Connery would carry through to the end of his career.

*

In relatively swift succession in the early 1990s, before his escapist blockbusters in the latter half of the decade, Connery moved into the American crime and legal system for two pictures that saw him, as an expert detective and experienced lawyer, portray a classic cinematic role he rarely ventured into: the investigator.

Rising Sun had quite the pedigree behind it. Based on a novel by Michael Crichton, with whom Connery had worked in the late 1970s on *The Great Train Robbery*, it was directed by Philip Kaufman – best known for his striking remake of *Invasion of the Body Snatchers* in 1978 and *The Right Stuff* in 1981, which went on to win an Academy Award for Best Picture. Not only that, but Connery would also be paired – for the first time since *Indiana Jones and the Last Crusade* – with one of the biggest Hollywood stars of that era: Wesley Snipes. Not to mention Harvey Keitel in a supporting role.

Connery portrays John Connor (no relation to *The Terminator*'s future saviour of mankind), a Zen-like LAPD detective and an expert in Japanese culture, who is partnered with Snipes' Lieutenant Webster 'Web' Smith to investigate the violent death of a call girl at the gala opening of Nakamoto, a Japanese business. They unearth a web of lies and corruption that involves senior Nakamoto executives, a corrupt United States senator and the forthcoming Nakamoto purchase of an American semiconductor company that could be behind what emerges as a growing number of deaths.

A criticism levelled at both Crichton's book and Kaufman's eventual film adaptation was one of anti-Japanese sentiment, which Crichton vociferously denied, and with this kind of controversy billowing behind it, *Rising Sun* was never going to have it easy. To make matters worse, the production was fraught with difficulty. Kaufman demanded multiple screenplay drafts from Crichton and his co-writer Michael Backes before both walked and Kaufman brought in David Mamet (who had worked on *The Untouchables* a few years earlier). Meanwhile, although Crichton had written Connor with Connery in mind (hence the similarity of the surname no doubt), he was furious at Kaufman's reimagining of Webster Smith from the Caucasian younger partner to a black detective, a decision encouraged by the studio after Snipes' success in *White Men Can't Jump*.

'Casting Wesley Snipes puts an additional burden on the picture,' said Crichton. 'In a movie about US–Japan relations, if you cast someone who's black, you introduce another aspect because of tension between blacks and Japanese.' This led to criticism of Crichton, while the film itself, because of Snipes' casting, became bogged down in what was perceived to be cultural stereotyping of African American and Japanese culture.

Amidst the backdrop of difficult production realities, script changes and even a studio edict that Kaufman commit to a two-hour cut (given his propensity for films of some length), Connery remains a Zen presence, as befits Connor. He is again the competent elder figure guiding the young buck to awareness and knowledge, and the dialogue reflects this aspect. In one scene, one of many where Connor is telling Web to pay attention to his wisdom, he describes himself, to Web's confusion, as his *sempai*: 'The *sempai* is the senior man who guides the junior man, the *kohai*. In Japan, the *sempai–kohai* relationship is presumed to exist when the younger man and the older man work together. Hopefully, they will presume that of us.'

Connery discussed how he backed the ethnic change in Web's character that led to Snipes' casting: 'I thought it was a very good idea. I thought it was an improvement cinematically and dramatically and presents another point of view. It ties into the racial aspect as well of the black/white cop . . . and it gives the whole beginning of the movie with Connor and Web conflict to work on from the beginning.'

There is a sense in *Rising Sun* that Connery's ability to adapt to numerous cultures, with roles that spanned nationalities and global locations, might have stretched a little thin. He looks the part – stylish and cool in black roll necks and Armani silks, betraying no inch of his advancing age – but when he begins talking about being part of a 'fragmented MTV rap video culture', especially opposite the youthful and urban Snipes, there is a cringe element. He is called upon at points to make long speeches about Japanese culture, which Kaufman believed he had the gravitas and charisma as an actor to pull off: 'Steve McQueen had it. Cagney had it and so did Cary Grant. If an actor has it, it means he can take stuff out of a supermarket freezer and there's something special about it. The fact is people are very attracted to the way he behaves. They have an empathy with him . . . and he has gravity under pressure.'

Dignity and character are what mark Connery's performances in films such as *Rising Sun* and, indeed, *Just Cause*, his next. They are why, even in a film as derided as *Rising Sun* – probably a low point for both Crichton and Kaufman, if not Snipes or Connery – a sense of belief in what the film is trying to do can be maintained. Film critic and Connery biographer Christopher Bray describes Connor as a character more in line with 007 than Connery's last portrayal of the spy in *Never Say Never Again*: 'Like Bond, Connor moves with ease through cultures that leave everyone else baffled. Unlike Bond, though, Connor is no elitist. Not for him the certainty that whatever he does is right and proper and good and true. For Connor is a cultural relativist – a man who knows that in order to get results you have to go along with the power structures of whatever it is you're trying to get the bulge on. In other words, he is rather more of a spy than James Bond ever was.'

*

Just Cause was an example of Connery flexing his muscles not just as a star but as a producer, with his production company Fountainbridge Films having injected cash alongside Warner Brothers into the adaptation of John Katzenbach's tough-edged novel about a miscarriage of justice. Connery insisted that close friend and art dealer Arne Glimcher – who had previously only directed one film, the little-known 1992 musical drama *The Mambo Kings*, featuring Antonio Banderas – direct *Just Cause*, despite his clear lack of experience. As the headline star, Connery had the power to make that happen.

The film sees Connery play Paul Armstrong, a liberal-minded Harvard professor, strenuously anti-capital punishment, who is persuaded by the grandmother of Bobby Earl Ferguson (Blair Underwood), a black man on death row in Florida for the rape and murder of a young girl, to investigate the case. Armstrong clashes with the detective (Tanny Brown played by Laurence Fishburne) who convicted Ferguson as he seeks to prove that the psychotic, imprisoned white killer Blair Sullivan (Ed Harris) is in fact the perpetrator. When all, inevitably, turns out to not be quite what it seems, Armstrong ends up in a fight for his life to protect his own family.

Just Cause is a wildly implausible vehicle for Connery on multiple fronts. For one thing, he is again the family man, but he has a daughter no older than ten (an early appearance by Scarlett Johansson) and the predictably much younger wife (Kate Capshaw). There is a clear sense that Armstrong should have been a character played by an actor a decade or more younger, in part due to the familial ties but also due to the film's descent into unlikely melodrama as the narrative progresses.

As with *Rising Sun*, Connery is playing an expert investigator who arrives on the scene with a deep knowledge of the subject matter but, equally, a questionable response to African American culture. *Just Cause* doesn't result in any kind of miscarriage of justice, the framing of an innocent black man for the kind of crime many such men are accused of in fits of racist hysteria in America. It opts instead for the 'twist' that Sullivan and Ferguson are in league, and the black man *did* kill the young white girl, with the story focusing on how Connery's liberal ageing lawyer is duped. The message is clear: if you grew up as a white person in the civil rights era and believed in progressive causes, you were wrong. The black man *is* to be feared.

Connery certainly doesn't seem to align with Armstrong's liberal mindset; when he was asked in press interviews if he agreed with those sentiments, he said: 'No, I'm more inclined towards the death penalty, but the character is vehemently opposed to it . . . as Hitchcock said, "It's only a movie".'

The intent behind *Just Cause* was perhaps to suggest a lack of traditional motive and reason behind murder. In a story where the audience starts to believe that the white saviour will rescue the obviously innocent black boy from the death penalty, it will turn out that the black boy was a killer, in the same way that Sullivan's serial killer suggests Armstrong's attempt to profile him is meaningless: 'Wanna know about my childhood and shit. Did my folks beat me, abuse me, sex me up? I tried telling 'em there ain't no formula for people like me. What we are dealing with here is just predisposition for an appetite. Good parents, bad parents. No cause and effect. It's just appetite.' This places

Just Cause closer to the nihilistic noir of David Fincher's recently released *Se7en* and perhaps the work of Thomas Harris, by this point memorably adapted by Jonathan Demme in *The Silence of the Lambs*. Glimcher wants the film to evoke Martin Scorsese's 1991 remake of *Cape Fear*, or even elements of Orson Welles' 1953 film *Touch of Evil*, but it lacks the psychological authenticity, tension or style to match them.

Connery, as with other roles where he is not on the surest of ground, attempts to coast through on florid dialogue such as 'If that's a confession then my ass is a banjo!', but he feels more out of his depth as Armstrong than he does John Connor. Had *Just Cause* stuck to any kind of principles and avoided descending into a ridiculous potboiler then it could have possibly made an adept comment on justice and the perception of black American criminality. In the end, Connery simply looks out of place in a film that plays into increasingly flawed and dangerous stereotyping.

Whether Connery sensed he was better off elsewhere is uncertain, but *Just Cause* was the last film of this type he ever made. As he moves into the latter part of the 1990s, he begins to adapt to the growing trends of the blockbuster age, moving back towards fantasy, towards action man escapism and, inevitably, back in his own way towards James Bond.

TEN

RENAISSANCE MAN

FIRST KNIGHT WAS not the first time Connery had been called upon to play a king. From Agamemnon in *Time Bandits* to Daniel Dravot's possessed 'king' of Kafiristan in *The Man Who Would Be King* and his fleeting moment as Richard the Lionheart in *Robin Hood: Prince of Thieves*, Connery understood the nature of regal power. He could have added the villainous Edward Longshanks to his resumé had he not turned down the role that Patrick McGoohan (his co-star decades before in *Hell Drivers*) played in Mel Gibson's *Braveheart* so that he could appear in *Just Cause*.

Connery was a natural choice for the totemic leader of a nation in Jerry Zucker's *First Knight*. This is not the classic myth of Arthur drawing the sword from the stone to become king of the Britons – so mercilessly lampooned in *Monty Python and the Holy Grail* – but rather an older King of Camelot who has brought peace to the realm and is now about the marry a beautiful younger bride in Guinevere (Julia Ormond). When Malagant (Ben Cross), a former Knight of the Round Table, attempts to kidnap Guinevere as part of a play for Arthur's throne, she is saved by Lancelot (Richard Gere), a dashing, sword-fighting vagabond who Arthur makes a knight and grows to trust. However, Lancelot and Guinevere – of a similar age – fall in love, and Arthur faces treachery within and without Camelot.

While it would have been unlikely to witness a younger Connery in the Lancelot role, which requires a floppy-haired, charming earnestness Gere has in spades (although, by this point, he too is a bit long in the tooth for such a role), *First Knight* tries to convince us that Guinevere might simultaneously desire to marry a king in his mid-sixties played by an actor who just half a decade earlier had been named the world's sexiest man, yet also have her heart stolen by the young buck who, as Connery has done for a decade of his career now, is mentored and guided by the elder. These two scenarios need to coexist for *First Knight* to work.

Though Connery received top billing, Arthur takes thirty minutes of the film to appear, and there is little doubt that the Lancelot and Guinevere love affair is the core of the film. While they might end up arrested for treason once Arthur discovers their romantic betrayal, Lorne Nicholson's script never intends the young couple to be the villains of the piece. It is a romance we are meant to buy into, just as readily as we are meant to sympathise with Arthur and hiss at the moustache-twirling pantomime of Malagant.

First Knight is the first picture in Connery's career to depict him as the tragic romantic hero who loses the girl. This is in sharp contrast to Bond and the earlier roles that made him. It even differs from *Indiana Jones and the Last Crusade*, in which he was still considered attractive enough for the beautiful blonde to take him to bed (even if she did turn out to be a Nazi). Arthur is charming, wise and kind, but he is also old and somewhat tyrannical – without the pressing terror of Malagant's intended rise, he is fully prepared to kill the two people he cares for the most when they betray him. He is left heartbroken when he realises Guinevere does not want him in the manner she wants the younger man.

Zucker is also at pains to depict Camelot, just as much as Guinevere, as the beautiful 'she' both male protagonists covet and adore. Lancelot pledges himself to Arthur's supposedly idyllic kingdom. Malagant doesn't just try to kidnap Guinevere, he wants to take control of Camelot. And when Arthur lies dying, in another example of an elder Connery falling as the tragic hero of the story, he forgives Lancelot the betrayal with his wife if he protects his one true love: 'My truest . . . my First Knight. Camelot is your home now. You are the future . . . the future of Camelot. You take care of her for me. Take care of her.'

First Knight feels like the first of numerous roles Connery subsequently took that begin to reconcile his age with the legacy of the cinematic figure he has been for decades. He claimed to be comfortable with Gere taking on the youthful, romantic, swashbuckling hero role before him. 'I looked and thought, "Let him get on with it." I've done plenty of that in my time and it was nice to play the elder statesman for once.'

How cyclical it would have been had Connery been reunited with his *Dr. No* director Terence Young for *First Knight*: Young had been slated to make the picture but died during pre-production. Connery would have started the process of facing his cinematic legacy with the man who, in no small part, helped him remove the sword from his own stone.

*

On a thematic level, not to mention numerous storytelling aspects in the world of fantasy and Arthurian myth, *Dragonheart* shares common DNA with *First Knight* – the two films just a year apart.

While animation had long been a staple of Hollywood filmmaking, the advent of CGI and live action cinema took one great leap forward in the early 1990s, particularly thanks to Steven Spielberg's *Jurassic Park*, which convincingly managed to have actors such as Sam Neill and Laura Dern interact on screen with living, breathing dinosaurs in a manner that decades on still refuses to age badly. Rob Cohen's *Dragonheart* takes this baton and runs with it in the creation of Draco, the last living dragon, in a sword-and-sorcery tale that sees Connery, for the first time in his long career, appear just as his voice rather than his physical presence.

Dragonheart is set in a fantastical, medieval, post-Arthurian England in which Einon (David Thewlis), the son of a cruel king who as a boy near death is saved by half of the heart of a dragon, grows to be even crueller than his father. Sir Bowen (Dennis Quaid), who tutored him, a knight of the 'old code' (Arthurian chivalry), becomes a dragon slayer, believing Einon was corrupted by the dragon heart. But when he encounters the dragon in question, who he names Draco after the constellation in the stars where the dragon believes their souls go after death, Bowen ends up partnering with Draco and a band of rebels to bring an end to Einon's reign.

When *Dragonheart* was first pitched by writer Patrick Read Johnson in the late 1980s (arguably before CGI had advanced enough to convincingly render Draco on screen), the emphasis was on Bowen and Draco's swindling of villagers – through fake dragon slayings – which Johnson described as 'Butch Cassidy and the Sundance Dragon', in a reference to the Paul Newman/Robert Redford classic Western. This changed as the story evolved by adding the nobility of Arthurian myth and the idea of Draco gaining redemption. That was the point Rob Cohen, who came on board as director after *Superman* and *Lethal Weapon*'s Richard Donner left six months into the project, sought Connery for Draco, believing that it was 'very important that [the dragon's] personality be derived from the actor who was going to play the voice . . . what [Connery] stood for in life as an actor and as a man that most related to what I wanted for Draco.'

Draco is as much charming crook as he is noble creature, despite having moral intentions he intends for Einon when he shares his heart with him. His relationship with Bowen is playful and rambunctious, with Connery chewing the scenery with relish, playing up Draco's affectations that the visual effects team worked into the CGI after studying hours of footage from the actor's performances to visually fit his style and make Draco as 'Connery-esque' as possible.

'We categorised every possible emotion,' explained Cohen. 'Sardonic, amusing, sceptical, critical, charming, seductive, angry – and pretty much assembled his emotional life on film and analysed how he used his expressions and mannerisms, which we transferred to laser discs.'

Dragonheart is, in this sense, unique. Though we might associate seminal animated pictures of the same era such as *Toy Story* with Tom Hanks or Tim Allen, the characters of Woody and Buzz are archetypal templates who those actors made their own. Draco is Connery, in many respects, and Connery is Draco. It is an animated performance unlike many others.

'It's not, you know, just like a voice-over, in that the logistics involved in making it are unbelievable,' said Connery of the complexities involved in playing the part. 'Just from the voice, they had to go and recreate digitally on the screen where the space had been left for me as the dragon. And from an original, Rob Cohen flew eighteen reels of film up to ILM [Industrial Light and Magic, the visual effects company], picked out all the scenes and gestures and these kind of things that he related to myself, and had them incorporated and choreographed them from Italy through Universal by satellite . . . it's the next generation's *Jurassic Park*.'

Dragonheart fits with *First Knight* in the sense that both films are about flawed heroic figures and the passing of torches onto a new era. Arthur dies as the last totemic figure of his age and Draco, as the last dragon, actively seeks death to move on and allow his soul to join the rest of his kind. Bowen, too, is haunted by King Arthur when Draco hides the band of heroes in Avalon – the great king also played by a legend, in the uncredited voice of Shakespearean stage titan Sir John Gielgud. *Dragonheart* exists in a future where chivalry is dead, the Knights of the Round Table are all in their tombs and noble heroes like Bowen are a rarity. Cohen's film is, ultimately, a story more about friendship than romance. Draco seeks release and begs Bowen to do it as a means of noble sacrifice. He, much like Arthur, becomes the tragic fallen hero who ascends to the stars and allows a better world to exist. In *First Knight*, it was Lancelot and Guinevere who would go on to rule in peace. Here, Bowen and fellow rebel Kara do the same – the evolution from Connery's Richard the Lionheart bestowing good wishes on the marriage of Robin and Marian.

Before his final two pictures Connery will come full circle with the screen persona he crafted in a very different way, by revisiting and recontextualising two aspects of the role that made his career and would become his legacy. He will once again become the hero and, in this case, the villain.

*

Michael Bay's *The Rock* arrived during the golden age of star-driven action pictures, which dominated popular culture and box offices across the 1980s into the 1990s.

Following the success of Bruce Willis in *Die Hard* and its numerous sequels, the one-man-army vehicles of Schwarzenegger and Stallone, and the cop-buddy duo films such as *Lethal Weapon*, *Stakeout*, the Bay-directed *Bad Boys* and so on, high-concept action had become the byword in Hollywood – and increasingly began pulling in older, esteemed movie stars to bolster their casts and viewing figures. Just a year before *The Rock*, Gene Hackman faced off against Denzel Washington in the tense, post-Cold War submarine thriller *Crimson Tide* (which would make a fine double bill alongside *The Hunt for Red October*), and a year later, John Malkovich would curdle the blood of audiences as Cyrus the Virus, a mass murderer, in Simon West's ludicrously enjoyable *Con-Air*.

Based on a speculative script from David Weisberg and Douglas Cook, which later included uncredited rewrites by everyone from

Jonathan Hensleigh to Aaron Sorkin, Quentin Tarantino and even Dick Clement and Ian La Frenais, Bay's film sees Nicolas Cage play the cheerfully earnest FBI agent and chemical weapons expert Stanley Goodspeed. When the famed San Francisco island prison Alcatraz is seized by Brigadier General Francis X. Hummel (Ed Harris), who threatens to release devastating biological weapons on the population unless reparations are made by the government to 83 marines who died under his command, Goodspeed must work with the most top secret political prisoner the United States have – John Patrick Mason (Connery). A former British SAS operative, who has been incarcerated for 30 years, Mason is the only man who has broken out of Alcatraz more than once. If he doesn't lead them into 'the rock' to stop Hummel in a matter of hours, tens of thousands could die.

As Cage combines zany theatricality with all-American heroism, Connery truly comes full circle in facing the role that made him. The role of John Mason is the closest Connery ever comes to playing James Bond outside the franchise while simultaneously fusing a character with his unique screen persona. The score favours Mason with a soft Highland theme on flute, when Hans Zimmer and Nick Glennie-Smith are not pounding the ears with their customary bombast. Mason is irascible (though, given his circumstances, who wouldn't be?) but even after decades in near-solitary confinement, he has lost none of his skill and acumen when it comes to tradecraft and combat. Mason was locked away by the FBI because he stole ultra-classified information on the Americans, and the film ends with Goodspeed, having been gifted the microfilm on which the information was stored, joking to his girlfriend, 'Honey, you wanna know who really killed JFK?'

Thus, Mason is established as a symbolic representation of the 1960s, the era when Connery set in stone his iconic status as James Bond. Mason quite literally knows the answer to the greatest American conspiracy of the 20th century. Had Connery never made another film after *You Only Live Twice* and then returned to make *The Rock* three decades later, the effect could well have been similar in depicting Mason as an avatar of the 1960s reconstituted. What is the first thing he does when released before heading for Alcatraz? He cuts off the long, straggly hair and unkempt beard (a look we have never seen Connery sport before), showers and shaves in a hotel while singing Scott McKenzie's 'San Francisco (Be Sure to Wear Some Flowers in Your Hair)'. The single was released in May 1967 – just one month before *You Only Live Twice* was released. He ends up impeccably tailored and looking every inch Connery at his most dapper. This is no coincidence. This is Bay and Connery working to reconstitute the spirit and shadow of the 1960s, and indeed Bond.

The film is at pains to make Mason a figure out of time, in a manner Mike Myers would gloriously lampoon just a year later in *Austin Powers: International Man of Mystery* (a film greatly indebted to *You Only Live Twice*). He is dismayed to learn 'the rock' has become a 'tourist attraction', and when freed from captivity, asks if his long hair and bushy beard are out of style. Goodspeed responds: 'Unless you're a 20-year-old guitarist from Seattle. It's a grunge thing.' Mason naturally has no idea what grunge is. Connery probably doesn't, either, but he does imbue Mason with a sharp wit, intelligence, style and, for his age, genuine hard-man skill.

The Rock is stylistically at odds with anything Connery has done before or after. The explosive camera work and frenzied editing are markedly different to that of the action-orientated pictures Connery had done over the decades. Bay, too, is unlike any director he worked with before: *The Guardian's* Alex Hess describes him: 'If you take cinema seriously, there's one certainty: Michael Bay is the enemy. Loud, brash and without an engaging character in sight, Bay's films are held up time and again as shameless and deplorable. They take place in an unreconstructed adolescent dreamworld where men are toughened warriors and women are an eye-candy bettered only by an exploding public transport vehicle. Hackneyed stereotypes are as commonplace as they are offensive. He is to vulgarity as a fish is to water – a living, breathing, profiteering manifestation of all that's wrong with Hollywood today.'

Yet Connery found a lot to like about the director's approach and choices. Bay discussed in the wake of Connery's death about how, when he was under pressure from the studio concerned about the film's progress, Connery came with him to the meeting – much to the executives' astonishment – and his assurances that Bay was doing a good job helped the production. This was before Bay's transformative (pun intended) success with one of the biggest movie franchises across the 2010s with *Transformers*, or indeed the monster success that was 1998's asteroid-bothering spectacular *Armageddon*. Connery operated as the mentor, the guide, both on and off screen.

'Michael Bay did *Bad Boys*, which I saw,' said Connery. 'I didn't care for it. There was a lot of American-type humour, which I have no problem with, that's just my personal choice. Then, when I was presented with the choice of doing *The Rock*, I looked at *Bad Boys* again, and there was no question that he had an eye for getting into scenes with a tremendous energy. And when the film was first shown, all these qualities were exposed. The problems that accompanied it, of course, were his lack of experience of dealing with actors and understanding the rhythm of a two-hour movie and where the breathing spaces – in terms of actors – come and where the characters are expressed. So there was a great deal of trauma in post-production about that, but eventually we got it right.'

When asked to expand on his experience with Bay as a director, Connery was politely supportive: 'Michael Bay had terrific experience in commercials and things and also he's very, very hip to the needs of stunts, especially you know with car crashes and all that kind of thing. He's not as conversant because he hasn't had the experience in the directing actors side, but I think the film is very well cast so they both complement each other because he did shoot all that stuff, so full marks.'

The Rock is haunted, in many respects, by the past. There is a brief but excellent ideological conversation between Hummel and Mason when they finally meet. Despite being captured, Mason tells him he thinks he's an idiot for the extremes he is deploying and Hummel quotes Jefferson: 'The tree of liberty must be refreshed from time to time with the blood of patriots and tyrants,' to which Mason retorts with Wilde: 'Patriotism is a virtue of the vicious.' How does Hummel respond? With brute force.

Is this how Bond, had Connery portrayed the character in his mid-sixties, would have responded to an ideological zealot like Hummel? Mason might not be ready to die for his country but nor, often, was Bond, despite existing, especially in the 1960s, as a blunt instrument to assure the upholding of the establishment and its neo-colonial values. Given Connery's own support of Scottish independence and his undisguised scepticism of the union – the fact that he was eventually knighted remains quite remarkable – it is fair to suggest that in hiring Clement and La Frenais to punch up his dialogue (as they memorably did in *Never Say Never Again*), Mason imbues just as much of Connery's own 1960s persona as he does Bond's. He is much more naturally suspicious and disrespectful of authority.

Age, too – as it frequently does with Connery's screen characters in this period – serves as a factor in Mason's depiction throughout *The Rock*. Before we meet the character, as he is discussed in hushed terms by the senior FBI and government figures who locked him up, Philip Baker Hall's justice makes the point that he is not the security risk he once was: 'Thirty years ago he was a highly trained SAS operative. He's my age now, for Christ's sake! I have to get up three times a night to take a piss.' Nevertheless, the audience is never in any doubt about Mason's prowess or virtue, even with these pointed mentions of his being long in the tooth. He more than holds his own and immediately slides into the category of the reluctant hero who the audience love, given how horrendous Hummel's hired mercenaries are. Seeing Mason beaten briefly by a younger man who calls him an 'English prick' is the only point where Connery's weathered years briefly show, and even then, the bigger ignominy is surely being called English!

In some ways, *The Rock* marked the end of an era for action movies of its ilk. Don Simpson, the other half of the famed Hollywood production pairing with Jerry Bruckheimer, passed away during production. The film would be dedicated to his memory. Subsequently, going into the 2000s, the emergent dominance of the 'franchise' picture as action gave way to science fiction and fantasy – *Men in Black, The Matrix, Lord of the Rings*. The heroic one-man action vehicle would begin a steady decline as modern filmmaking, alongside the growing rise and prevalence of the internet, would fashion an entirely fresh cinematic culture that Connery would never quite embrace.

The Rock, in that sense, was arguably Connery's most successful final film, both in terms of the box office and critical reception. 'Michael Bay is nothing if not right for this material, thanks to his many prize-winning television commercials,' wrote Janet Maslin in *The New York Times*. 'Much of *The Rock* is shot and edited with flagrant salesmanship, from the film's blue backlighting to its sheets of rain, masses of flowers and other decorative touches. Even the green beads of poison gas look good . . . As for Mr. Connery, he lends this material immense class even when delivering facile wisecracks or speaking in the cheap vernacular of the screenplay. His presence is foolproof even when the dialogue is beneath him.'

John Mason is not a role that especially challenges Connery, and he would have at least one more performance in him that ranks among his best, but Mason does exist as a symbolic example of the screen presence millions imagined Connery to be. He knew, in many respects, he was playing James Bond again. And Bay's film, through a much deeper American social and cultural prism than even the American-influenced Bond franchise, has the kind of reverence for Connery the actor and Connery the icon that we saw in *Robin Hood: Prince of Thieves* and *Dragonheart*. It is the signature screen role of his late career. Underlying a role filled with caustic remarks, sarcastic one-liners, grumpy retorts and masculine flexes, Connery imbues Mason with heart. His one wish in being free from prison is to spend time with the daughter born just after he was locked away and who he has never met. Set to the Scottish strings of Mason's theme, he sets Goodspeed – who he has come to trust and admire – on his quest to learn the secrets of the decade he embodied and vanishes. Bay considered a sequel featuring Connery as Mason on the run from the government but abandoned it. He perhaps understood, for once, that ambiguity and enigma were more poetic.

Mason is Connery's last great on-screen hero. He becomes Bond again. He becomes legend.

*

This is why it is both surprising, and perhaps also makes sense, that he chose to play a Bond-type villain in his next film, 1998's *The Avengers*.

Though a title better known in the 21st century thanks to the dominance of the Marvel Cinematic Universe as a seminal comic-book picture, *The Avengers* was in fact the cinematic revival of one of numerous popular 1960s television series reimagined for 1990s blockbuster cinema. While *The Rock* was part of a trend for in-your-face, marquee-dominated action spectaculars, *The Avengers* leaned closer to the future the MCU would fully establish – franchise-baiting properties based on revisionist, modern approaches to classic stories, less reliant on titanic box-office names and more on the known and beloved intellectual property involved.

The Avengers, therefore – at the time – made complete sense. Enough people remembered the original spy series from Sydney Newman, which ran across the entirety of the 1960s, to make a film treatment attractive. Patrick Macnee (who gets a cameo in the new version as, pointedly, an invisible man) and a pre-*On Her Majesty's*

Secret Service Diana Rigg as superspy John Steed and his partner, Mrs Emma Peel, investigate for 'the Ministry' (British intelligence) crimes ranging from plain espionage to the bizarre and fantastical across multiple seasons, shifting, appropriately, from black and white to colour through the 1960s. Along the way, Steed became a dapper, bowler-hat wearing, Savile Row-styled trailblazer (at the same time as Connery was bringing a similar sartorial style to the big screen as 007) and Mrs Peel was much admired, especially in Britain, for her fashion and dynamic character.

Ralph Fiennes – cresting a wave of acclaim for 1996's Oscar-winning *The English Patient* – and Uma Thurman, a 1990s icon for her turn in Tarantino's *Pulp Fiction* (1994), combined as the new Steed and Mrs Peel. On paper, this made sense. Fiennes – tipped at points as a potential Bond – fitted the mould of the debonair English gentleman, while Thurman – though American – had a statuesque glamour that evoked Rigg. What became clear almost immediately in Jeremiah Chechik's film, however, was a truly diabolical script and the two actors' complete lack of chemistry; their performances count as some of the most stilted and cringe-making committed to celluloid.

Which brings us to Connery, who towers over the picture as climate-controlling supervillain Sir August de Wynter. Having taken over the Prospero weather shield, which covers Britain (developed by scientist Mrs Peel), Sir August plans to use it to blackmail the British government. 'From now on, you will buy your weather from me!' he barks, berating a council of politicians in a kilt and full traditional Highland dress, having boomed, 'Now is the winter of your discontent!' – one of many ripe lines and abominable puns Chechik's film deploys in lieu of anything akin to characterisation and narrative coherency.

Connery discussed in press interviews what drew him to the part: 'It had a kind of sense of style about it, and the scripts I read at first – I read the first one and I knew then that Ralph was playing Steed, and that Uma Thurman was playing Emma Peel. Which made a major difference about whether one would do it or not. Unless these two work, no matter how good or bad your villain is, the piece doesn't work. And they're perfect and even better than I had imagined when I read it.'

Somewhat prophetic words given how poorly Fiennes and Thurman worked as a partnership; as a result, this is, arguably, Connery's worst on-screen performance. Without question, it is the hammiest. De Wynter is first seen in his gigantic mansion playing organ music as a range of passionate emotions play across his face. The nature of the role is, ostensibly, that of a classic 1960s Bond villain. In one sequence, de Wynter holds a conference of his scientists (all dressed as giant bears, Connery included, in a questionable visual nod towards the whimsy of the original series) and tells them his master plan, offering whoever wishes to leave the chance to do so. When two conscientious objectors speak up, de Wynter immediately kills them. The scene is deliberately designed to evoke Bond films such as *Goldfinger* or even *A View to a Kill* and establish de Wynter as the kind of demented, eccentric supervillain 007 would traditionally have to stop. There is even a scene in which de Wynter chains Mrs Peel to a torture device, evoking the iconic moment of Connery's Bond tied up beneath a giant laser.

Connery looked vaguely embarrassed when discussing the outlandish outfits he wore in the film at the time: 'Well, the teddy bears were an extraordinary idea and, you know, it gets into the teddy bear's picnic and all the themes and different colours, and you've never seen anything until you've seen a table with eight . . . teddy bears.'

Well, quite . . .

Costumes aside, in his first interaction with Mrs Peel, he grabs her aggressively by the throat before kissing her hand and whispering sweet nothings into her ear. He later drugs her, places her on a bed, begins to remove her clothing and is very clearly about to rape her before Eileen Atkins' cheery old lady spy interrupts him at the door. This is hardly Christopher Lee's suave Scaramanga or even

Telly Savalas's swaggering Blofeld. For one of the very few times in his career, Connery's on-screen charm fails him. De Wynter simply comes across as a dirty old man. At one point, he tells Mrs Peel: 'Take India. You can have a good 10 inches overnight over there. You know . . . one should never fear . . . being wet.' He is certainly not talking about the weather here. Such moments do nothing to dispel the issue of Connery's misogyny.

Connery was furious when a film that had been hacked to bits by Warner Brothers after difficult test screenings (which resulted in the loss of 30 minutes of footage, much to Chechik's chagrin) opened to scathing reviews, and he said at the time: 'If ever there was a licence to kill, I would have used it to kill the director and the producer.'

Despite all of this, it is likely that Connery relished playing the role of supervillain rather than superhero, wary as he was of such typecasting over the years. Villainous roles had been in relative short supply throughout his career, thanks to his on-screen charisma being best enjoyed by audiences in heroic archetypes; he had long ago detached from the kind of toxic masculine figures he displayed in Hitchcock's *Marnie*, *Woman of Straw* and *The Offence*, all strident attempts to escape 007. De Wynter, however, is a sleazy and quite egregious example of those same dubious archetypes fused with a camp grandiosity, a histrionic villain who could only exist in a fantastical, kitsch world.

The Rock and *The Avengers* serve as examples of some of the best and worst work of his career as he edges ever closer to retirement and the reconciliation of his long-standing persona as that of the world's sexiest man.

*

At the end of the 1990s, Connery remained a commanding screen presence despite approaching pensionable retirement age for any other profession, and after the ludicrous *Avengers*, he made two pictures that display the continued contrast between his screen personas.

Playing by Heart, released in the summer of 1998, is the lesser known of the two. Written and directed by Willard Carroll, best known to this point for writing children's film series *The Brave Little Toaster*, the film takes a cue from the work of Robert Altman; it is set in Los Angeles, features a sprawling ensemble of seemingly unconnected characters and explores different facets of love, marriage and commitment. Despite Carroll's relative inexperience, he managed to assemble a remarkable cast that included Gena Rowlands, Gillian Anderson, Angelina Jolie, Ellen Burstyn, Jon Stewart, Dennis Quaid and Madeleine Stowe.

It was unusual for Connery to appear in such a wide ensemble picture, à la *Short Cuts*; for one thing, he receives alphabetical star billing behind Anderson and Burstyn. Yet he was keen to play Paul, one half of a successful, award-winning cookery show filmed in the home he shares with his wife of decades Hannah (played by Gena Rowlands), whose own secrets of infidelity begin to spill out, threatening the sanctity of a marriage he has perhaps not paid enough attention to. Connery agreed to make the picture for a minor fee, forgoing a lot of his luxuries on set, and encouraged the rest of the cast to do the same to ensure Carroll stayed within the modest budget he had to make the film. As Carroll remarked: 'Sean Connery continued his total democratic cooperation in the ensemble piece. He was the most generous actor, although he's a larger-than-life star.'

After the grandiose action of *The Rock* and the fantasy world of *The Avengers*, Connery sought a role that was quieter and more introspective, and Carroll noted how taken he was by the script: 'He called and said he loved the idea of portraying an intimate, passionate relationship between people in their twilight years.'

It seemed that, at last, Connery wanted to play a romantic lead who reflected his real age, a far cry from de Wynter's lechery or even King Arthur's desire for a much younger bride. In Rowlands was a beautiful woman of equivalent age who Connery could convincingly play opposite in a role that decrypted and reinforced the strength of long-term marriage.

There is a sense in *Playing by Heart* that while Connery is keen to explore an older age love affair, and as usual try to play a character who isn't perfect, he also wishes to remain something of a dignified older gentleman who will be forgiven for his indiscretions. Connery himself struggled through his first marriage to the woman who bore his son, and indeed his second marriage to Micheline – who he was with from the early 1970s through to his death – survived a very public affair in the late 1980s with much younger singer-songwriter Lynsey de Paul. He was not a man without his failings, but *Playing by Heart* never truly holds Paul's feet to the fire. Carroll's picture draws in the myriad threads of his narrative to an interconnected reveal where Connery gets to play the warm father figure to three beautiful, grown-up daughters in Anderson, Jolie and Stowe – the kind of women he might otherwise be romancing in more mainstream fare.

This is not to say his innate sex appeal is not in evidence. Anderson, at this point part of the cultural zeitgeist thanks to her role as Dana Scully in *The X-Files*, said of him: 'In person, Sean projects the same energy as he does on screen. It's not just sexual. It's radiant, intriguing and powerful and you can sense it the moment he walks into a room.' Many of the cast he worked with, who had grown up with him as a major screen presence, considered him a living legend in this and other regards, including his work ethic. He set the tone for the cast and crew.

Playing by Heart was funded by Miramax Films. Owned by producers Bob and Harvey Weinstein (the latter would become *persona non grata* in Hollywood decades later after his conviction for sexual assault triggered the #MeToo movement), Miramax rode high on the independent film movement of the 1990s that challenged the blockbuster orthodoxy of the major studios, producing pictures as celebrated and varied as *Pulp Fiction*, *Shakespeare in Love*, *Clerks* and *Sex, Lies and Videotape*. It fostered the career of many young filmmakers whose work became synonymous with the popular culture of that decade, notably Quentin Tarantino, Kevin Smith and Steven Soderbergh. While Carroll would not subsequently have a career in film to match, Connery's involvement in such low-budget, character-driven fare suggested his awareness of how the cinematic landscape was beginning to change as the century drew to a close.

Across a career filled with hard-bitten grouches and action-man archetypes, *Playing by Heart* stands as one of Connery's 'gooiest' roles, one where he gets to dance with his partner in his twilight years as a soft jazzy score plays. Was he content to evolve into this figure now and put his days as the charming, romantic hero behind him? The answer, provided by his next picture, was no. He had one last roll of that dice in him.

*

'Oh! What a tangled web we weave when first we practice to deceive' is a quote famous not from Shakespeare, as often believed, but the Scottish author Sir Walter Scott's poem 'Marmion: A Tale of Flodden Field' from 1808. *Entrapment* gives these words to Connery's last devilish romantic figure, international art thief Robert 'Mac' MacDougal.

Though Paul deceived his wife in *Playing by Heart*, deception takes place on an entirely other level in Jon Amiel's slick action blockbuster, which epitomises the high-concept picture at the tail end of the millennium. Mac, highly skilled and elusive, is being hunted by New York insurance investigator Virginia 'Gin' Baker (Catherine Zeta-Jones) after the theft of a priceless Rembrandt, planning to 'entrap' him by inveigling herself into his life as a fellow thief. Gin, however, is just as crooked and plans a much bigger heist in Kuala Lumpur, just as the clock strikes twelve on the year 2000, but Mac begins to suspect she is playing both sides.

Entrapment is chiefly remembered for what critics and audiences considered one of the most unconvincing screen romances of recent years between Connery and Zeta-Jones. The latter was on the rise, having charmed British television audiences in the early 1990s as David Jason's daughter in the sunny, bucolic *The Darling Buds of May* and recently played opposite Antonio Banderas in Martin Campbell's big-budget *The Mask of Zorro*. A year away from her much publicised marriage to Michael Douglas, Zeta-Jones was fast emerging as one of the most desired A-list Hollywood actresses of her age, in more ways than one.

That same year, Connery's former two-time collaborator John McTiernan released his remake of Norman Jewison's sizzling thriller *The Thomas Crown Affair* (1968), with current 007 Pierce Brosnan stepping in for Steve McQueen and Rene Russo for Faye Dunaway. *Entrapment* in some respects feels like a reaction to McTiernan's attempt to make an espionage caper driven by the sex appeal, and sexual attraction, of both lead actors – not to mention a similar plot in the investigator hunting down the cool art thief and falling in love with him. If Brosnan and Russo didn't quite sizzle like the era-defining McQueen and Dunaway, they at least smoked as two of the hottest actors around. Connery and Zeta-Jones had to work hard to achieve any credible chemistry as Mac and Gin, and not just, one suspects, thanks to the age gap. Their relationship feels more like a father–daughter dynamic, complicated by matters of forced attraction.

It doesn't help that Amiel's film, in working to create a sense of old-school, dashing escapism, crafts a pair of ludicrous characters. Mac is, in some ways, one of Connery's strangest roles. A legendary art thief, he lives in splendid isolation in a Scottish castle and comes armed with his own set of 'rules' that include the baffling 'I'm never late. If I'm late, it's because I'm dead.' One senses Mac has never tried to catch a train in the UK.

There is also the familiar whiff of misogyny about Mac, in how he treats Gin, that was evident in *The Avengers*. In operating as her mentor figure in the world of larceny (yet another positioning of Connery as the wise old sage à la *The Name of the Rose* or *Rising Sun*), Mac ends up less a romantic equal and more of an older, domineering, possessive partner. It is hard to imagine Gin, albeit a rather disturbed individual herself, falling for him in the way she does, certainly on a sexual basis. Amiel's camera also indulges in the 'male gaze', particularly in the training sequences when Zeta-Jones slinks around in a leotard as Connery looks on – or tries not to. These are moments when the forty-year age gap between them looks wider than ever.

Connery discussed at the time, when asked about some of *Entrapment*'s more challenging stunts including dangling off the tallest building in the world in Kuala Lumpur, how he wanted the focus to be more specifically on this questionable relationship: 'I was doing the ones on the cables – that's all modern technology, when you talk about special effects in film, and in actual fact it was one of the problems in the initial film, there was too much of that sort of stuff in it. And one wanted to get closer to the relationship of the kind of older guy with a young modern woman. So we got away from that.'

Entrapment, a glossy and rather disposable caper, presents a pre-millennial world that neither Connery nor Mac seem to entirely understand. Mac is confounded by the concept of stealing billions of dollars via a computer transfer. 'Where's the good, old-fashioned loot?' he asks, incredulously, and it could be coming from the mouth of either man. Gin's intended heist will happen on the stroke of midnight at the millennium, and Connery's character rings in the 21st century hanging from the wire of one of the world's tallest buildings, the spectre of a figure still chasing a persona no longer available.

The last film Connery made in the 20th century was one in which he deceived himself more than anyone else – in stark contrast to the dignified screen actor in *Playing by Heart* who perhaps understood that in embracing his age, embracing the role of one of cinema's greatest, most magnetic icons who had grown past being the romantic hero or action star, that he could enter a whole new era with roles that didn't need to rely on the audience's impression of who Connery was. Some of these opportunities he had already missed. Some he would turn down around this time. He departed the 20th century a legend, yet he would go on to make two more major motion pictures in the next century – the one that would signal his curtain call – that challenged what he could do as a performer and reinforced the heroic status he could never quite escape.

ELEVEN

NEVER SAY NEVER

CHRISTMAS 2001 SAW the release of a blockbuster unlike any other – Peter Jackson's *The Lord of the Rings: The Fellowship of the Ring*, the first of a planned trilogy adapting J. R. R. Tolkien's celebrated fantasy saga that would be released over subsequent years. The books had been considered unfilmable for decades, with only one (animated) attempt at adaptation, but Jackson would craft them into three of cinema's greatest achievements – and Connery was very nearly part of it.

Although already famous as a knight of the realm for services to theatre over decades, not to mention to modern cinema audiences as Magneto in the *X-Men* franchise, Ian McKellen cemented his role in movie history as Gandalf, the ancient wizard who guides young Hobbits Frodo Baggins and Samwise Gamgee on their quest to take the power of the One Ring to the fires of Mount Doom. It is hard to imagine anyone else in the role after the fact, but McKellen claims that before him the producers courted both Anthony Hopkins and Connery. Producer Mark Ordesky confirms this: 'We did make an offer to Connery but he said no. We never got an answer until years later, but apparently he read the material and just didn't get it.'

The idea of Connery as Gandalf, smoking a long pipe, bellowing, 'You shall not pass!' and sacrificing himself nobly (until the next film) in the Mines of Moria, is a tantalising vision. There is little doubt Gandalf could have been his last, great magisterial role, and in a career dotted with fantasy pictures, it would not have been entirely out of character. Yet he refused.

Having been reputedly offered $30 million plus 15% of the gross earnings, it was a decision that cost Connery north of $450 million. He chose instead to make what would be his last picture, *The League of Extraordinary Gentlemen*. Connery admitted it was a decision based upon gut reaction and remained gracious about it: 'I read the book. I read the script. I saw the movie. I still don't understand it. Ian McKellen, I believe, is marvellous in it.' His honesty is admirable, but it is fair to say that Connery did not always make the wisest choices during his long career. It would be the first of two wizards he would say no to in the early 2000s, ceding that of Albus Dumbledore in the adaptation of J. K. Rowling's *Harry Potter and the Philosopher's Stone* to his friend Richard Harris. Turning down the role of Gandalf was his last, biggest mistake, but over the years there were many other fascinating refusals or pictures that simply never came to pass that might have yielded incredible screen returns.

Back in 1964, in the wake of *Marnie* and on the eve of *Goldfinger*, Connery was approached by the greatest director of the classic American Western, John Ford, to play the lead role of Sean O'Casey in a biopic of the Irish dramatist called *Young Cassidy*, but the filming dates didn't work, and Ford also ended up dropping out due to ill health. It signals Connery's interest in the kind of historical figure he would later play in *The Molly Maguires*. In 1965, while his wife Diane was filming in Rome, his *Dr. No* collaborator Terence Young contacted him to suggest he and Diane might be a good fit to star opposite each other in *The Amorous Adventures of Moll Flanders*.

Having witnessed the toxic marriage of his friend Rex Harrison and fellow actor wife Rachel Roberts, Connery was reticent. He was concerned the result might end up in disaster, and his typically sexist response at the time was: 'I want a wife to go to bed with, not a script conference.' He would also turn down Young's offer to play another husband in 1967, that of his future *Robin and Marian* co-star Audrey Hepburn, in the chiller *Wait Until Dark*. (Efrem Zimbalist took the role and was nominated for a Golden Globe.)

Another disappointing refusal was the lead role in Michelangelo Antonioni's *Blow-Up* in 1966, and he also said no to a key figure of the British New Wave, Tony Richardson, in his retelling of the famed Crimean War conflict, *The Charge of the Light Brigade*. He would have played a captain in Louis Nolan, raised in Edinburgh, of Irish heritage and critical of the deployment of his cavalry. Connery would presumably have felt comfortable with the character's Scots-Irish background and enjoyed his anti-authoritarian nature.

Other projects that never got off the ground included *The Immortal Queen*, from a script by *The Hill*'s Ray Rigby, in which Connery would have appeared opposite his future co-star in *Murder on the Orient Express*, Vanessa Redgrave, as Mary, Queen of Scots. He would have played James Hepburn, the fourth Earl of Bothwell. Nothing came of Connery starring opposite Rachel Roberts in a take on Ibsen's tragicomedy *The Wild Duck*, either. He would likely have played merchant Hakon Werle with whom Roberts as Gina Ekdal has an affair. It was eventually made in 1983 with Jeremy Irons and Liv Ullmann.

Beyond the 007 *Warhead* project mentioned earlier, Connery's most intriguing never-made project in the 1970s was the adaptation of William McIlvanney's *Laidlaw*. The novel focuses on D.I. Jack Laidlaw as he hunts the killer of a teenager amidst the violence and bigotry of 1970s Glasgow. A prize-winning book, the first in a series featuring the character, it has been described as the instigator of what became known as the crime genre of 'tartan noir' and it was an inspiration for Ian Rankin's Rebus novels. Fellow Scottish crime novelist, Doug Johnstone, examines the impact: '*Laidlaw*'s eponymous detective is an existentially troubled individual with a strong moral compass and a stronger sense of socialist justice. The Glasgow he stalks is a brutal place, rife with depravation and poverty, yet depicted with dark humour and perceptive, poetic prose. The plot reads like a cliché today, but that's because McIlvanney was first to do it. The murderer of a teenager has to be found and, well, that's it. But McIlvanney subverts expectations, and gives away whodunnit early on, focusing instead on the psyches of characters that represent different facets of Glasgow, and by extension Scotland. In a time when English crime writers were still copying Agatha Christie, McIlvanney took the hard-boiled ethos of Raymond Chandler and Dashiell Hammett and applied it to the working classes of the city around him.'

Upon reading the novel, Connery actively sought McIlvanney out in the hope of adapting the text for the big screen, but the project sadly fell apart as the writer described years later: 'I had this great idea, so I began writing it. But before you get yourselves over-excited, I never finished it. Connery's still waiting.' The role of Laidlaw would surely have been one of Connery's career-best performances – a remarkable complement to his earlier work in *The Offence* that would have connected him to the Scottish roots he increasingly sought to evoke in his work and provided him with challenging, raw, down-to-earth subject matter at a time in his career when he was mostly appearing in escapist, big-budget disposable fare in which he coasted with the charisma audiences expected from him.

*

As the 1980s turned, with Connery's cinematic stock the lowest it had been for years, he signed with a new agent in Creative Artists Agency's co-founder Michael Ovitz, who turned out to be a powerfully influential force in Connery's life throughout what – the 1960s aside – would be the most successful and lucrative period of his career. Connery liked the man's forward-thinking approach, that he didn't rest on old glories, and was impressed by his modesty given the industry he was in, noting: 'He wasn't making any monumental claims. He said that he wanted an office that would have the best writers and directors, with the best actors and actresses. He foresaw the idea of packaging. Putting together creative and talented people was very much in his game plan.'

Ovitz understood that Connery's career needed more daring choices, but the actor remained resistant to numerous projects. He rejected larger-than-life British impresario Lew Grade's overtures to appear as the lead in *Saturn 3*, the 1980 science-fiction picture directed by Stanley Donen, revolving around a distant future where an overpopulated Earth relies on scientific research from stations manned across the solar system. Connery would have played Adam, opposite former Charlie's Angel Farrah Fawcett as his colleague and lover Alex, who must prevent a treacherous military officer, Benson, from controlling a sentient robot. (The role was earmarked for Connery's friend and *The Man Who Would Be King* co-star Michael Caine.) Though Connery would soon venture into science fiction with *Outland*, avoiding Donen's film was perhaps a wise choice. It eventually starred Kirk Douglas and Harvey Keitel – and was panned.

Ovitz also lobbied him for a picture Caine *did* end up making, Brian De Palma's neo-noir *Dressed to Kill*, playing Dr Robert Elliott, a New York psychiatrist who becomes embroiled in the murder of a housewife and with the prostitute who witnessed the crime. Influenced by Hitchcock's *Psycho*, and a forerunner to the boom of 1980s erotic thrillers such as *Body Heat* and Adrian Lyne's *Fatal Attraction* and *9½ Weeks*, Connery would have strayed here into more emotional and intriguing territory. This is also true had he performed in a very different film, *Annie* – with John Huston – that would have seen him appear in his first musical project since *Darby O'Gill and the Little People*. Albert Finney would end up playing the role of Daddy Warbucks earmarked for Connery, as he would in perhaps the greatest missed opportunity of Connery's career towards the end of both men's lives. More on that later.

'The British are coming, the British are coming!' Colin Welland memorably proclaimed at the 1982 Academy Awards ceremony after picking up his Oscar for best screenplay for *Chariots of Fire*. Directed by Hugh Hudson, against all expectations, it turned out to be an Oscar darling and an early 1980s boon for the ailing British film industry. The music by Vangelis became instantly iconic. Connery loved the script but said no to the smaller role of Olympic Committee member Lord Birkenhead (played eventually by Nigel Davenport, who also ended up playing the Earl of Bothwell in Charles Jarrott's 1971 *Mary, Queen of Scots*), as he felt the picture would be a minor event.

Though written with Robert Mitchum in mind, Connery was just one of many considered for the role of future detective Rick Deckard in Ridley Scott's *Blade Runner* before Harrison Ford, his future *Indiana Jones* co-star, was immortalised in the part. It coincided with the success of *The Untouchables*, following his career resurgence and Academy Award, at which point Ovitz began fielding numerous offers. Connery also said no to a reunion with Terry Gilliam as the titular character in his eccentric 'imagination' trilogy entry *The Adventures of Baron Munchausen*, eventually played with entertaining brio by theatre darling John Neville.

He turned down two roles that went to another icon of the 1960s, Peter O'Toole: first, that of opportunistic Peter Plunkett in Neil Jordan's supernatural comedy *High Spirits*, the owner of an Irish castle who tries to invent hauntings to attract tourists only to find the real spirits are unhappy about the scheme; second, Bertolucci's *The Last Emperor*, where he would have played kindly teacher Reginald Johnston, who guides John Lone's boy Emperor of China in the post-First World War era towards a Western education. The first rejection by Connery was wise, the second less so.

Equally compelling would have been his involvement in Barbet Schroeder's *Reversal of Fortune* in 1990, another role that Jeremy Irons eventually took on opposite Glenn Close and won the Best Actor Oscar for. As socialite Claus von Bülow, arrested for the attempted murder of his wife, it could have seen Connery tread the same psychosexual arena he never managed to tread in *Dressed to Kill.* In a similar vein, a year later he was offered the role of wife-beating husband Martin Burney opposite his *Never Say Never Again* co-star Kim Basinger in *Sleeping with the Enemy*, but director Joseph Rubin couldn't afford his fee. Patrick Bergin starred opposite Julia Roberts in the end. Another role that never came to pass was as the Player King in the film adaptation of *Indiana Jones and the Last Crusade* contributor Tom Stoppard's play, *Rosencrantz and Guildenstern are Dead.* This was due to a biopsy he had on his throat to remove spots from his larynx, which the notoriously private actor sought to keep out of the papers and caused animus between he and Stoppard, clueless as to why he had dropped out shortly before shooting.

Long before *The Lord of the Rings*, Connery resisted the advances of many cinematic franchises that sought to pull him away from his defiantly singular career and into the orbit of iconic roles heavily beloved by fandoms. *Indiana Jones*, perhaps thanks to the cachet of Steven Spielberg, was a rare outlier in this regard. In 1987, William Shatner – not just the main star but the director of the latest big-screen *Star Trek* adventure, *The Final Frontier* – wanted him for the role of Sybok, the emotional half-brother of Leonard Nimoy's legendary Vulcan Spock, who intends to steal the U.S.S. *Enterprise* and travel through the Great Barrier at the centre of the galaxy, convinced that he will find God there. As Shatner's daughter Lisabeth recounts: 'From the beginning, my father had envisioned Sean Connery in the role of Sybok. Not only did he have tremendous respect for Connery's acting talents, but he knew that Connery's presence in the film would draw in large foreign box-office business. Since *Star Trek* movies have traditionally done poorly overseas, this would have been a great bonus. Unfortunately, my father was deeply disappointed to learn that Connery had just accepted another part for the same time period when *Star Trek V* would be filming, and would be unavailable.'

Said film was, probably, *Indiana Jones and the Last Crusade* – by far the wiser choice given *The Final Frontier*'s critical drubbing, despite the spectacle it would have been to see Shatner, Nimoy and Connery sharing scenes. As a second prize, Shatner named the planet containing 'God' Sha-Ka-Ree after the actor, so Connery does have a place in the legacy of *Star Trek* after all.

He resisted joining John McTiernan for a third time for the director's second take on the *Die Hard* franchise, *Die Hard with a Vengeance* (actually the third film in the saga), where he would have played Simon Gruber, the international terrorist brother of Alan Rickman's memorable Hans Gruber from the first picture, and staged a gold bullion robbery under the guise of a game of revenge against Bruce Willis's NYPD cop John McClane for killing his brother. Jeremy Irons – in what was fast becoming a habit – assumed the role that would have been a fun performance from Connery. It is not hard to imagine him playfully intoning, 'Simon says . . .' while wreaking havoc on New York City.

As a new millennium beckoned, *The Matrix* arrived in 1999, with Keanu Reeves' stylish kung-fu hero Neo, a narrative that fused Hong Kong action cinema with Greek myth and philosophy, and startling, revolutionary special effects. The Wachowski Brothers (now sisters) created a world in the Matrix, a computer simulation run by a dominant artificial intelligence which had wiped out most of humanity centuries before. Inside, Neo is guided by Morpheus (Laurence Fishburne), a mentor who introduces him to the deeper level of reality behind the Matrix.

Don Murphy, producer of *The League of Extraordinary Gentlemen*, claimed Connery had told him: 'I was offered *The Matrix* – twice – and I turned it down because I didn't understand it.' Connery also reportedly said no to the role of the Architect, one of the creators of the Matrix, who in the sequel, *The Matrix Reloaded* (2002), appears in one oft-lampooned scene as a 'God' figure in the machine who, in complex liturgical fashion, explains Neo's programmed destiny. As film critic Chris Evangelista says, 'In retrospect, this makes more sense. The part was played by Helmut Bakaitis, who, with his white hair and beard, looked a little like Connery. It's a lot easier to swallow Connery as the exposition-laden Architect than Morpheus.' What is much harder to imagine is Connery uttering the Architect's dialogue, which is, to say the least, mechanical. (Bakaitis, admirably, manages to pull it off.)

He reputedly also said no to a reunion with Spielberg on another film that revolutionised CGI, 1993's *Jurassic Park*. He was offered the part played so well ultimately by Richard Attenborough of park owner John Hammond – another white-haired, white-suited 'God' figure tainted by hubris. This would have been a much more appropriate role than the Architect for Connery. The thought of Connery delivering 'Welcome . . . to Jurassic Park' as John Williams' beautiful score soared in behind him is a rousing thought.

There is one final role in a film just as seminal to modern cinema, and especially to Connery's career, that it would have been fascinating to see him take on – a part that would have seen Connery emerge from retirement after almost a decade, now in his eighties, for something tailor-made not just for his talents as an actor, but for the man himself. The role: Kincade, the gamekeeper. The film: 2012's *Skyfall*.

In truth, Connery returning to the James Bond franchise as an old man was never more than a tantalising 'what if?', as director Sam Mendes explained when asked if the idea was considered: 'There was a definite discussion about that – way, way early on. But I think that's problematic. Because, to me, it becomes too . . . it would take you out of the movie. Connery is Bond and he's not going to come back as another character. It's like, he's been there. So, it was a very brief flirtation with that thought, but it was never going to happen, because I thought it would distract.'

While Mendes may be correct about the effect it might have had on *Skyfall*'s climax, it would have made for an incredible cinematic moment. Kincade was the gamekeeper and steward of Skyfall, the ancestral home of the Bond family, deep in the Scottish Highlands, a place 007 is forced to return to with his boss M (Judi Dench) as they are hunted by sinister, vengeful villain Raoul Silva (Javier Bardem). Bond, M and Kincade turn Skyfall into a fortress before Silva storms the glen, and Mendes stages an outstanding, explosive *Straw Dogs*-inspired climax.

Kincade was played by Albert Finney, another icon of the 1960s, and he brought a wonderful sense of grumpy yet kind-hearted capability to the last act, calling Daniel Craig's Bond a 'jumped-up little shit' and so on. Imagine, however, Connery in the role of an old Scottish gamekeeper, dressed in tweeds and sporting a shotgun, who helps 007 defend his family home. Would this not have been the perfect, full-circle conclusion to Connery's illustrious career? Would Bond fans not have delighted in seeing him spar with Craig and become, essentially, the father figure to Bond?

In a career of roles as paternal mentors, certainly in later years, Connery's Kincade might have been the ultimate expression of such an idea. And considering how *Skyfall* was a billion-dollar hit that revitalised the franchise, set Craig on course as perhaps the most successful 007 since Connery himself, and added a level of cinematic prestige to what had become a series in danger of lampooning itself, Connery might have ended his life on screen in a far more prestigious and fitting way than he actually did.

It was not meant to be. Had Mendes not discussed it publicly, the rumour might have ended up apocryphal. Yet, amongst all Connery's missed opportunities and 'what if?' projects, his return to Bond might have been his most momentous. Although, in fact, he did return to 007 later in life, for one of the lesser-known projects he undertook after his final screen performance, and in a manner that no one could ever have predicted.

*

In the early 1990s, following tabloid speculation that he had throat cancer, Connery decided to answer these critics in unique style.

Appearing on David Letterman's show, he made his entrance in a genuine jetpack, flying down to the stage in a moment that evoked the pre-credits sequence of *Thunderball,* set to the James Bond music. For an actor known not only for his cantankerous nature, but also for his undisguised antipathy to the Bond franchise and those in control of it during his involvement, Connery's decision here appeared to be a pointed reminder that he was always, deep down, James Bond, that he knew it, and in his own way had accepted it.

Connery, a few years later, discussed an incident that took place at his villa in Spain. 'I was going upstairs. I heard my own voice coming from one of the rooms. My grandchildren were watching *Goldfinger.* So I sat down with them and watched for a bit. It was interesting. There was a certain elegance, a certain assurance to it that was quite comforting. There was a leisureliness that made you not want to rush to the next scene. Of course, I also saw things that could have been improved.'

Was this a sign that Connery had begun to re-evaluate his role in the franchise? Roger Moore, his successor and long-time friend, described him as being 'more sanguine' about the character as the years passed, and though he was still reluctant to revisit the role and character, not contributing to events, interviews or features to the same degree as the Bonds that followed him, he perhaps understood that audiences loved him, first and foremost, for the stamp he made on culture as 007.

This might explain the choice he made in 2005, following his official retirement from filmmaking, that he would play James Bond once more – in a video game remake of his second 007 adventure, 1964's *From Russia with Love,* providing the voice for gamers who could play Bond themselves in an expanded version of that original story. Connery said when the project was announced: 'As an artist,

I see this as another way to explore the creative process. Video games are an extremely popular form of entertainment today, and I am looking forward to seeing how it all fits together.'

This was a pedigree project: it would the last Bond videogame by Electronic Arts who had previously produced successful PlayStation versions of Pierce Brosnan films *Tomorrow Never Dies* and *The World is Not Enough*, plus an original Brosnan-voiced adventure in 2004's *Everything or Nothing* (in the main, good enough to pass as the fifth Brosnan Bond movie audiences sadly never got). Bruce Feirstein, who had co-written multiple Brosnan Bond movies and *Everything or Nothing*, came aboard to fashion the game's script. Level designs were based on original designs by Ken Adam. Likenesses of original film actors including Robert Shaw, Lotte Lenya and Desmond Llewelyn were used. The designers even worked to replicate Connery's physicality in the way Bond moved, which the actor seemed fascinated by. The game was designed to bulk out Ian Fleming's original plot and the original Richard Maibaum screenplay, providing an experience for Bond fans both old and new.

Connery, in retirement, agreeing to play Bond once again was a startling development. This, after his declaration in the mid-1990s that 'I couldn't play him now. It'd be silly even to contemplate. I've outlived him.' At that stage, video gaming was incredibly popular but still in its technical infancy, with the revolutionary PlayStation just about to hit the market. A decade on, PlayStation 2 had followed the Nintendo 64 in being a gaming sensation and the technology was affording, as Brosnan did during his Bond tenure, the opportunity for actors to reprise roles in the medium of audio for the millions of young gamers enjoying these active experiences. They included Connery's own grandchildren, who were the primary reason he agreed to play Bond again in this format, excited as they were to have their granddad back in his signature role.

His family's enthusiasm, the fact that EA were returning to *From Russia with Love* (the favourite 007 film of three Bonds, Dalton, Craig and Connery) and the tantalising possibility of revisiting the era that defined him seem to be the reasons behind his decision to return to 007. He said as much: 'I don't think it's dated at all going back to the '60s. This'll be something almost like starting all over again.'

Starting over seems to be a recurring theme, certainly post-*Diamonds Are Forever*. He swiftly became disenchanted, after *Goldfinger*, with the formulaic nature of the increasingly outlandish series, and only took on *Diamonds* as a means of exploring more intimate, diverse projects. From then on, he was drawn into Kevin McClory's obsession of remaking *Thunderball*, resulting eventually in *Never Say Never Again*. Notably, in his good-natured appearance on the *Late Show with David Letterman*, he doesn't wheel on in an Aston Martin or rappel in as he did Blofeld's volcano base – he descends to the stage, strapped into a jetpack *Thunderball*-style. Connery seemed interested in recapturing the magic of 1960s Bond, even if he perhaps never quite understood the phenomenon it became and remains.

In truth, there is little more than kitsch value to Connery's return to Bond in the game. You can hear the weathered years in his voice – he was 75 when he recorded the dialogue. The game never replicates the experience of either Fleming's book or Young's film: it places itself within an ongoing fascination with the 1960s that we saw in 1990s blockbuster remakes of classic properties from that era – such as *The Avengers* – and soon after, the success of series such as *Mad Men* which adroitly replicated both the timeless cool and troubled toxicity of those turbulent times. Bond even got in on the act two years later for the 100th anniversary of Fleming's birth, with Sebastian Faulks' 1960s-set novel *Devil May Care*, a book many believed would have made a perfect Connery-starring adaptation had it been written at the time.

Ultimately, *From Russia with Love* the game is all about finality in terms of how it relates to Connery. It was his final adieu to Bond. He came almost full circle with the character, returning to the very early days, the days before he became too heavily embroiled in the difficult contract battles over pay with Eon Productions which heavily soured the experience for him. It was the final time he ever uttered famous lines such as 'shaken, not stirred' or 'Bond, James Bond' before his death.

While it might have been the last time he played 007, it would not be the last time his unmistakable voice was heard.

*

In 2003, the same year Connery bowed out of the silver screen, Public Broadcasting Service (PBS) aired a sprawling project called *Freedom: A History of US*, a sixteen-episode documentary series hosted by news anchor Katie Couric based on a series of novels by Joy Hakim about the story of America and the freedom it so cherishes as a nation. As the official website states: 'Freedom is what has drawn to America countless human beings from around the world; it is what generations of men and women have lived and died for; it is, in a profound sense, our nation's highest calling. This is also the story of the chief obstacles to American freedom – the "unfreedoms" that have littered our national story, and in some cases have called its very integrity into question. But despite all the mistakes and all the tragic setbacks, there is an overarching positive message to this series. This is a history of the United States as the unfolding, inspiring story of human liberties aspired to and won.'

In adapting Hakim's books, the series draws a line from the New York terrorist attacks on 9/11 back to the story of American independence and the formation of the United States in 1776, subsequently moving through the nation's struggle to unite its states, the evils of slavery and the tragedy of the Civil War through the two world wars and into the early 21st century. A galaxy of Hollywood stars lent their voices to the most influential figures in American history by reading letters or transcripts alongside the unfolding historical examination – everyone from Tom Hanks as Abraham Lincoln to Whoopi Goldberg as Harriet Tubman and Robin Williams as General Ulysses S. Grant.

Connery serves as one of the few non-American cast members to lend his voice to John Muir. Born in 1838 in Dunbar, Scotland, Muir was a naturalist, botanist, philosopher and adventurer who campaigned for the preservation of the American wilderness in the wake of the Gold Rush and the embers of the Civil War. As biographer Steven Holmes noted: 'Muir has profoundly shaped the very categories through which Americans understand and envision their relationships with the natural world.' The official website for Scotland itself notes how Muir, despite being a key figure in the establishment of some of America's most beloved national parks, never forgot his Scottish roots: 'He held a strong connection with his home country throughout his life and was frequently heard talking about his childhood spent amid beautiful and natural East Lothian countryside. He returned to Scotland on a trip in the 1890s and visited the places of his youth that were etched in his memory.'

It is not difficult to understand why Connery would have been happy to lend his voice to such a beloved Scottish-American traveller. Did he consider himself along similar lines? He was bedded in American culture thanks to his Hollywood roles, lived in the Bahamas, and was equally a 'son of Scotland'. He had been honoured by the British government in recent years, having after much lobbying on their part finally accepted a knighthood in 2000, and to underline his position as a true Scottish-American, Connery also received the 22nd Annual Kennedy Center Honor for his lifetime contribution to arts and culture soon after. (Not to mention his Academy Awards, BAFTAs, the Ordre des Arts et des Lettres from Franch and some honorary doctorates along the way.)

Yet Connery consistently made Scotland an important part of his career. His production company, Fountainbridge Films, founded in 1992, was committed to bringing more film work to Scotland, working to develop a major film production studio in Edinburgh, and had produced several of his more recent blockbusters such as *Just Cause* and *Entrapment*. And while he closed the organisation in 2002, when he went into retirement, Connery perhaps felt a kinship with a man like John Muir – a man of two worlds who, in his own way, helped shape both.

*

In 2012, *Sir Billi*, known as *Guardian of the Highlands* in the United States, was billed as the first CGI animated film made in Scotland. Connery's name and (unrecognisable) face were emblazoned on the poster used to publicise his brief emergence from retirement to play Sir William 'Billi' Cedric, an elderly veterinarian who lives with his talking pet goat on the outskirts of a quaint Scottish town called Catterness. He becomes embroiled in a bizarre plot involving corrupt policemen, a submarine and illegally captured beavers. The plot doesn't really matter.

Sascha Hartmann's animated adventure gained the kind of press attention such a modestly budgeted film would never have garnered had it not boasted the voice talent of Connery, whose 80-plus years at this point were beginning to show in his performance as Sir Billi.

Connery was effusive when asked about the film: 'I read it in its original form and we went along step by step and thankfully we made the actual recordings in the Bahamas. And then I witnessed all the kind of up-to-date stuff and I must say Sascha and his team, with Tessa [Hartmann, writer] there, they've really done a marvellous job.'

The herculean effort to convince Connery to be involved in another film is therefore partly explained by his not having to leave his Bahamian home.

Savaged by critics (*Variety* 'woefully anaemic', *The Scotsman* 'mirthless', Rotten Tomatoes 0%) and sporting incredibly crude animation and a range of wince-inducing performances from otherwise talented character actors such as Alan Cumming and Miriam Margolyes, *Sir Billi* must stand as the final example of Connery playing to the 007 gallery.

Hartmann's film is full of in-jokes about not just the Connery era but the entire Bond series. Sir Billi drives a classic Aston Martin DB5 – a car chase in the hills evokes both *Goldfinger* and later *Goldeneye* – and Cumming, who played Boris the computer hacker in the first Brosnan Bond film, pastiches Brosnan's first stunt as 007 when he jumps off the side of a dam with a harness. A Scottish flag parachute jump is thrown into the mix to echo Roger Moore's Union Jack jump in *The Spy Who Loved Me*, and Patrick Doyle's score briefly utilises notes from John Barry's *Thunderball* score.

Serving perhaps as the cherry on the Bond pastiche cake is the inclusion of Dame Shirley Bassey performing the theme song, having belted out the title tracks for two Bond adventures. 'The thing about this title song was I had a vision and thought at the end of the day if we've got Sean Connery involved then we need to have the lady!' said Hartmann.

As with *From Russia with Love* the game, Connery seemed to enjoy the nostalgia of revisiting those early years of Bond, and through his brief work on the PBC documentary voicing John Muir, he sought to invest in his native country. He no longer lived there, his parents had long since passed away, and his connections to those youthful Edinburgh days had faded, but Connery had maintained a strong interest in Scottish culture and politics throughout his career.

As early as 1967, Connery was calling for Scottish national independence. He wrote to SNP candidate George Leslie: 'I am convinced that with our resources and skills we are more than capable of building a prosperous, vigorous and modern self-governing Scotland in which we can all take pride and which will deserve the respect of other nations.' The SNP asked him to stand as a candidate, but Connery refused to be so tightly drawn in, instead using his voice, and platform, to be a vocal proponent for Scottish independence, contributing to the party funds over many years and fostering close relationships with figures such as the former SNP leader Alex Salmond. It was unclear why Connery did not provide support during the 2014 independence referendum in person: rumours swirled about poor health but his brother stated that it was because of his tax-exile status. (The Scots voted in favour of remaining in the United Kingdom by 55% to 45% after an unprecedented turnout of 85%.)

Sir Billi was likely a well-intended way for Connery to connect with his heritage from afar, but it is regrettable that it stands as an ignominious final contribution to cinema. His only two 21st-century live-action feature films – his final contributions to an industry he had watched transform from a post-war studio system into a corporate, franchise-dominated behemoth that would only expand in his retirement – exemplify Connery's career-spanning push–pull between the popular and the personal.

*

On 27 January 2010, the most reclusive, and to many the greatest, American author of the 20th century died in New Hampshire, aged 91 – Jerome David Salinger.

Known principally for his 1951 novel *The Catcher in the Rye*, a text that inspired everyone from John Lennon to his killer Mark David Chapman (obsessed with the character of Holden Caulfield, he was calmly reading the book at the crime scene before his arrest), Salinger was a private man. Like his female contemporary Harper Lee, he published only one novel in his life, following the book up with several short stories and novellas in the 1960s. He refused interviews. He litigated against people trying to release follow-ups to his work. He turned down tens of millions of dollars from Hollywood to transform *The Catcher in the Rye* into a movie or television show.

Filmmaker Shane Salerno spent ten years working to capture Salinger's legend in his documentary *Salinger*, released after the writer's death. He described why. 'I loved his work, and how he had the world at his doorstep, and said no thanks. He somehow understood in 1951 the corrosive effect that fame and money could have on his writing. He was singular, and in this internet age where people pursue their 15 minutes of fame, nobody did what Salinger did: living in the woods in New Hampshire, writing to please only himself. The biggest challenge was, how far do you pull back the curtain on a mythic figure while preserving his legacy?'

This same question drives Gus van Sant's *Finding Forrester*, released in 2000. Set in contemporary New York, the film focuses on a bright black kid from the Bronx, Jamal Wallace (Rob Brown). He is a basketball player but also a talented writer. When he is dared to sneak into the local apartment of a recluse, William Forrester (Connery), he strikes up a testy friendship when Forrester shows interest in his work. When Jamal gets a basketball scholarship to an exclusive private school, he learns that Forrester wrote *Avalon Landing*, a Pulitzer Prize-winning masterpiece. Forrester recognises the brilliance in Jamal's work, and Jamal, ultimately, proves to be the one person in 50 years who can bring Forrester back out into the world.

When discussing the film, Connery talked about the importance of the written word in the story and how it can change lives for the better: 'You have no idea how many people were talking about how they were affected. The literacy and the literature that's not being read now, what they really miss . . . there's one chap that was talking about his daughter saying now that's she gotten on to reading, it's changed her. And she's changed his life and her life and their kind of relationship because suddenly she's got something internalising going on. It's so pleasing to hear people are moved by it and caught by it, because you're right. Who would imagine in that setting, the Bronx, this guy and this guy would become friends?'

The storytelling, and the way Connery plays Forrester, proves that van Sant's film – similar thematically to his early Oscar-winning film with Robin Williams as the professorial figure, *Good Will Hunting* – is demonstrably influenced by Salinger, as well as John Kennedy Toole, who killed himself due to the perceived failure of *A Confederacy of Dunces*, only for it to win the Pulitzer. It is the ultimate emeritus role for Connery, fusing his on-screen persona with the man behind the performer. Forrester is grumpy and does not suffer fools gladly, but he retains a brilliance and wisdom that he is willing to impart, doing so with increasing charm as the film thaws out the character thanks to Jamal's calm yet challenging approach. As he says to Forrester at one point: 'What's the reason in having a file cabinet full of writing and keeping the shit locked so nobody can read it?'

Though it was discovered during filming that Connery could not even type, an analogue man in an increasingly digital age with the internet taking off and the fear of Y2K in the rear-view mirror, he nonetheless convinces as Forrester thanks to how unlikely the dynamic is with Jamal. It also sees Connery skirting the edges of black culture in a different manner to *Rising Sun*.

Connery agreed that the core of the film was the relationship between William and Jamal: 'It's nice, it's something that we don't do that many films about, an actual relationship. And friendship. And the title also has many connotations. Like finding Forrester, he finds himself. Then Jamal finds him. And then they find each other, and they're finding out that they have something for each other.'

Here Connery looks and sounds every inch his age. His sarcastic cry of 'You're the man now, dog!' to Jamal served as a formative internet meme, even spawning a website of the same name that to this day serves as a hub for meme culture. Connery would be long retired before the age of social media, Tumblr and the prevalence of the GIF, but he remains even after his passing frequently deployed whether for Bond, *Forrester* or *The Rock*. An online immortal, he has been cemented in a world he never really understood, a world where pictures like *The Matrix* captured the zeitgeist, and, in that sense, it is easy to understand why Forrester would have appealed as a character.

'I'm not playing Salinger,' he explained, 'but his ghost was always near at hand. Forrester closets himself in his apartment with the books and his royalty cheques. He hated celebrity. He shunned fame. I myself have avoided many of the pitfalls of fame by choosing not to live in Los Angeles. The story took hold of me from the first reading and I knew I had to avoid being sentimental. I wanted people to believe the relationship between Forrester and the young boy could actually develop.'

Even without the latent Scottish nationalism that emerges from Forrester at the end of the picture, Connery portrays a figure at odds with not just the traumatic past he has buried, but the rapidly changing modern world, in a century built more out of chaos than certainty. He snaps back at Jamal during a fractious exchange: 'There are no reasons! Reasons why some of us live and why some of us don't! Fortunately for you, you have decades to figure that out!'

What he tries to instil in Jamal is instinct, the kind of determined impulse of character that Connery showed and imbued in many of his roles. 'No thinking,' says Forrester. 'That comes later. You must write your first draft with your heart. You rewrite with your head. The first key to writing is . . . to write, not to think!' In this sense, Forrester represents the old school. He represents the kind of man, a kind of thinker, who is rapidly becoming extinct. It is telling that van Sant visually tries to bring Connery full circle in using a youthful image of the actor first seen in 1958's *Another Time, Another Place*, on the set of Forrester's apartment. He is working to capture an old-world, almost otherworldly, sense of timelessness to Forrester and in many ways to Connery, who was now 70 and entering a pantheon of actors still working at the time, such as Paul Newman and Gene Hackman, who emerged from an era of enormous social and political change and from the embers of post-war Hollywood and the studio system.

Production designer Jane Musky talked about how they worked to evoke this sense of a world long lost in the design of Forrester's home: 'We wanted the apartment to look like a kind of Never Never Land to Jamal, who comes from a normal street environment and lives in cramped quarters. Because it had to carry so many scenes, we decided to make the apartment oversized, almost palatial, so that the camera could move around in it freely. Also, Sean Connery is a big man, so everything there – the chairs, the table, the bed, they're all oversized too. We had to achieve 40 years of layering so that the apartment had the proper authentic texture. It wasn't supposed to be a fire hazard, you know, strewn with papers and all sorts of junk.'

Forrester is in marked contrast to the celebrated writing professor Dr Robert Crawford (played by F. Murray Abraham, in a similar, antagonistic part to the one he performed opposite Connery in *The Name of the Rose*), who tries to stymie Jamal's academic knowledge and achievement despite not possessing either the talent or awareness of Forrester and Jamal. It is to defend Jamal's ability, and decency, that Forrester – a living legend many presumed was already dead – emerges from his living sarcophagus to return to academia. He reads from unpublished work that to a dilettante like Crawford is equivalent to a lost gospel, as a means of displaying to Jamal the importance of their friendship. In this case, the mentor learns from his charge, rediscovering a zest for life and coming to terms with the tragic loss of his brother, through the younger man's integrity. It then transpires that Forrester is quoting not his words, but Jamal's. Crawford's petty officiousness and undercurrent of white privileged elitism is exposed for what it is.

There could easily be accusations that Forrester acts as a white saviour to rescue the gifted black boy on trial, and it is probable that such a fantasy tale – of the talented black youth being raised up as the next great American writer – might play with a shade more cynicism in a divisive, right-wing American landscape and with the Black Lives Matter movement growing in stature. Would Jamal, had his story been real, as a man in his late thirties, now stand as one of the important black writers of his day – a Ta-Nehisi Coates or Colson Whitehead – pouring scorn on such a clichéd feelgood tale? Maybe, but *Finding Forrester* is nevertheless an example of how Connery was prepared to start passing on the torch. He gives up his position as the great American literary genius, and gifts it both to the younger generation and a man of colour. It feels like a hopeful sign of the world to come.

As we witnessed in previous Connery films since the 1980s, the actor was not averse to a screen death. Forrester's demise is different. It's not a hero's death, such as Ramírez in *Highlander*, or the tragic demise of a flawed man like Malone in *The Untouchables*. This is the bittersweet ending for a haunted creative master who only discovered life at the very end, as he relates in a parting letter to Jamal: 'Someone I once knew wrote that we walk away from our dreams . . . afraid that we may fail, or worse yet, afraid we may succeed. While I knew so very early on that you would realise your dreams . . . I never imagined I would once again realise my own. Seasons change, young man. While I waited until the winter of my life to see what I've seen this past year . . . there is no doubt I would have waited too long, had it not been for you.'

It should, by rights, have been Connery's final screen performance, if life was fair and reflected the symmetry of fiction. To a Scottish reverie, riding off on his bike, Forrester emerging from his chrysalis after decades entombed – a living relic of the 1950s and 1960s reconstituted at the millennium – to discover the joy of life one last time should have been the poetic departure of a titan of the silver screen.

Alas, there was one final curtain call to come. It's an extraordinary tale.

*

Where *Finding Forrester* dealt with the pinnacle of literary endeavour by exploring the great American novel, *The League of Extraordinary Gentlemen* only exists thanks to a less esteemed art form, albeit one which in recent decades had gained cultural and critical traction. The comic book, or in this case, the graphic novel.

At the end of the millennium, writer Alan Moore and artist Kevin O'Neill debuted *The League of Extraordinary Gentlemen*, a colourful and exuberant set of volumes set in the late 19th century and bringing together numerous classic Victorian characters not protected by copyright law to form a group, a league, for British intelligence with a range of powerful skills and abilities, to protect the world from outlandish threats. It would see the vampiric Mina Harker (wife of Jonathan Harker from Bram Stoker's *Dracula*) alongside Jules Verne's Captain Nemo and H. Rider Haggard's Allan Quatermain face down arch-villains including Sax Rohmer's Fu Manchu and Sir Arthur Conan Doyle's Professor James Moriarty. A dieselpunk fusion of Victorian history, Gothic literature and superhero exuberance, *LXG* – as it became known – was a huge, long-running success that lasted in comic-book form for twenty years. A film adaptation was inevitable.

The film version of *LXG* is set in 1899, as a mysterious villain called the Fantom and his terrorist group kidnap German scientists as part of a plan to plunge Europe into war. British intelligence, led by M (Richard Roxburgh), seek out an aged, retired Quatermain (played by Connery) at his colonial Kenyan residence to lead up the 'League', including the vampiric Dr Mina Harker (Peta Wilson), swaggering American gunslinger Tom Sawyer (Shane West), Rodney Skinner as an invisible gentleman thief (Tony Curran), Dorian Gray (Stuart Townsend), Dr Henry Jekyll (Jason Flemyng) and Captain Nemo (Naseeruddin Shah), to stop the Fantom from destroying Venice and starting a global conflict. Inevitably, not all turns out to be what it first appears.

While Moore's book emphasises Mina as the protagonist, romantically attaching her to Quatermain, the film (to appease Connery's star presence) places the wizened colonial adventurer as the leader of the League, despite him arguably lacking many of the superpowered skills of his brethren. Sawyer was intentionally developed as the younger heroic love interest to offset Connery's increasing age, a concern that wasn't present just three or four years earlier in *Entrapment* opposite a much younger female co-star. Connery, equally, is given plenty of fist-balling action sequences against younger male stars, much as we saw him hold his own in *The Rock*. There is a desire to play him both as the old soldier but at the same time retain the vigour of Connery as an action man.

To what degree, however, is Connery playing James Bond again one final time? Is he some amalgam of Bond and an elderly Indiana Jones? Quatermain is perhaps the signature colonial adventurer of 19th-century fiction: protagonist of Haggard's 1885 adventure *King Solomon's Mines*, he is a professional big game hunter in South Africa whose life from a youth to an old man is evoked across numerous African adventures. Haggard's texts are riddled with what can now be considered racist tracts of the Victorian age, from belief in the superiority of the white man and an admiration for warrior races such as the Zulu, although they also contain disdain for certain racist pejoratives and a questioning of the traditional Christian faith. Quatermain is, without doubt, a creature embedded in the 19th century as Connery was in the 20th.

Yet he ends up working for M, a character known in Moore's books as Campion Bond – the direct grandfather of 007 – and clearly based on the establishment figure from Ian Fleming's work. He is sought out in retirement and told expressly that 'stories of your exploits have thrilled English boys for decades' and 'the empire needs you' – the same empire his 007 in *Dr. No* worked for, treading the Commonwealth in Jamaica to stop another crazed supervillain. 'But the question is . . . do I need the empire?' Quatermain replies. Connery seems to be enjoying, at such an age, reprising the kind of adventurer he once was on screen. Yet he also seems jaded by some of the traditional aspects of it, such as romance when Mina enquires as to whether her beauty distracts him. 'My dear girl, I've buried two wives and many lovers . . . and I'm in no mood for more of either.' Hearing this come from Connery is remarkable. It is an admission that he can no longer, as he perhaps sought to in *The Rock* and *Entrapment*, recapture the screen persona he once had.

As *Finding Forrester* dialled into William's quasi-parental relationship with Jamal, so too does *LXG* with Quatermain and Sawyer. The young man is reckless and hot-headed, suave and swaggering, an American Bond in all but name. Quatermain, in guiding and training him as they hunt the Fantom, advises temperance in Sawyer as he trains him to shoot: 'You have to feel the shot. Take your time with it. You have all the time you need. All the time in the world.' This he does. Sawyer's world is the one to come. Quatermain's is behind him. In this, he shares a similarity to Forrester. They are both men who are lost, trapped in their isolated, dusty old houses, with only their memories. 'I am not the man I once was,' Quatermain admits. *LXG*, like *Finding Forrester*, is Connery playing a version of his cinematic character finding a reason to exist one last time.

Here, he is a man who now rejects his symbolic representation of empire. Quatermain becomes attached to Sawyer given how he lost his own son, who would be around the same age, in a futile attempt to help Queen and Country. 'After that, I washed my hands of England and the empire and . . . the legend of Allan-bloody-Quatermain.' Perhaps Connery found some affinity in a man who washed his hands of his own legend and legacy. This is certainly, in many respects, what Connery sought to do with the Bond character and archetype he represented. He wanted to venture into new territory, but he remained forever haunted. Only by confronting it, as Connery did with *Never Say Never Again* and later with his *From Russia with Love* voice work, did he perhaps exorcise the demon.

LXG ends up placing Connery within a paradigm where he can no longer save the world alone. The only picture he made in the wake of the 9/11 terrorist attacks in 2001 – an event that pushed American cinema into a fearful, reactionary space for a decade or more – *LXG* sees Quatermain and his team unable to prevent the Fantom destroying Venice, which collapses into the ocean below. When he is unmasked, revealing that M and the Fantom were both covers for his real identity – Sherlock Holmes' nemesis Moriarty – the villain promises that no matter what the League do, they are powerless to stop the century ahead: 'War will come, sooner or later . . . as inevitable as summer into autumn.' 'There'll be others like me, Quatermain. You can't kill the future.' Moriarty's plot to pit the superpowers of the 19th century against each other is little different from the 20th-century plots Connery's Bond, and all those who followed him, would foil. He turns out to be right in his pessimistic assumption, post-9/11, that he was just the vanguard.

It is a century neither Quatermain, nor Connery, would truly experience. Quatermain succumbs during the battle to stop Moriarty, passing on the torch to Sawyer much as Forrester did to Jamal. As it was Quatermain's final adventure, so *LXG* was Connery's. The shoot in the Czech Republic was hellish, with seven million dollars' worth of set being washed away in a flood that delayed production, and Connery clashing almost violently at points with director Stephen Norrington – best known for helming *Blade* with Connery's former *Rising Sun* co-star Wesley Snipes in 1998 – who didn't even turn up for the premiere.

'I knew if I did [walk off set], it would never restart,' said Connery. 'The only one he [Norrington] was scared of was me . . . He said, "Do you want to hit me?" I said, "Don't tempt me." The experience had a great influence on me; it made me think about showbiz. And I have had other problems: people who raise money on me, then cut me out of it.'

When asked where Norrington might be, Connery – opting not to hide his loathing of the man – quipped, 'Check the local asylum.' Though the film turned a profit, critics were scathing. Unlike many such comic-book adaptations of the time, no sequels were forthcoming. No critical re-evaluation of the film has ever taken place.

Norrington never directed another picture, and Connery decided the experience was enough. He described himself in interviews as 'fed up with all the idiots', adding: 'There is a widening gap between those who know about movies and those who green-light movies. Then the s**t hits the fan. The one thing you can't say in Hollywood is "I don't know". You appear in a film and then you realise the director has directed f*** all.'

He quit *Josiah's Canon*, a planned heist adventure to be directed by Brett Ratner, where he would have headed a gang who break into a bank vault to recover Jewish gold secreted from the Nazis at the end of the Second World War. Probably an *Ocean's Eleven/ Mission Impossible*-style picture, with Connery reprising a role similar to Mac from *Entrapment* – a gentleman thief grandmaster, it would have seen him cruise on the kind of charm that defined him as he edged into his seventies. He announced in 2006, however, that he had quit for good and later quipped that 'retirement is just too much fun'. Yet strangely, while *The League of Extraordinary Gentlemen* is a disappointing climax to such a grand career, his role as Quatermain, and behind it that of Forrester, are perhaps fitting endings for Connery. The hero. The mentor. The star. His was a century, much like for Quatermain, that had passed.

At one point in *LXG*, a character asks Quatermain if he is indestructible, and he replies: 'Well, a witch doctor did bless me once. I had saved his village. He said Africa would never allow me to die.' The final shot of the film, as the League members bury their fallen leader in Africa and head off into their new century, teases a supernatural recovery for Quatermain. A bolt of lightning hits his grave as the screen cuts to black. Did the gods and spirits of Africa reanimate their fallen son? Would Quatermain become immortal and enter the 20th century to rejoin the League and save the continent he considered his home?

Maybe. And while Sean Connery never made another live-action film before his death, the power of cinema had by this point immortalised him. He had himself become legend. And his legacy would live on long past his presence on the big screen.

EPILOGUE

IMPERFECT MAN, PERFECT STAR

AS OCTOBER ROLLED into November of 2020, and the COVID-19 pandemic still raged across the globe with billions unvaccinated, millions working from home, and with countless more in hospitals, the world of entertainment still found the time and space to mourn the passing of Sir Sean Connery.

One of his oldest friends, Michael Caine, commented: 'Sean was a rare combination of being a great star and a brilliant actor. He proved this first in James Bond. The second [time] he proved [this was] when we both were in *The Man Who Would Be King*. We had a great time together. I haven't seen him for quite a long time and I've missed him, but today, I really miss him. I am grateful for the time we spent together. A wonderful man.' Colleagues from across his career expressed their sadness: from Tippi Hedren, his *Marnie* co-star: 'An elegant man, a brilliant actor and an overall amazing individual . . . Not to mention extremely attractive.' His co-star on *The Untouchables*, Kevin Costner: 'He was the biggest star that I ever worked with and I will be forever grateful to be linked with him on film. Sean Connery was a man's man who had an amazing career.'

Tributes came from all walks of life, such as Nicola Sturgeon, First Minister of Scotland: 'It was a privilege to have known Sean. When I last spoke to him it was clear even then that his health was failing – but the voice, the spirit and the passion that we all loved so well were still there. I will miss him. Scotland will miss him. The world will miss him.'

Hugh Jackman praised him: 'I grew up idolizing #SeanConnery. A legend on screen, and off.'

Fellow Bond, Pierce Brosnan, gave his own tribute: 'Each man in his turn looked to you with reverence and admiration as we forged ahead with our own interpretations of the role. You were mighty in every way, as an actor and as a man, and will remain so till the end of time.'

Connery's death came just three years after the passing of the James Bond who succeeded him, Sir Roger Moore, one of Connery's oldest friends and never the rival he was painted as by the British tabloids. They formed an unofficial triumvirate with Caine that helped blaze a trail for British actors who broke into Hollywood at the end of the studio system, and on the fringes of transformative cinematic movements, while always remaining stars. Of the three, it was Connery who shone brightest. Moore never quite escaped 007. Caine was perennially trapped in the bus teetering over the cliff edge at the end of *The Italian Job*, no matter his future career success. It was Connery who reinvented himself, sometimes successfully and sometimes not, across numerous generations.

Film critic Matt Zoller Seitz encapsulated the aura of the man: 'Connery's flinty-eyed dangerousness made him an emblem of an ancient brand of masculinity – one that would become increasingly questioned during the second half of his life and in the decades following his retirement. Like certain film stars from before his time (like John Wayne) and after (think Mel Gibson), Connery continues to fascinate and excite despite (or because of) knowledge that the image and the man had a lot in common.'

This suggests a merging of star and character that many of the most iconic and successful actors in cinema history have always been forced to balance. Connery was focused, often serious, at times cantankerous, and respectful about the men who directed him (he was never directed by a woman) and the work they did, but at points he considered fame – if not fortune – a noose around his neck. He always remained dogged by the controversy of his remarks from the 1960s, fuelled again by comments in the 1990s, about his attitude towards domestic violence and violence towards women more generally. Writer Annie Brown wrote a piece, in the wake of his death, calling for Connery not to be eulogised as a great man: 'What is the grace period we should give a dead wife beater before we condemn his abuse? In the sixties Connery was married to Australian actress Diane Cilento, who later claimed in her autobiography that he abused her physically and mentally – something the Bond actor denied. Given the weight of Connery's own words, there is no reason to disbelieve her tales of being locked in a toilet, whimpering on a bath mat, terrorised by a violent, tempestuous man.'

Would Connery have survived the age of so-called 'cancel culture'? Perhaps. Perhaps not. He would probably have had little time for it. Yet this is not to say the man and his work should not be reconsidered through a modern perspective, unfair as it may be to classify a historical figure – certainly an actor, writer or director and so on – as needing to hold to the moral values of our own age. Connery, as we have seen, was forged during inter-war poverty, witness to among the most tumultuous decades in human history in his lifetime, and like many such performers or entertainers of his time was a man of multitudes. As journalist Martyn McLaughlin wrote in *The Scotsman*: 'None of this contradiction and darkness inherent in Connery's character dulled the brightness of his star. Maybe because they helped create it. He was, after all, the emblem of a particular strain of masculinity that was once revered. Nowadays, it is openly questioned, and fading fast from view. In the age of #MeToo, it seems inconceivable that his star would ascend under the same circumstances. But then, no young actor nowadays would begin their working life at the age of nine, rising at 5am from the squalor of a cramped tenement to deliver milk in a handcart. Connery was, in many ways, an imperfect man. But he was, and will remain, the perfect star.'

While writing this book, I have often wondered why Connery had such an impact on me as a child growing up in the 1980s and 1990s, why he became my favourite screen actor. His Bond films were never even my personal favourite as a child; I always preferred the exuberant camp of Moore's comedic Bonds, and how Brosnan later fused a similar style with modern, blockbuster action sequences. Yet something about Connery the actor and the man, appealed in an era just before the age of the internet, of social media, of the rapid cultural and political change it would render, and the swift advance of gender identity and women's rights that were never going to square with Connery's image, singed into the mind of multiple generations since *Dr. No*, of powerful, unashamed alpha maleness.

To me, he was as much Henry Jones Sr or John Mason as he was James Bond, but there is little doubt that 007 covers his entire life and professional career like a blanket whether he wanted it to or not. Might he have been able to enjoy such a position within popular culture had he not felt the producers of the Bond series remunerated him unfairly over the years he was associated with the character? Or had he truly managed to gain the kind of critical acclaim as a serious performer that he deep down craved? He never fully came to terms with James Bond, first and foremost, being his legacy, even if by the end of his career he had made some peace with it. That strikes me as an eternal shame given the joy he gave, and continues to give, to millions of people in his portrayal of the world's greatest secret agent.

Hugh Jackman would not have been the only young man to grow up idolising Connery as a performer. He exists within a pantheon of actors, now approaching middle age or retirement and working in cinema and television today, who embody a similar blend of the charisma and power Connery brought to the screen. Harrison Ford's portrayal of Indiana Jones, itself endlessly copied by lesser pictures and filmmakers, takes more than a small cue from the suave danger of Connery's 007. Dwayne 'The Rock' Johnson combines a similar all-purpose charm with the 'superman' brawn of the 1980s and 1990s man-mountain action heroes Connery held his own against. Tom Cruise, himself divisive and single-minded, has retained the kind of star power, no matter what kind of role he portrays, across nearly as many decades as Connery himself. In a cinematic landscape fuelled by franchises and intellectual property, those few stars whose name can carry a picture, who remain singular, unique figures in a sea of corporate dominance, all of them take something from how Connery and his films bridged entire eras and from a man who often refused to compromise.

Similarly, as we have seen, for all his stardom and international reach, he never lost touch with his roots. He invested in Scotland and its own legacy, financially supporting government schemes and cheering on sporting successes; he was a regular at Wimbledon and the US Open supporting his fellow Scot and friend Sir Andy Murray. Had he lived to his own century, might he have one day seen Scotland vote for the independence he so wished would happen and campaigned for across decades? It is possible. He passed away at the beginning of what will be a critical decade for the world, for Scotland. The future of the country he grew up in, worked in and lived in may well end up radically changed from the Fountainbridge he was born in.

This book was never meant to be an autobiography. We only ever know a person, as fans and audiences, from a distance. Who Connery was as a man is largely for those who knew him, who worked with him, who befriended and loved him. For the rest of us, we have his body of work, who he was on screen, and what he gave us as an actor and performer. The work will never be forgotten – the great, the good and the bad.

Perhaps the man who best inhabits Sean Connery's legacy for a new century, Daniel Craig, to many the most iconic 007 since the 1960s, should get the final word in how he ended his own eulogy to a titan of cinema, an actor who spanned generations, and a man who inhabited the spirit of an age now lost to history: 'Wherever he is, I hope there is a golf course.'

SEAN CONNERY FILMOGRAPHY

FILM

Year	Title	Role
1954	*Lilacs in the Spring*	extra
1957	*No Road Back*	Spike
	Hell Drivers	Johnny Kates
	Action of the Tiger	Mike
	Time Lock	2nd Welder
1958	*Another Time, Another Place*	Mark Trevor
1959	*Darby O'Gill and the Little People*	Michael McBride
	Tarzan's Greatest Adventure	O'Bannion
1961	*On the Fiddle*	Pedlar Pascoe
	The Frightened City	Paddy Damion
1962	*The Longest Day*	Pte. Flanagan
	Dr. No	James Bond
1963	*From Russia with Love*	James Bond
1964	*Goldfinger*	James Bond
	Marnie	Mark Rutland
	Woman of Straw	Anthony Richmond
1965	*The Hill*	Joe Roberts

	Thunderball	James Bond
1966	*Un monde nouveau*	Himself
	A Fine Madness	Samson Shillitoe
1967	*You Only Live Twice*	James Bond
	The Bowler and the Bunnet	Himself (and director)
1968	*Shalako*	Shalako
1969	*The Red Tent*	Roald Amundsen
1970	*The Molly Maguires*	Jack Kehoe
1971	*The Anderson Tapes*	Duke Anderson
	Diamonds Are Forever	James Bond
1972	*España campo de golf*	Himself
	The Offence	Detective Sergeant Johnson
1974	*Zardoz*	Zed
	Murder on the Orient Express	Colonel Arbuthnot
	Ransom	Nils Tahlvik
1975	*The Dream Factory*	Himself
	The Wind and the Lion	Mulai Ahmed er Raisuni
	The Man Who Would Be King	Daniel Dravot
1976	*Robin and Marian*	Robin Hood
	The Next Man	Khalil Abdul-Muhsen
1977	*A Bridge Too Far*	Maj. Gen. Roy Urquhart
1979	*The First Great Train Robbery*	Edward Pierce
	Meteor	Dr. Paul Bradley
	Cuba	Robert Dapes
1981	*Outland*	Marshal William T. O'Niel
	Time Bandits	King Agamemnon
1982	*G'olé!*	Narrator
	Five Days One Summer	Douglas Meredith
	Wrong Is Right	Patrick Hale
1983	*Sean Connery's Edinburgh*	Himself
	Never Say Never Again	James Bond
1984	*Sword of the Valiant*	The Green Knight
1986	*Highlander*	Juan Sánchez Villalobos Ramírez
	The Name of the Rose	William of Baskerville
1987	*The Untouchables*	Jim Malone
1988	*The Presidio*	Lt. Col. Alan Caldwell
	Memories of Me	Himself
1989	*Indiana Jones and the Last Crusade*	Henry Jones, Sr.
	Family Business	Jessie McMullen
1990	*The Hunt for Red October*	Captain Marko Ramius

	The Russia House	Barley Blair
1991	*Highlander II: The Quickening*	Juan Sánchez Villalobos Ramírez
	Robin Hood: Prince of Thieves	King Richard the Lionheart
1992	*Medicine Man*	Dr. Robert Campbell
1993	*Rising Sun*	Capt. John Connor
1994	*A Good Man in Africa*	Dr. Alex Murray
1995	*Just Cause*	Paul Armstrong
	First Knight	King Arthur
1996	*Dragonheart*	Draco
	The Rock	John Patrick Mason
1998	*The Avengers*	Sir August de Wynter
	Playing by Heart	Paul
1999	*Entrapment*	Robert MacDougal
2000	*Finding Forrester*	William Forrester
2003	*The League of Extraordinary Gentlemen*	Allan Quatermain
2012	*Sir Billi*	Sir Billi
	Ever to Excel	Narrator

TV

Year	Title	Role
1956	*Dixon of Dock Green*	Joe Brasted
	The Condemned	Performer
	Sailor of Fortune	Achmed
1957	*The Jack Benny Programme*	hotel porter
	Blood Money	Harlan 'Mountain' McClintok
	Anna Christie	Mat Burke
1958	*Women in Love*	Johnnie
	The Boy with Meat Axe	Performer
1959	*I Captured the King of the Leprechauns*	Michael MacBride
1959/60	*ITV Play of the Week* (four episodes)	Various roles
1960	*Colombe*	Julien
	An Age of Kings	Harry Percy (Hotspur)
	Without the Grail	Innes Corrie
1961	*Adventure Story*	Alexander the Great
	Anna Karenina	Count Alexis Vronsky
	Macbeth	Macbeth
1969	*Male of the Species*	MacNeil

| 2003 | *Freedom: A History of US* | John Muir |
| 2007 | *Modern Greeks: C.P. Cavafy* | Narrator |

VIDEO GAMES

| Year | Title | Role |
| 2005 | *James Bond 007: From Russia with Love* | James Bond |

ACKNOWLEDGEMENTS

MY THANKS TO Peter Burns for being a champion of this book, a supportive collaborator and someone who challenged me to make it the best it could be. My equal thanks to my editor, Alison Rae, who chiselled the book into what it is today.

Thanks to Carl Sweeney and Russ Hugo. This book might have initially been a podcast series but my great discussion with Carl and Russ helped me see the book's potential.

And as always, my greatest thanks to my wife Steph, an island of patience and support in a sea of time spent huddled away writing.

BIBLIOGRAPHY

Adams, David. 'Sean Connery Back as Bond'. IGN. May 19, 2012.

Archerd, Army. 'Spelling set for busy millennium'. *Variety*. Jan 14, 1999.

Archyde, 'With his accent to cut with a knife, we took Sean Connery for a Pole', Nov1, 2020.

Bart, Peter. "War Is 'Hill,' Mate!". *New York Times*. 10 Jan, 1965.

Billi Productions. 'Sean Connery interview'. 2006.

Bradshaw, Peter. 'Sean Connery: a dangerously seductive icon of masculinity'. *The Guardian*. Aug 25, 2020.

Bray, Christopher. *Sean Connery: A Biography*. Pegasus. 2012.

Brew, Simon. 'Sean Connery, and his Highlander II contract restrictions'. *Film Stories*. Jun 2, 2020.

Brody, Richard. '"*Marnie*" Is the Cure for Hitchcock Mania'. *The New Yorker*.

Aug 17, 2016.

Brooke, Michael. 'British Film in the 1940s'. BFI Screenonline.

Brown, Annie. 'Don't canonise Sean Connery - he was a coward and a bully'. *Daily Record.* Nov 4, 2020.

Canby, Vincent. 'Crack *Orient Express* Clicks as Film: The Cast'. Nov 25, 1974.

Carter, Jimmy. 'Sean Connery talks the Rock/Dragonheart with Jimmy Carter'. Ask Jimmy Carter. 1996.

Chapman, James. *License to Thrill: A Cultural History of the James Bond Films.* B Tauris & Co. 2008.

Chowdhury, Ajay & Sweet, Matthew. *Some Kind of Hero: The Remarkable Story of the James Bond Films.* The History Press. 2018.

Clarke, Cath. 'How we made the original *Murder on the Orient Express*'. *The Guardian.* Nov 13, 2017.

Cohen, Rob. *The Making of Dragonheart* (DVD). Universal Studios.

Corliss, Richard. 'What's Old Is Gold: A Triumph for Indy'. *Time Magazine.* May 29, 1989.

Crawley, Tony. 'Sean Connery interview'. *Starburst Magazine* No. 42. 1981.

Desowitz, Bill. 'The author of *James Bond Unmasked* reminisces about his rare interview with Connery in 2002.' *Indiewire.* Oct 31, 2020.

Duffy, Elle. 'Sean Connery dead: Tributes for James Bond actor after death at 90'. *The Herald.* Oct 31, 2020.

Drury, Sharareh & Beresford, Trilby. 'Daniel Craig, Pierce Brosnan, Sam Neill, George Lucas and More of Hollywood Pay Tribute to Sean Connery'. *Hollywood Reporter.* Oct 31, 2020.

Ebert, Roger. 'The Next Man'. Roger Ebert. Nov 17, 1976.

Ehrlich, David. 'From Swashbucklers to Supermen: A Brief History of Action-Movie Heroes'. *Rolling Stone*. Sept 1, 2015.

Electronic Arts. 'Sean Connery: Making of *From Russia With Love* (Video Game)'. *From Russia With Love* game. 2005.

Entertainment Weekly. '*League of Extraordinary Gentlemen*'. Apr 25, 2003.

Evangelista, Chris. 'Why Sean Connery Turned Down '*The Matrix*', But Not The Role You Think He Did'. *Slashfilm*. Aug 18, 2021.

Ferguson, Jim. 'Studiola's Jim Ferguson interviews Sean Connery star of *Finding Forrester*'. *Asian Connections*. Aug 12, 2003.

Fleming Jr, Mike. 'Secret J.D. Salinger Documentary & Book, Now Revealed (Mike Has Seen The Film)'. *Deadline*. Jan 29, 2010.

Geoghegan, Kev. "Lost' Sean Connery play recording unearthed by director'. BBC. Jun 2, 2014.

Gleiberman, Owen. '*Medicine Man*'. *Entertainment Weekly*. Feb 21, 1992

Gordon, Lawrence. *Family Business* trivia. IMDB.

Gow, Gordon. 'A Secretive Person'. *Films and Filming*. March 1974.

Greig Fulton, Niall. 'Who Was John Hopkins?'. Ed Film Fest. May 22, 2017.

Harrison, Mark. 'Beyond Bond – The Acting Legacy of All the 007s'. Den of Geek. Aug 10, 2018.

Hakim, Joy. 'About the series'. PBS. 2002.

Hammond, Clive. 'Sean Connery's furious admission on final film appearance: 'Was a nightmare!'. *The Express*. Jun 20, 2022.

Hess, Alex. 'My guilty pleasure: *The Rock*'. *The Guardian*. Apr 14, 2014.

Holmes, Steven. *The Young John Muir: An Environmental Biography.* Univ. of Wisconsin Press. 1999.

Hood, Phil. 'How we made *Highlander*: 'Connery opened his homemade whisky on the plane'. *The Guardian*. Jul 5, 2016.

Huntley Film Archives. 'Sean Connery on *The Avengers* Teddy Bear Scene'. 1998.

Hutchinson, Tom. 'Sean Connery, back in Bondage – interview'. *The Guardian*. 28 Dec, 1971.

Jameson, Fredric. 'History and the death wish: *Zardoz* as open form'. *Jump Cut* no. 3, 1974.

Johnstone, Doug. 'How William McIlvanney invented tartan noir'. *The Guardian*. Aug 11, 2013.

Jones, Allison. 'Darling Buds of LA'. *Birmingham Post & Mail*. 1999.

Kael, Pauline. '*The Untouchables*'. *The New Yorker*. Jun 29, 1987.

Kenny, Glenn. 'Prince of the City'. *DGA*. Fall 2007.

Leonelli, Elisa. 'Sean Connery and Me'. *Cultural Daily*. Nov 11, 2020.

Lewin, David. '*Playboy* Interview: Sean Connery – A candid conversation with James Bond's acerbic alter ego'. Nov 1965.

Lindbergs, Kimberley. '*Woman of Straw* (1964)'. *Cinebeats*. Aug 25, 2020.

Loder, Kurt. 'Great Scot: Nobody Pushes Sean Connery Around'. *Rolling Stone*. 27 Oct 1983.

London Celtic Punks. 'Film Review: *The Molly Maguires* (1970)'. Jun 5, 2015.

Lumet, Sidney. *Making Movies*. Vintage Press. 1996.

Maslin, Janet. 'Sean Connery is Seasoned James Bond'. *The New York Times*, 7 Oct 1983.

McClennan, Patrick. '007 star Pierce Brosnan hails Sean Connery for "leading the way for us all who followed"'. *Radio Times*. Nov 1, 2020.

McLaughlin, Martyn. 'Sir Sean Connery: An imperfect man, but the perfect star'. *The Scotsman.* Oct 31, 2020.

Miller, Angela. L. Berlo, Janet Catherine. Wolf, Bryan J. & Roberts, Jennifer L. *American Encounters: Art, History, and Cultural Identity.* Washington University Libraries. 2018.

Montreal Gazette, The. 'Does Sean Connery still have that old 007 magic?'. Jul 10, 1971.

Moore, Sam. '"Harvey Weinstein would threaten to get Tarantino to direct": An oral history of The Lord of the Rings at 20'. *The Independent.* Dec 15, 2021

Moral, Tony Lee. *Hitchcock and the Making of Marnie.* Scarecrow Press. 2005.

Movieline Staff. 'The Extreme Sport of Being John McTiernan'. *Movieline.* Aug 1, 2001.

Musky, Jane. '*Finding Forrester*'. *Film Education.*

Nikita. 'Entretien avec Alberto De Martino'. *Nanarland.* Feb 16, 2007.

Ng, Alvin. '"You're just Out of Practice": James Bond, the Incompetent Womaniser in *Thunderball* (1965), *Moonraker* (1979), *GoldenEye* (1995) and *Casino Royale* (2006)'. Jul 2019.

Parker, John. *Sir Sean Connery: The Definitive Biography.* John Blake. 2021.

Parker, Ryan. '*Robin Hood: Prince of Thieves* Nearly Featured John Cleese as King Richard'. *Hollywood Reporter.* Jun 14, 2021.

Parker, Sean. 'Sean Connery Turned Down *Indiana Jones 4* Because the Role Was Too Small'. *Hollywood Reporter.* Jan 18, 2018.

Pattison, Michael. 'Diamonds Aren't Forever: Close-Up on Sidney Lumet's "*The Anderson Tapes*". *Mubi.* Dec 26, 2017.

Payne, Robert. M. 'Total eclipse of the Sun'. *Jump Cut* no. 40, March 1996.

Pelan, Tim. 'The Marshall and the Space Miners – In Peter Hyams' *Outland*, No One Can Hear You Punch Out'. Neo Text.

Pelan, Tim. 'Gang Wars, the Prohibition Menace: Brian De Palma's *The Untouchables*'. *Cinephilia & Beyond*.

Pfeiffer, Lee & Phillip, Lisa. *The Films of Sean Connery*. Citadel Press. 2002.

Rees Shapiro, T. 'Sean Connery, who brought James Bond to life on film, dies at 90'. *The Washington Post*. Oct 31, 2020.

Ritman, Alex. 'Terry Gilliam Says Sean Connery Was Originally Written Into *Time Bandits* as a Joke, Yet "Saved My Ass" on Fantasy Film'. *Hollywood Reporter*. Nov 2, 2020.

Roxborough, Scott. '*The Name of the Rose* Screenwriter on Sean Connery's Most Un-James Bond Role'. *Hollywood Reporter.* Nov 2, 2020.

Ryan, Mike. 'Sam Mendes, *Skyfall* Director, On Bringing Humor Back To James Bond & Flirting With The Idea Of Casting Sean Connery'. *Huffington Post.* Nov 5, 2012.

Scene By Scene. 'Episode 1: Sean Connery'. BBC. May 10, 1997.

Seitz, Matt Zoller. 'Bonded and Unbound: Sean Connery, 1930-2020'. Roger Ebert. Oct 31, 2020.

Sellers, Robert. *The Battle for Bond*. Tomahawk Press. 2008.

Sinyard, Neil. *The Films of Richard Lester*. Barnes & Noble. 1985.

Shatner, Lisabeth. *Captain's Log: William Shatner's Personal Account of the Making of Star Trek V the Final Frontier*. Pocket Books. 1989.

Smith, Brian. 'Sir Sean Connery IS Sir Billi in his last official film appearance'. *From Sweden With Love.* Sept 11, 2013.

Smith, Dinita. 'James Bond: Agent of Cultural Change'. *Las Vegas Sun.* Jan 29, 1998.

Sollosi, Mary. 'The stars of *The Untouchables* look back, 30 years later'. *Entertainment Weekly.* Jun 5, 2017.

Spielberg, Steven. 'The Making Of *Indiana Jones And The Last Crusade*'. *Empire Magazine.* Oct 8, 2012.

Stewart, Jackie. 'Sean Connery remembered by Jackie Stewart'. *The Guardian.* Dec 13, 2020.

Svetkey, Benjamin. 'From the archives: Sean Connery reflects on his career'. *Entertainment Weekly.* Sep 21, 2021.

Testard, Jacques & Tristan Summerscale. 'Interview with William Boyd'. *The White Review.* Jun 2011.

Thompson, Howard. 'Screen: *Operation Snafu*: Comedy and New Stage Show at Paramount'. *The New York Times.* May 22, 1965.

TV-AM. Sean Connery – *Russia House* interview. 1990.

von Dassanowsky, Robert. '*Casino Royale* at 33: The Postmodern Epic in Spite of Itself'. *Bright Lights Film Journal.* Apr 1, 2000.

Warner, Brian. 'The Story Of How Sean Connery Gave Up $450 Million By Turning Down *Lord of The Rings*.' *Celebrity Net Worth.* Oct 31, 2020.

Williams, Owen. 'Directors Special: Peter Hyams Goes Film-By-Film'. *Empire Magazine.* Jul 24, 2014.

Wygant, Bobbie. Sean Connery interview. The Bobbie Wygant Archive, 1979.

Wygant, Bobbie. Sean Connery interview – *Rising Sun*. The Bobbie Wygant Archive, 1993.

Wygant, Bobbie. Sean Connery interview – *Entrapment*. The Bobbie Wygant Archive, Apr 24, 1999.

YouTube. '1968 - Sean Connery about filming with Brigitte Bardot in *Shalako*'. Mar 20, 2015.

YouTube. 'Connery: Close Up TV special'.

YouTube. 'The legacy of the original James Bond', 60 Minutes Australia.

YouTube. Sean Connery on Parkinson, 2003.

YouTube. Sean Connery on the Late Show with David Letterman, 1993 & 2000.

YouTube. Film '83 *Never Say Never Again* Special Interview Sean Connery.

YouTube. *The Guardian* Lectures: Sean Connery Talks to Iain Johnstone about *Never Say Never Again* 1984.

YouTube. Bill Boggs interviews Sean Connery – Complete Version.

YouTube. Sean Connery on His Immortal James Bond: 'You Have to Work Very Hard to Make Something Look Easy'.

YouTube. Connery, Channel 4 documentary.

YouTube. Before Bond: Sean Connery's early years, BFI.

YouTube. BBC – Sean Connery: In His Own Words.